POETIC INDIVIDUALITY
IN THE
MIDDLE AGES

POETIC
INDIVIDUALITY
IN THE
MIDDLE AGES

New Departures in Poetry

1000—1150

PETER DRONKE

OXFORD

AT THE CLARENDON PRESS

1970

Oxford University Press, Ely House, London W. 1

GLASGOW NEW YORK TORONTO MELBOURNE WELLINGTON
CAPE TOWN SALISBURY IBADAN NAIROBI DAR ES SALAAM LUSAKA
ADDIS ABABA BOMBAY CALCUTTA MADRAS KARACHI LAHORE
DACCA KUALA LUMPUR SINGAPORE HONG KONG TOKYO

PRINTED IN GREAT BRITAIN
AT THE UNIVERSITY PRESS, OXFORD
BY VIVIAN RIDLER
PRINTER TO THE UNIVERSITY

PREFACE

THIS book has grown out of the attempt to analyse the literary implications of a group of texts that have occupied me increasingly in the last five years, and which I have come to regard as key-texts in the total picture of eleventh- and twelfth-century European poetry. My investigations began with individual works rather than with a theory about individuality: thus the chapter on *Ruodlieb* was first completed as a lecture for Queen's University, Belfast (May 1966), and that on Hildegard as a lecture to the Medieval Academy of America (April 1967). Nevertheless, I should like the book to be read not as a discussion of separate works but as a study that tries to illuminate different facets of a single central problem, relying on a single (though many-branched) approach and argument.

The common problem of poetic innovation and experiment to which these texts contribute inevitably demands constant reference to the realm of inherited literary convention and traditions, of the typical in medieval poetry, which has been adumbrated with such authority and so richly illustrated by Ernst Robert Curtius. By concentrating on a different mode of approach to individual poems, I have attempted in one respect to complement Curtius's great study, to sharpen the focus upon the spontaneity and independence of poetic creation that existed alongside, as well as within, established traditions.

I should like to acknowledge warmly a research grant from the Alexander von Humboldt Foundation, which enabled me to study Hildegard's Wiesbaden manuscript, and to write about *Semiramis*, in the winter of 1966, and several generous travel grants from the University of Cambridge, with the help of which I have been able to look at manuscripts in Rome, Paris, and Dendermonde.

Preface

My deepest thanks to the scholars who have criticized parts of this book in typescript: Marie-Thérèse d'Alverny, Marcelle Thiébaux, Bernhard Bischoff, Sir Roger Mynors, and—*hoc non deficit incipitque semper*—Ursula Dronke.

P. D.

February 1969

CONTENTS

LIST OF WORKS CITED
IN ABBREVIATION

AH	*Analecta Hymnica Medii Aevi*, ed. G. M. Dreves, C. Blume, H. M. Bannister (55 vols., 1886–1922)
ASPR	*The Anglo-Saxon Poetic Records*, ed. G. P. Krapp, E. V. K. Dobbie (6 vols., 1931–42)
Bächtold-Stäubli	*Handwörterbuch des deutschen Aberglaubens*, ed. H. Bächtold-Stäubli, E. Hofmann-Krayer (10 vols., 1927–42)
Beiträge	*Beiträge zur Kunde der lateinischen Literatur des Mittelalters*, ed. J. Werner (2nd ed., 1905)
Blaise	A. Blaise, *Dictionnaire latin-français des auteurs chrétiens* (2nd ed., 1962)
Briefwechsel	Hildegard von Bingen, *Briefwechsel*, tr. A. Führkötter (1965)
Cabrol–Leclercq	*Dictionnaire d'archéologie chrétienne et de liturgie*, ed. F. Cabrol, H. Leclercq (15 vols., 1907–53)
CB	*Carmina Burana*, ed. A. Hilka, O. Schumann (1930 ff.)
CC	*Die Cambridger Lieder / Carmina Cantabrigiensia*, ed. K. Strecker (1926)
CCM	*Cahiers de civilisation médiévale*
Deutsche Vjs.	*Deutsche Vierteljahrsschrift für Literaturwissenschaft und Geistesgeschichte*
Du Cange	*Glossarium Mediae et Infimae Latinitatis*, ed. C. Du Cange, L. Favre (5th ed., 10 vols., 1883–7)
Echtheit	M. Schrader, A. Führkötter, *Die Echtheit des Schrifttums der heiligen Hildegard von Bingen* (1956)
ELLMA	E. R. Curtius, *Europäische Literatur und lateinisches Mittelalter* (2nd ed., 1954)
Forcellini	*Lexicon Totius Latinitatis*, ed. Æ. Forcellini, F. Corradini (4 vols., 1864–87)
MÆ	*Medium Ævum*
MARS	*Mediaeval and Renaissance Studies*
MGH	*Monumenta Germaniae Historica*

MLREL	P. Dronke, *Medieval Latin and the Rise of European Love-Lyric* (2nd ed., 2 vols., 1968)
NE	*Notices et extraits des manuscrits de la Bibliothèque Nationale et autres bibliothèques* (1787 ff.)
Novum Glossarium	*Novum Glossarium Mediae Latinitatis ab Anno DCCC usque ad Annum MCC*, ed. F. Blatt (1957 ff.)
PBA	*Proceedings of the British Academy*
PBB	*Beiträge zur Geschichte der deutschen Sprache und Literatur* [*Paul und Brauns Beiträge*]
P.G.	*Patrologia Graeca*
Pitra	J. B. Pitra, *Analecta Sacra, Tom. VIII: Analecta Sanctae Hildegardis* (1882)
P.L.	*Patrologia Latina*
PLM	*Poetae Latini Minores*, ed. Vollmer, W. Morel (6 vols., 1910–35)
Poetae	*Poetae Latini Aevi Carolini* (*MGH*, 1881 ff.)
Proverbia	*Proverbia Sententiaeque Latinitatis Medii Aevi*, ed. H. Walther (5 vols., 1963–7)
RE	*Realenzyklopädie der klassischen Altertumswissenschaft*, ed. A. Pauly, G. Wissowa (1893 ff.)
RP	*Romance Philology*
SP	*The Anglo-Latin Satirical Poets and Epigrammatists of the XIIth Century*, ed. T. Wright (2 vols., 1872)
Thorndike–Kibre	L. Thorndike, P. Kibre, *A Catalogue of Incipits of Mediaeval Scientific Writings in Latin* (2nd ed., 1963)
ZfdA	*Zeitschrift für deutsches Altertum*
ZfrP	*Zeitschrift für romanische Philologie*

I

POETIC INDIVIDUALITY · QUESTIONS

THE questions raised in this study have been stimulated in many ways by a reconsideration of the medieval work of Ernst Robert Curtius,[1] and of the assumptions and methods that impelled it. The extraordinary range and penetration of Curtius's work is evident; his wealth of detailed insights into medieval literature is perhaps unparalleled in this century. In considering why an author chose particular expressions and images, why certain ways of developing his theme rather than others, Curtius was often able to adduce historical reasons of a kind that made earlier accounts seem haphazard and unsatisfying. At the same time, the distinctive rigour of Curtius's investigations has on occasions prompted me to a further question: I have wanted to ask, what aspects of medieval literature are less susceptible of understanding along Curtius's lines? Are any medieval works incompatible with his approach, and if so, why? That Curtius's studies should be able to open into such questions is one of their great merits: it is because his insights are not random but related to an exceptionally lucid and stringent set of premises. These premises, however, are not stated together outright in any one place in Curtius's writings. So I shall begin by trying to isolate some of them for closer observation.

First, his concept of a poetic tradition. For Curtius a poetic tradition, at least for the Romance lands in the Middle Ages,

---

[1] My chief concern has been with *Europäische Literatur und lateinisches Mittelalter* (2nd ed., 1954), and with the three essays 'Zur Literarästhetik des Mittelalters', *ZfrP* lviii (1938), 1–50, 129–232, 433–79. The medieval essays collected in Curtius's *Gesammelte Aufsätze zur romanischen Philologie* (1960) are also relevant to the discussion. When quoting from *ELLMA*, I cite the English translation by Willard R. Trask (1953), with page-references to the German edition in square brackets. I have translated citations from Curtius's other writings myself.

would seem to be exclusively a literary tradition—that is, a
written, never an oral, one. For him this implies a somewhat
'Cartesian' view of poetic development: everything in the
poetic tradition can be analysed in terms of 'clear and distinct
ideas', and can be led back to a set of phenomena equally clear
and distinct. Thus in the final chapter of *Europäische Literatur
und lateinisches Mittelalter* Curtius offers an account of how
vernacular literature began in the various Romance languages:

> French literature begins in the eleventh century with religious
> narrative poems. The pearl among them, the *Song of St. Alexis*
> (*c.* 1050), is the well-considered composition of a scholarly poet
> who knew the devices of rhetoric and had read Virgil. . . . Latin
> culture and poetry precede, French follows. Latin loosed the tongue
> of French. Because France was the pillar of *studium*; because the
> *artes*, with grammar and rhetoric in the lead, had their headquarters
> there—that is why the flower of vernacular poetry blooms first in
> France.[1]

French poetry, however, 'begins' not in the eleventh century
but in the ninth, with the *Song of St. Eulalia*.[2] Are we to imagine
that in the two centuries between *Eulalia* and *Alexis* no vernacular French poetry was composed—or rather that, because
there was still no vernacular *reading*-public, the French
poetry that flourished in those centuries was rarely written
down, and hence has not survived in our literary records? Is
it possible that the *Eulalia* lyric stood as an isolated achievement
in its own day? It moves with a serene assurance that hardly
suggests a beginner's work, or a work that has no predecessors
in its own poetic idiom. Was it Latin poetry that here loosed
the tongue of the French poet? If we assume he knew Prudentius' poem on Eulalia, how to account for the significant
departures from Prudentius in narrative detail,[3] and for the

---

[1] *ELLMA* 383–4 [387–8].
[2] Text with facsimile in R. M. Ruggieri, *Testi antichi romanzi* (2 vols., 1949),
no. 21.
[3] In Prudentius (*Peristephanon*, III) Eulalia is tortured by a praetor, not by
the Emperor Maximian; whereas flames burn her to death in the Latin poem,

startling difference in narrative technique (what the Latin poem tells in over two hundred lines, the vernacular compresses into less than thirty)? Or shall we assume that the French poet knew the ninth century Latin *Eulalia* sequence? In content the two lyrics have virtually nothing in common.[1] Only the precise similarity of the sequence form in the Latin and the French would suggest a debt; only the assumption that the sequence at its beginnings was essentially a learned Latin, not vernacular form, would suggest that the French was the debtor. But this assumption, as Handschin and Spanke argued more than thirty years ago, is questionable on many grounds.[2] The possibility that here it was the vernacular poet who loosed the tongue of the Latin remains open.

With the earliest surviving lyrical compositions in Provençal, this possibility becomes still more attractive. Like the French *Eulalia*, the song *Mei amic e mei fiel* has a formal and melodic counterpart which is Latin.[3] But the difference in poetic quality —in the vernacular, a vivacious scene brought to life wittily and succinctly, in the Latin, a string of religious clichés, verbose and without progression—is so marked that the formative poetic influence of the Latin is here out of the question. The vernacular accomplishment is too great to have been achieved *in vacuo*—we can here say with certainty that this poet presupposes a vernacular lyrical tradition that has not survived in writing: he is relying on a range of lyrical idiom in his native tongue that is more sophisticated and more adroit than the eleventh-century authors of Latin hymns in southern France could emulate. So, too, in the lyrical play of the *Sponsus*,[4]

they are unable to hurt her in the French one, so that the French poet devises a new form of death for her, by beheading.

[1] The Latin sequence (ed. P. von Winterfeld, *ZfdA* xlv. 133–47) contains only a brief allusion to Eulalia's mode of death, no narrative of her *passio*.

[2] Cf. my discussion 'The Beginnings of the Sequence', *Beiträge zur Geschichte der deutschen Sprache und Literatur* (Tübingen), lxxxvii (1965), 43–73.

[3] The Latin and French are printed together by A. Roncaglia, *Cultura Neolatina* ix (1949), 67 ff.

[4] I cite from the critical edition by D'Arco Silvio Avalle, *Sponsus* (Documenti di Filologia 9, 1965).

surviving in the same manuscript as *Mei amic*, the vernacular
lines have a poetic intensity beside which the Latin often seem
lifeless, an assurance beside which the Latin look awkward.
Compare the haunting refrain-line, the Foolish Virgins' cry
of wretchedness that they could not keep awake—

> Dolentas, chaitivas, trop i avem dormit!

with the more diffuse and conventional

> A! misere,   nos hic quid facimus?
> Vigilare   numquid potuimus?

Or consider the eight somewhat stilted and repetitious lines
in which the Wise Virgins refuse the request of the Foolish for
a share of their oil:

> Nos precari,   precamur, amplius
> desinite,   sorores, otius.
> Vobis enim   nil erit melius
> dare preces   pro hoc ulterius. [. . .]
>
> Ac ite nunc,   ite celeriter,
> ac vendentes   rogate dulciter
> ut oleum   vestris lampadibus
> dent equidem   vobis inertibus.

These reveal their hardness and scornfulness, but not as effectively as their three vernacular lines, where they snap at their
sisters:

> De nostr'oli   queret nos a doner?
> No·n auret pont, alet en achapter
> deus merchaans   que lai veet ester.

Whatever hypothesis one adopts about the relation between
the Latin and the Provençal parts of this play, it is the Latin
that reveals a poet who is relatively a beginner, it is the Church
that is 'cashing in' on the poetic and dramatic gifts already
evident and established in a vernacular tradition, which until
then had not been set down in writing. The strength of this
tradition can be gauged also by considering the characterization: what could have prompted this poet to present the Wise

Virgins as nastily as if they were Goneril and Regan, the Foolish as lovingly as if they were Cordelia? I know of nothing in the learned, exegetical tradition that could account for this. Surely this conception is popular in inspiration, the result of a non-theological imaginative penetration of the parable.

As to the final sentence from Curtius that I quoted—did the flower of vernacular poetry bloom first in France? This can be said only if one assumes there is no poetic tradition that is not a written tradition. Curtius applies the same premise even more drastically to Spain: 'Spain had hardly any share in the Latin Renaissance of the twelfth century. . . . Spanish literature, then, begins more than a century later than French.'[1]

Since this was written the 'beginnings' of Spanish literature have come to look rather different. A group of lyrical stanzas in a Romance vernacular have come to light from Spain which are of the same type as the much later preserved *cantigas de amigo* of the peninsula. Nine of these stanzas can be shown with certainty to be at least as old as the eleventh century, and there is decisive evidence that Romance stanzas *of this type* existed in Spain already before 900.[2] The conclusion to draw is not that vernacular poetry blooms first in Spain, not France, and to search for a new historical–sociological explanation of why this should be so; it is rather that the concept of a poetic tradition is defective if it assumes that the earliest extant poetic records show the earliest poetry in an absolute sense. For the dramatic tradition in Spain, a consideration of the *Auto de los reyes magos* (usually dated *c.* 1150)[3] imposes a similar conclusion: its salient dramatic features—the individualization of the three magi in their soliloquies, their hesitation and open scepticism concerning the birth of Christ, their attempt to devise a test for him, Herod's soliloquy with its closed, destructive scepticism, the comic squabbles of Herod's learned men—cannot be paralleled

---

[1] *ELLMA* 385–6 [389].

[2] For evidence see especially the edition by Klaus Heger, *Die bisher veröffentlichten Harǧas und ihre Deutungen* (1960), pp. 1–55.

[3] Ed. R. Menéndez Pidal, *Revista de archivos, bibliotecas y museos*, Época 3, IV (1900).

either in the Latin magi plays of the time or in the Latin exegetical tradition.[1] Could a vernacular poet have achieved such a richness of dramatic invention had he not had an oral tradition within which to work, a vernacular audience capable (through long practice) of appreciating the kind of intellectual subtleties and verbal wit that he would give them? Perhaps even more strikingly this emerges from the first surviving Anglo-Norman play, the *Mystère d'Adam* (also *c.* 1150): the extent of this poet's mastery, in his vernacular, of sophisticated dialogue and profound characterization through dialogue, make it impossible to regard his as a 'first attempt' or isolated experiment.

For Italy again Curtius makes such a simplification: 'Italian poetry does not begin until *c.* 1220.'[2] And yet there survive three remarkable poems—the *Ritmo cassinese*, the *Ritmo laurenziano*, and the *Elegia giudeo-italiana*—which according to the most recent scholarship are to be dated *c.* 1200. My point here is not to quibble over twenty years: it is to look at the implications of these three poems. They are totally unlike one another in tone and content, and totally unlike anything that is preserved in thirteenth-century Sicilian or Tuscan poetry. For not one of the three has a specific learned model ever been suggested (though the *Ritmo laurenziano*, in its 'goliardic' tone and metre, seems to me related to the humorous begging-songs of the Archpoet and Hugh Primas). In the *Ritmo cassinese* and the *Elegia* Leo Spitzer[3] has demonstrated a degree of artistry and

---

[1] It has been suggested (Winifred Sturdevant, *The Misterio de los Reyes Magos* (1927), pp. 74 ff.) that the 'testing' motif in the Spanish play may derive from Old French poetic versions of the *Gospel of the Infancy*. But there, too, it would seem to reflect a popular, not learned, tradition; it is significant that Paul Meyer, publishing extracts from these versions, observed 'Les manuscrits offrent chacun des divergences considérables de rédaction', and indeed none of the numerous extant *written* versions is early enough to be a possible source for the Spanish play (*v.* Sturdevant, pp. 36–8; cf. also R. B. Donovan, *The Liturgical Drama in Medieval Spain* (1958), pp. 70–3).

[2] *ELLMA* 387 [391].

[3] 'The Text and Artistic Value of the Ritmo cassinese', *Romanische Literaturstudien* (1959), pp. 425–63; 'The Influences of Hebrew and Vernacular Poetry in the Judeo-Italian Elegy', *Twelfth-century Europe and the Foundations of Modern Society* (ed. M. Clagett / G. Post / R. Reynolds, 1961), pp. 115–30.

literary awareness that once more precludes any possibility that such poems represent the actual beginnings of vernacular composition in Italy. (And indeed when Raimbaut de Vaqueiras, between 1197 and 1202,[1] inserted an Italian stanza in his polyglot *descort*, he cannot conceivably have been the first love-poet to think of composing in Italian). Curtius, however, having fixed *c.* 1220 as an absolute beginning, asks 'Why so late?', and continues:

> To answer it is surprisingly easy if one looks at Romania as a whole. In twelfth-century Italy jurisprudence, medicine, and the epistolary style flourish. But the study of the *auctores* languishes, and with it Latin poetry and poetics.

But the development of the epistolary style in twelfth-century Italy arose, as the polemics of the time show, in conscious reaction to an older, more humanistic rhetoric, concentrating on study of the *auctores*, that Italy had known in the later eleventh century.[2] At that time Anselm of Besate and, above all, Alberic of Monte Cassino show an approach to the problems of Latin style perhaps more sensitive and more expert than any to be found in twelfth-century France. Eleventh-century Italy, too, has its share of Latin poets, of whom Alphanus of Salerno was probably the most humanistically cultivated, Peter Damian the most gifted. Was there, then, a flourishing tradition of vernacular poetry in eleventh- and twelfth-century Italy? I see little reason to doubt it—but not necessarily for reasons such as Curtius would give, as that the Latin literary culture of the time could have brought this about. My reasons for supposing such a tradition are less direct: the existence, for instance, of an early eleventh-century Latin song from northern Italy, *Foebus abierat*,[3] where a woman encounters

---

[1] Cf. J. Linskill, *The Poems of the Troubadour Raimbaut de Vaqueiras* (1964), p. 21.

[2] Cf. F.-J. Schmale, *Adalbertus Samaritanus Praecepta Dictaminum* (*MGH*, 1961), esp. pp. 8 ff., and my study 'Medieval Rhetoric' in the forthcoming *The Literature of the Western World* (ed. D. Daiches and A. K. Thorlby), vol. ii.

[3] Ed. *MLREL* ii. 334–41; on the provenance, see the Preface to the Second Edition, ibid. i. x.

her lover's ghost—a song whose content unmistakably draws on a native fund of ballad; or again the existence of the Arthurian archivolt at Modena (generally dated early twelfth century), suggesting that narratives—and quite possibly poetic narratives—of Arthurian legends had already then captured the imagination of people in Italy. (Could they have done so had they been performed there solely in the Breton tongue?) The extent to which such earlier Italian poetry may have been influenced by contemporary Latin literature is obviously not ascertainable.

It seems to me a faulty premise, however, to assume a necessary and deterministic relation at any time between the learned poetic techniques and the practice of individual poets, learned or unlearned. Thus Curtius, to give one example, outlines seven rhetorical devices for arousing pathos that Macrobius had seen in the *Aeneid,* and shows that each of these can also be found used in the *Chanson de Roland.* He draws the conclusion that these are constituent parts of a tradition of literary techniques, i.e. of a scholastic poetic analysis and of instruction in poetic composition, which already appears fully formed in Macrobius and maintained itself throughout the entire Middle Ages. Macrobius has the conviction that Vergil in composing poetry let himself be guided by the rules of rhetoric. The medieval poets themselves did so without exception.[1]

This last sentence is explicitly contradicted by some of the rule-givers themselves who were most influential in the Middle Ages. Thus Augustine argues:

If there is an acute and ardent imagination, eloquence will come more readily to those who read and hear the eloquent than to those who pursue rules for eloquence. . . . And yet in the discourses and oratory of the eloquent, the rules of eloquence are found to be fulfilled, rules that they did not have in mind in order to be eloquent or while they were being so, and whether they had learnt those rules or had not even met with them. They fulfil them because they *are* eloquent; they do not employ them in order to be eloquent.[2]

---

[1] 'Literarästhetik', p. 451.   [2] *De doctrina christiana* IV. iii. 4–5.

In the same spirit Geoffrey of Vinsauf, eight centuries later, affirms at the outset of his *Poetria Nova* that rules for composition must not be external, that it is only 'the heart's intrinsic measure' which can determine what techniques of expression are right for any given poem: 'it is the inner man who prescribes the design, ordering its unfolding with sureness'.[1] Is it conceivable that 'the medieval poets . . . without exception' should have ignored this view of the function of the rules?

Regarding the seven specific rhetorical devices for arousing pathos, it seemed worth while to try an experiment: could these devices also be found used in a similar way in an heroic poem composed outside the western, Graeco-Roman tradition, in a poem, too, that was manifestly not learned or clerical in its principal inspiration? With this question in mind I chose to look at the Armenian epic romance *David of Sassoun*[2] (the kernel of which is today thought to be of the tenth century, though some portions may go back to considerably older traditions still),[3] and found that at least six of the seven devices have what seem (on the basis of a recent scholarly translation) to be precise counterparts there.[4] This does not of itself invalidate Curtius's interesting observation with regard to the *Roland*: Turoldus may well have learnt these particular techniques as

---

[1] *Poetria Nova* (ed. E. Faral, *Les Arts poétiques du XIIe et du XIIIe siècle*), ll. 43–9.

[2] *David de Sassoun*, ed. and tr. F. Feydit (Collection Unesco, 1964).

[3] Ibid., p. 14.

[4] To give one example for each (cf. 'Literarästhetik', p. 451):

    1. 'Apostrophe of inanimate or unspeaking objects, as of a weapon or a horse':

> 'Cours, Poulain, cours!
> Taille, petite Épée, taille!' (*David*, p. 305).

    2. *Addubitatio*:

> Le roi regarda aux alentours. Que vit-il?
> Des troupes répandues partout, plus nombreuses que les astres dans les cieux (*David*, p. 57).

    4. Hyperbole (cf. 2 *supra*):

> Sanasar appliqua une gifle sur la figure du bourreau,
> Que la tête s'envola et que le tronc resta debout. (*David*, p. 69).

[*note 4 continued overleaf*

part of his learned, clerical training in composition. But grant-
ing it to be true in Turoldus's case does not mean it is inevitably
true of medieval poets. With gifted poets there are, as Augustine shrewdly observes in the context of eloquence, several other
possibilities: they can have an intuitive rhetorical mastery by
which they 'obey the rules' without knowing that they do so;
they may have learnt the rudiments of these rules long before,
and forgotten about them consciously ever since; they may
never have been interested in theoretical discussion of their art
and none the less been sensitive readers of poetry or retentive
listeners.

The concept of a body of learnt literary techniques, in short,
cannot be used unconditionally. This is a possible way for poets
towards certain modes of expression, but by no means a necessary one.

To conclude the discussion of this first point, I would venture
three suggestions:

(i) A poetic tradition is a wider concept than Curtius allows.
Often it extends beyond the earliest written records. The poetic
and historical records must be questioned so as to elicit what
oral poetry may have existed behind them, and what continues
through the centuries to exist alongside them.

(ii) A poetic tradition may be conditioned by the learned
assimilation of literary techniques, but is not always, or wholly,
or necessarily so. The races, whether Romanic or Germanic,

[*note 4 continued*]

    5. *Exclamatio ex persona poetae*:
        'Sauvez-moi des mains de ce peuple arménien,
        Et je vous sacrifierai quarante génisses.'
        (Oui-da! Et pourquoi les idoles viendraient-elles à ton secours?)
        (*David*, p. 72).
    6. The address of the narrator using the *cernas* formula:
        Il vous appliqua une de ces ruades au calife
        Qu'il alla faire trois pirouettes
        L'une derrière l'autre et s'affaler sur la place. (*David*, p. 101).
    7. *Sententiae*:
        La vieille leur dit: 'Pourquoi ne vous accepterais-je pas, mes enfants?
        L'hôte est une créature de Dieu.' . . .
        'Vivons ensemble. Le pain est à Dieu.' (*David*, p. 135).

that inhabited France, Spain, and Italy, are all known to have revered poetry and the poet from the earliest times. This itself makes it improbable that vernacular composition in these lands should have begun only at a late period and under the stimulus of learned influence.

(iii) A poetic tradition has no deterministic power over the poets of individual talent who take that tradition as their point of departure.

A second major point for discussion arises out of Curtius's concept of the topos. At the outset of the English edition of *Europäische Literatur und lateinisches Mittelalter*, he advanced a claim to an exceptionally precise method for the study of literature: 'I have attempted to employ [philology] with something of the precision with which the natural sciences employ their methods. Geometry demonstrates with figures, philology with texts. But philology too ought to give results which are verifiable.'[1] This claim he saw substantiated particularly in his study of topoi:

A technique of philological microscopy permitted us to find identical structural elements in texts of the most varied origins— elements which we were justified in regarding as expressional constants of European literature . . . our principal object was to obtain a more accurate knowledge of the structure of our literary material by the use of precision methods which were sound both empirically and systematically.[2]

What are the criteria for empirical soundness in the revealing of these structural elements? One at least, I suggest, is that the discovery and classification of each instance be completed by an awareness of its function in context, and by a recognition of the individuality—or lack of it—in the artistic use to which it is put. That is, I believe the method as such gives the scholar no privileged access to his text: the extent to which the results are accurate depends on two gifts that must be conjoined —the ability to see likenesses of structure or expression in

[1] *ELLMA*, p. x.
[2] Ibid., p. 228 [235]. On the concept of the topos, cf. also the acute observations of María Rosa Lida de Malkiel, 'Perduración de la literatura antigua en Occidente', *RP* v (1951–2), esp. 113 ff.

disparate contexts; and the ability to give a total response to each context, reintegrating the comparative observations so that they are seen in a just proportion to the wholes in which the structures observed occur. The first gift can express itself in what is, relatively speaking, a 'precision method'; the second can express itself only through literary sensitivity. It is not 'verifiable' in the same way as the first: the philologist's total response is not a demonstration, completed, like the geometer's, with a Q.E.D., but an invitation to the reader to perform a new, unpredictable experiment—to test the philologist's 'data' against his own response to the context where they occur. Analytic study must constantly be accompanied and complemented by integrative, contextual understanding; the first is accurate only in so far as the second is sensitive.

To attempt to show in detail what can go empirically wrong with the method of analysing topoi, and why it can go wrong, I should like to reconsider four of Curtius's own examples. The first is the invocation of nature:

Medieval poetry was far too lacking in independence to give a living development to the topos which it had received from pagan late Antiquity. The Christian poet knows, of course, that nature was created by God. He can therefore address its component parts as creatures of God or of Christ. . . . The medieval poet does not invoke nature, he enumerates its component parts, and does so according to the principle, 'The more the better!'[1]

The first sentence quoted here is evidently not empirical. It is an *a priori* judgement. Is it borne out, I shall not ask by 'medieval poetry', but by the one instance that Curtius here cites in some detail? He cites six lines:

Omnis factura Christi: sol, sidera, luna,
Colles et montes, valles, mare, flumina, fontes,
Tempestas, pluvie, nubes, ventique, procelle,
Cauma, pruina, gelu, glacies, nix, fulgura, rupes,
Prata, nemus, frondes, arbustum, gramina, flores,
Exclamando: vale! mecum predulce sonate.

[1] *ELLMA*, pp. 92–3 [102].

These are part of a brief love-lyric of eighteen lines, a poet's plea to the woman he loves.[1] It is presented as a wholly personal prayer: the last line is an aside saying 'Do not show others what I have sent to you alone.' What is the function of the six lines of incantation in this lyric? Not enumeration for its own sake, but to bring to a climax the torrent of love-hyperboles that had begun in the second line of the poem: already there, when the beloved is called *fons vivus*, the language of human love takes on sacred associations; these pervade the poem more and more, until finally all the elements of creation are asked, not to 'bless the Lord' as in the psalm and the canticle, but to bless the human beloved. For, the poet now affirms explicitly, his love for her is imbued with just this sense of leaping up to the divine that the elements and creatures have in the canticle; the 'extreme' that he seeks in her love is not simply a physical fulfilment but an eternal oneness.

Whether the poet's summation of elements is excessive or artistically right is debatable; but it is clear that the way he uses the 'invocation of nature' topos is by no means 'lacking in independence'; nor is it governed by the principle 'The more the better!' It is a more daring principle, that not even an accumulation of sacred language is too much or too high to express the highest aspirations of a man's sexual passion.

A second example concerns the topos of invoking the Muses. Here Curtius judges that Milton

is as unsuccessful as Tasso or Prudentius in filling the Christian Urania with life. She remains the product of an embarrassing predicament. Milton and Tasso both came to grief over the deceptive phantom of 'Christian epic'. The Christian cosmos could become poetry in Dante's journey to the otherworld, and after that only in Calderón's sacred plays.[2]

Are the generalizations of the last two sentences based empirically on the preceding observations about Milton's Muse? And

[1] Ed. and tr., *MLREL* i. 249–50. The lines cited by Curtius are not, as his reference suggests, 'stanza 11' of a longer poem.
[2] *ELLMA*, p. 244 [250].

are these observations themselves empirically founded? The formulation in the first sentence cited would lead me to doubt it. It assumes that Milton, having inherited the topos of a Christian Muse, was then confronted with the problem of filling this topos once more with life. But considering the invocations in *Paradise Lost* makes me believe that Milton began not with a factitious convention that he hoped to vary effectively, but with an experience of more-than-worldly illumination in the course of his composing, an experience that grew more intense with the onset of his blindness, and that he felt acutely none of the conventional modes of divine invocation could fully convey. The Spirit whom he bids

> what in me is dark
> Illumine, what is low raise and support (I. 22–3);

the Light that, when the poet can no longer see the 'human face divine', can yet be summoned to

> Shine inward, and the mind through all her powers
> Irradiate; there plant eyes; all mist from thence
> Purge and disperse (III. 52–4);

the Muse whom he can still implore

> In darkness, and with dangers compassed round,
> And solitude (VII. 27–8);

or who even

> deigns
> Her nightly visitation unimplored
> And dictates to me slumbering (IX. 21–3):

these expressions are not, it seems to me, so many failed attempts at filling an old convention with life. Rather, they are repeated, fragmentary attempts at a single personal image, to evoke a rare or unique experience of the suprahuman element in poetic composition. They 'fail' only in so far as they are inevitably fragmentary, in so far as the poet must, if the experience is not to be wholly incommunicable, rely on approximations already familiar to his readers.

Another kind of problem is raised by Curtius's illustrations of a 'summation schema' that he finds in late Antiquity (Tiberianus) and again in sixteenth- and seventeenth-century Italian and Spanish: it consists of summing up in the concluding stanza of a poem the comparisons that feature in the preceding stanzas. Between Antiquity and the Renaissance Curtius finds only one instance of this schema, in a lyric by Walafrid Strabo (†849):[1]

That he should himself have invented the summation schema is unthinkable, *because it is irreconcilable with the imitative style of Carolingian Humanism.* He must, then, have had late Antique forerunners. Presumably there were others beside Tiberianus. Perhaps they are lost.[2]

I can bring no new evidence of other medieval uses of this schema, nor can I show that Walafrid invented it afresh, without ancient models. But I venture to ask, on the basis of the evidence Curtius offers, whether before the sixteenth century this indeed *is* a schema—or a coincidence? What can be seen in Renaissance Italy and Spain as a mannerism that poets imitated from one another, seems in the two isolated earlier

---

[1] Walafrid's stanza (which mentions again eight images developed in the preceding ones) runs:

> Haec carnem, stolidissime,
> nostram respiciunt, homo,
> consuetam male vivere:
> puppis, pluma, focus, sphera,
> pullus, flumen, avis, fera,
> haec attende sagaciter.

I believe the possibility should not be ruled out that Walafrid may have been stimulated to such a device by vernacular didactic verse that he knew, rather than by Latin. (Could a fertile didactic poet in the learned tongue at this time have been completely immune to his own vernacular tradition of didactic-gnomic verse, of which the roots are very ancient and the rhetorical devices often highly developed?) It is worth noting that the Norse *Hávamál* (ed. J. Helgason, *Eddadigte*, i. 16 ff.), for instance, shows several striking schemata of accumulation and summation in sts. 81–7—sts. 85 ff. are, like Walafrid's, swiftly enumerated examples of inconstancy—even though none of the devices as such is precisely similar to the Latin. So, too, in *Skírnismál* (*Eddadigte*, ii. 23 ff.), the runes cut by Skírnir (st. 36) represent a 'summation' of aspects of his curse (sts. 26–35).   [2] *ELLMA*, pp. 290–1 [294] (italics mine).

instances something that needs no ghost come from the grave to account for it. To conclude a poem[1] by recapitulation of one's principal comparisons is no profound or mysterious proceeding. Is the only reason against assuming coincidence 'the imitative character of Carolingian Humanism'? However one may define Carolingian Humanism, Carolingian poetry (which is at issue here) is at least no monolith: Walafrid's contemporary and friend, Gottschalk, and the somewhat younger Notker Balbulus, were the boldest innovators in lyric since Antiquity;[2] nor is Walafrid himself, in his choice of forms and content, wholly devoid of individuality. He is the first poet since Antiquity to compose in a wide range of lyric metres, both classical and rhymed, and the first medieval poet to attempt an otherworld vision in poetic form. To have hit unaided upon the notion of summarizing the exempla in a poem would scarcely have been beyond him.

A fourth type of problem emerges with Curtius's exposition of the topos of the pleasance (*locus amoenus*). After discussing ancient pagan examples he continues:

> In the Middle Ages the *locus amoenus* is listed as a poetical requisite by lexicographers and writers on style. We encounter a great number of such pleasances in the Latin poetry which flourished from 1070 onwards. . . . The philosophical epic of the latter part of the twelfth century incorporates the *locus amoenus* into its structure and develops it into various forms of the earthly paradise. In his *Anticlaudianus* Alan of Lille describes the dwelling place of Natura. . . . It is the 'place of places' ('locus ille locorum'), hence the optimum of the *locus amoenus*.[3]

Such a conception of this topos ignores important qualitative differences. A number of early Christian poets (e.g. Dracontius, Avitus)[4] had already attempted to transform the pagan

---

[1] Strictly speaking, Walafrid's poem continues with two further stanzas that are unrelated to the 'schema'.

[2] Cf. my discussion in *The Medieval Lyric* (1968), pp. 32–44.

[3] *ELLMA*, pp. 197–8 [204].

[4] Dracontius: *PLM* v (ed. F. Vollmer, 1914), 8 ff.; Avitus: *MGH, Auct. Ant.* VI. ii (ed. R. Peiper), 208 9.

locus amoenus into a Christian earthly paradise. Alan stands in this tradition, but attempts something very different: to portray not Eden but a place that has a precise cosmological meaning, which is a perfect expression of the essence of the goddess Natura who inhabits it. All Alan's images are chosen with this meaning in view: his *sedes Nature* partakes, like the goddess herself, of change and changelessness; it has the specific beauty of the transient and that of the eternal; it fuses reality and miracle, nature and art.[1] It unites and fulfils all the disparate potentialities in creation, and is the source of all these:

> Iste potest solus quicquid loca cetera possunt;
> Quod minus in reliquis melius suppletur in uno.

Thus it is *locus locorum* not in the banal sense of being the best *locus amoenus*, but in the philosophical one of being *forma formarum*—exemplar and fount of forms—for the created world.

Alan's complex image has left the topos of the 'lovely spot', the device enjoined by writers on style, far behind. And yet there is one poet in late Antiquity who had likewise attempted to invest the familiar *locus amoenus* images with cosmological meaning: Lactantius, in his *De ave phoenice*. He sets the Phoenix in a grove that in its details exemplifies the bird's own earthly-heavenly nature, its share in time (by its cycle of death and renewal) and in eternity (by subsisting endlessly through death and renewal).[2] Lactantius in the fourth century and Alan in the twelfth create an image that is related to both the pagan poets' 'lovely spot' and the Christian poets' Eden, but is neither.

I have used these illustrations to try to show four kinds of empirical danger that the analysis of topoi may involve:

(i) the topos that, considered in isolation, may seem aimless and lacking in independence, can turn out to have a striking individual function if its context is observed;

(ii) the consideration of a topos may be only of partial

[1] *Anticlaudianus* (ed. R. Bossuat, 1955), i. 55 ff.
[2] Cf. B. Stock, 'Cosmology and Rhetoric in *The Phoenix* of Lactantius', *Classica et Mediaevalia*, xxvi (1965), 246–57.

relevance to the poet's comprehensive intention in the passages where the topos is used;

(iii) the questions, what constitutes a topos, where is a schema followed and where freshly invented, cannot be decided on *a priori* grounds;

(iv) the attempt to trace the continuance of a topos can lead to a blurring of qualitative distinctions, distinctions that may be crucial for deciding which structures or expressions truly belong together, and which are only loosely analogous.

To describe the analysis of topoi as 'a technique of philological microscopy', a 'precision method', may be misleading: as a method it is as precise or imprecise as the literary sensibility of the person using it. The extent to which it is 'sound empirically' depends on the delicacy with which the user can judge where and how it is relevant. Does it none the less have certain intrinsic advantages over other kinds of attempt at literary understanding? That I think is the question involved in the second part of Curtius's claim, that this is a method which is 'sound systematically'.

Curtius's most detailed comments that have a bearing on this occur in a passage in the essays 'Zur Literarästhetik des Mittelalters':

The historical study of topoi can also make a contribution to the understanding of individual works and isolated texts. It makes possible a distinction between what is individual and what is typical, but also between what is popular and what is learned. One can understand a medieval text—whether of historical, philosophical, or other nature—only if one has investigated whether it stands within the tradition of a topos. . . .

Recent stylistic research (*Stilforschung*) seeks in the style the individuality of the author. This is justified for the modern period, which begins with the literary revolution of the eighteenth century, or more precisely, with the importation of the English theory of 'original genius'. This assumption, however, is valid only to a limited degree for ancient literature and for the more recent literature before 1750. Eduard Norden once said 'What is individual in Roman literature shows itself not so much in the formation of something

new as in the particular development and transformation of what
was given.'[1] This is true *mutatis mutandis* also of medieval literature
and its continuance in Renaissance and Baroque. Stylistic research
in the sense of an investigation of individual styles is therefore
(*daher*) only possible if the study of topoi has prepared the way.[2]

That the historical analysis of topoi can contribute valuably
to the comprehension of individual works is clear. To what
extent it can itself help to distinguish between the individual
and the typical within the work is less certain—what if the
individuality lies precisely in the way that the typical is used?
Nevertheless, a skilled and flexible analysis of the topos, such
as Curtius himself provides on many occasions, may well help
to illuminate this problem too. To establish a distinction, in
discussing topoi, between the popular and the learned is a still
trickier matter. To what extent can the topos of the learned
poet and the 'oral formula'[3] of the unlearned coincide? Cannot
an oral tradition at its highest level be the product of great
'learning' on the part of the oral poets—as the Germanic and
Celtic cultivation of poets' wisdom and knowledge shows? In
the case of devices equally prevalent in learned and unlearned
poetry, such as *adynata* (lands sink in the sea, stones float, rivers
run backwards),[4] or expressions of 'outdoing' (heroes, or
rulers, or palaces putting all previous ones in the shade),[5] or
again the devices for increasing pathos in heroic poetry, which
I discussed above, the problems become particularly acute:
what is learned tradition here? what is oral tradition? what
polygenesis? Such questions cannot be decided by the analysis

[1] 'Das Individuelle in der römischen Literatur zeigt sich nicht sowohl in der
Prägung von Neuem, als vielmehr in der besonderen Aus- und Umprägung
von Vorhandenem.'
[2] 'Literarästhetik', pp. 139–40.
[3] Cf. most recently M. V. Curschmann, 'Oral Poetry in Medieval English,
French, and German Literature', *Speculum*, xlii (1967), 36–52, with excellent
bibliography.
[4] Cf. E. Ól. Sveinsson, 'Kormakr the Poet and his Verses', *Saga-Book* xvii. i
(1966), 44–53; *ELLMA*, pp. 94–8 [104–8]; F. R. Schröder, 'Adynata', in
Edda, Skalden, Saga (1952), pp. 108 ff.
[5] Cf. *ELLMA*, pp. 162–5 [171–4].

of topoi alone. For only a limited number of works, learned or unlearned, can be adequately described as 'standing within the tradition of a topos': many would be better described as *using* topoi to a greater or less extent, and more, or less, consciously.

If, as regards *Stilforschung*, we here limit ourselves to considering expressive individuality in poetry, I find it hard to believe that there should be any essential difference between the questions to be asked of the poetry before 1750 and the poetry after that date. Norden's dictum in this context is ambiguous: it seems unlikely that he meant that the truly new formations (as in lyrics of Catullus) reveal individuality less well than the transformations of the traditional (as in the *Aeneid*). Perhaps he was suggesting that the formation of something new is a much rarer event in the history of poetry than the development or transformation of something traditional, and that it is the second therefore that provides a better field for the investigation of individuality. But this could well be true not only of classical literature and of the survival of the classical tradition in Europe, but of all literature at all times. Does it perhaps seem less true of certain periods and places—such as archaic Greece—simply because so comparatively little has been preserved? And is the difference between the formation of something new and the development of something given a difference of kind, or only of degree? Can we, finally, agree with Curtius that for the study of ancient and medieval poetry the study of the typical must have *priority* over the study of the individual? Or must they not rather complement each other constantly? Would it not be difficult, for instance, to comprehend Catullus' individuality as love-poet without considering what he has in common with the earlier love-poetry that he knew—and equally difficult to perceive precisely what Catullus shares with earlier love-poetry without his own uniqueness thereby emerging the more sharply? Each of these aspects of comprehension must constantly rely on the results won by the other, and itself help to refine those results. At the same time,

the questions of individuality of expression cannot be divorced
from those of the poet's total intention in his poem.

If we were to give an absolute priority to the investigation
of the typical, is there not a danger that we should see the
poetry of the Middle Ages in terms of its most stereotyped
minds and imaginings, rather than in terms of its most fruitful, unpredictable ones? Under such conditions *Toposforschung*
would tend to show us, not the mode of living of images and
expressions, but more often their mode of dying. *Toposforschung*
is systematically sound only if controlled by an awareness of
questions such as these: what proportion of any literary work
does this method help to account for? What proportion of any
outstanding literary work? Is not the significance of *Toposforschung* commensurate with the significance of content of
what is investigated? To discuss the topoi 'old woman and girl'
or 'goddess Natura'[1] as Curtius does, for instance, is to bring
illumination to focal images in European literature. His discussion of eulogistic topoi (the orator 'finds no words' that can
fitly praise the person celebrated; 'all' share in the amazement
or joy or grief on his account; 'the whole earth sings his praise',
etc.),[2] though equally expert, belongs by contrast to the foot-
notes of literary history. Are the images of 'old woman and
girl' and 'Natura', and the various devices for praising rulers,
topoi in quite the same sense? Are they best treated by quite
the same method? The two images are important because of
their *content* of imagination and idea, and are susceptible of a
systematic historical analysis. The panegyric flourishes are
virtually devoid of content—do they not prompt the question,
to what extent could such flourishes have been hit upon independently by sycophants in any age, even without the help of
ancient models?

Toposforschung, to conclude, can be systematically sound, but
cannot be systematically complete. It opens out into questions
of other kinds, and challenges a study begun from a seemingly

---

[1] *ELLMA*, pp. 101–27 [112–37].
[2] Ibid., pp. 159–62 [168–71].

opposite, but complementary, approach.[1] By this approach
questions such as these could be asked: where can we find evidence of conscious experiment in medieval poetry? Can we at
times determine that a poet is rejecting the stylistic or thematic
conventions known to him for the sake of a new kind of poetic
achievement? Can we ever put our finger on poetic individuality, when our knowledge of the sources and traditions behind
the poet is manifestly incomplete?

The works singled out for closer investigation are, deliberately, not ones that Curtius has discussed: rather, ones that
present particular difficulties and anomalies in terms of his
method and assumptions. They are works, that is, showing a
number of remarkable features that cannot be accounted for
by anything in the poetic tradition up to their time—as far as
the written records can tell us. Thus they raise, first of all, the
question with which I began: to what extent is it justifiable,
or necessary, to surmise a wider tradition than these records—
both of oral composition that was never committed to writing,
and of written literature that has been lost? This problem is
particularly acute for the two eleventh-century works I discuss, *Ruodlieb* and *Semiramis*. How far would it be legitimate
to postulate, before the one, oral poetry of a kind irretrievably
lost, before the other, profane Latin writing of a kind different
from any that survives? It is possible to demarcate in what ways
we do not have a context for these two poems; how far is it
necessary to 'invent' such a context?

The questions about the nature of the poetic tradition lead
over into the second range of questions, about the nature of
the typical and untypical in poetry. However flexible our concept of the poet's tradition, however rich our knowledge
of what it is and might have been, certain things suggest themselves intuitively as being untraditional. Can detailed study of

---

[1] To make a beginning, it seemed best to attempt this work on a small
scale, and with a very limited range of 'specimens' for detailed consideration.
There could be no question of matching Curtius's outstanding mastery and
range of material in the investigation he chose to conduct.

a poet and his imaginative procedures ever make such intuitions well founded? If it is possible to show features that are characteristic of one poem or one poet, can we not hope to make certain inferences from what is characteristic to what is distinctive, or even unique? Such attempts at disclosing individuality in poems and poets may in turn contribute to a wider conception both of the poetic tradition and of the methods of studying it.

In the study of poetic individuality, these methods will inevitably reveal their limitations; I believe this is equally true if the stress is on the literary context or on the social and historical one. The period from which I have chosen to illustrate is one that has often been said to show 'the emergence of the individual' in medieval Europe. It is true that from about 1050 we can observe in the West, and especially in France, a ferment of intellectual and imaginative activity in every sphere, in a fullness that is unparalleled—except perhaps in Islam—in the two preceding centuries. This ferment is, to a large extent, susceptible of historical and sociological explanation; itself, it helps to account for the sheer range of poetic individuality, the abundance of poetic experiment, in this age. And yet the emergence of the individual in poetry has no intrinsic connection with this age rather than with another, and can be accounted for historically only as much—or as little—as imaginative genius ever can. If it were in my competence to treat of them in detail, other kinds of experiment, other strivings by poets for the truly individual artefact, could I think be as convincingly demonstrated from poetry of the eighth century (*The Dream of the Rood*), or of the ninth and tenth (among the early scaldic poets—Torf-Einarr or Egill Skallagrímsson), as from the period I have chosen. In Latin, even a 'lean' century such as the tenth can show us at least three authors—Rather, Liutprand, Gerbert[1]—whose prose is so individual an expression of their being that scarcely a paragraph in their writings

---

[1] Cf. E. Auerbach, *Literary Language and its Public in Late Latin Antiquity and in the Middle Ages* (English ed., 1965), pp. 134–79.

could be attributed to anyone but themselves. The same holds
even of a seventh-century Latin document, the fantastic autobiography of St. Valerius.[1] The compelling practical advantage
of selecting works from the period 1000–1150 for closer discussion is that we have a far more detailed map of works for
contrast and comparison than we have for the previous centuries. Even when comparisons are not elaborated, it is relatively less difficult to indicate a range of contours and reliefs.
For similar reasons it seemed advisable to choose Latin rather
than vernacular texts for a first investigation of this kind. At
least some vernacular poems from the same period could have
taken us—or a scholar qualified to discuss them—to the heart
of the same problems; yet the imponderables in such a discussion would have been much greater still.

Ruodlieb (discussed in Chapter II) is an epic romance in the
learned tongue, yet for the nature of its language scarcely any
parallels have been found. In themes and conception it owes
almost nothing to ancient epic; nor has it anything in common
with the manneristic Latin 'epic' panegyrics of the ninth and
tenth centuries. In Latin verse hagiography only Hrotsvitha's
Gongolfus[2] suggests certain parallels: here too, as Werner Braun
has valuably shown,[3] we see the ideals of graciousness and
courtliness, even the ideals of the warrior's and hunter's life,
fused with the Christian goal of *caritas*. Perhaps still more
important in relation to *Ruodlieb* is the way in which Hrotsvitha, in the compass of a fairly brief narrative (a little less than
six hundred lines) was able to achieve an elegant fusion of
diverse genres. This has not to my knowledge been observed
before: Hrotsvitha's poem brings together a merry wonder-
tale (the enchanted fountain, bought by the saint, that leaves
its place to follow him—an episode of the same order as Ruodlieb's magic fishing); an exemplary story of the 'noble revenge',
when Gongolfus forgives his wife's infidelity; a serious romance

---

[1] Cf. G. Misch, *Geschichte der Autobiographie*, II. ii. 317–55.
[2] Ed. P. von Winterfeld, *Hrotsvithae Opera* (*MGH*, 1902), pp. 35–51.
[3] *Studien zum Ruodlieb* (1962), pp. 38–41.

theme—wife and lover together murder the husband; and finally a high-spirited fabliau theme, showing the ludicrous punishment of the wanton woman. All these are combined without incongruity.[1] It is this range and power to combine narrative material drawn apparently from various genres that the *Ruodlieb* poet shows supremely.[2] At the same time, in the breadth of conception of his poem, as in its dramatic riches and sophistication, he leaves the world of verse hagiography, even that of *Gongolfus*, far behind. In *Ruodlieb*, even where a particular tradition can be suspected, the poet's embodiment of that tradition is tantalizing: the king's maxims of proverbial wisdom that are given to Ruodlieb are, both in tone and content, far from the *Proverbia Sententiaeque Latinitatis Medii Aevi*: in their crisp cynicism—which is humour rather than wit— they are closer to those in the Norse *Hávamál*. The last completed episode of the poem has thematic affinities with one of the most widespread narrative topoi of oral epic and balladry, the wooing of a bride (*Brautwerbung*)—yet this wooing is here satirized with a Boccaccian lightness of touch. Even when the poet uses a well-known literary topos—a set description of old age, or a greeting of the formulaic 'tot-quot' type—the language he brings to it, or the dramatic context for which he uses it, makes of the established device something wholly untypical.[3]

At the same time, *Ruodlieb* shows certain essential resemblances to the twelfth-century courtly romances: the poet has a sense of the joys and splendours of a glamourized court, a delight in describing costly gifts, beautiful clothes, jewellery, horses; a delight in gracious behaviour—in the elaborate

---

[1] The episodes themselves are given in the Merovingian *Vita* that is Hrotsvitha's source—yet this prose narrative is flat and uninventive by comparison with her poem. The extent to which she transformed the prose artistically, and in many ways changed its emphasis, has been carefully analysed by Walther Stach, 'Die Gangolf-Legende bei Hrotsvith', *Historische Vierteljahrsschrift*, XXX (1935), 168–74, 361–97.

[2] I am not suggesting a direct debt of the *Ruodlieb* poet to Hrotsvitha— the very limited diffusion of Hrotsvitha's work makes this relatively unlikely.

[3] See discussion below, pp. 52–3, 62.

deference of courtiers, as when asking leave to depart from their host, in the generosity of princes, in the magnanimity of the 'noble revenge'. Yet these resemblances also throw certain differences into relief: unlike the courtly romances, *Ruodlieb* avoids detailed descriptions of fighting—there are no long scenes of battles, jousts, tournaments. The *Ruodlieb* poet, too, is more inclined than most romance authors to dwell with affectionate fullness on the non-aristocratic characters in his story—his wayward but repentant country wife, his shrewd and gentle peasant. Particularly in this dramatic comprehensiveness *Ruodlieb* shows us the emergence of a new kind of poem—it is not merely new in being an unexpectedly early instance of a genre that grows familiar a century later. I attempt to show that at times the newness is of such a nature that we can say with some confidence it is due to an individual genius and will to experiment, rather than to supposed traditions we can no longer ascertain.

Semiramis, the poetic dialogue studied in the third chapter, challenges our customary notions of medieval 'imitation' of classical poetry. Traces of the poet's reading of the ancients are far more apparent here than in *Ruodlieb*; superficially, too, his theme could be seen as a variation on Ovid's telling of the Europa myth. What I hope will emerge from detailed analysis is the extent to which such an explanation would be only superficial, how far we have here no imitation but a startlingly free creation of a fabulous ancient world. Once again, as for *Ruodlieb*, links with ninth- or tenth-century Latin poetry seem almost wholly absent. Even more important, the form of the work is unparalleled in earlier medieval Latin, and raises the problem of the existence of a clerical but profane dramatic tradition different from anything that the extant literary monuments show.

Abelard's cycle of *planctus*—and especially that of Israel over Samson, which is my chief point of focus in the fourth chapter —raises problems of yet another kind. A man who is not only philosopher and poet, but professional theologian, presents a conception of Old Testament figures that often contradicts or ignores everything that theologians had said about those figures in the past. And the poetic–dramatic techniques of his *planctus* can scarcely be explained in terms of the Latin literary tradition any better than their human implications in terms of the exegetical. The lyrical *planctus* was already a many-sided and fertile genre, both vernacular and Latin, when Abelard came to compose his cycle, yet his contribution to the genre is unique.

From the ninth century onwards[1] we know of (i) vernacular *planctus* to be sung by women: a woman laments at parting from the lover who belongs to a people hostile to her own (*Wulf and Eadwacer*), or at being unjustly outcast from her husband's land (*The Wife's Complaint*); in the brief lyrical stanzas preserved in the Mozarabic *kharjas*, girls lament the absence of the man they love, or that he has abandoned them; among the older Irish secular songs is *The Lament of the Old Woman of Beare* (*c.* 800), and in Welsh the rending lyrical laments ascribed to the girl Heledd, weeping over the deaths of her brothers (*c.* 850). Latin melody-titles from the ninth and tenth centuries—*planctus sterilis, planctus Bertanae*—point to the existence of early lost Latin women's laments, a type that flowers in the eleventh century in the exquisite *Levis exsurgit zephirus*, and the grimmer lament of a nun, *Plangit*

---

[1] Anglo-Saxon laments: ed. G. P. Krapp and E. V. K. Dobbie, *The Exeter Book* (*ASPR* iii, 1936), pp. 179, 210, 134, 143, 178. Norse: Egill, Sigvatr: ed. F. Jónsson, *Den Norsk-Islandske Skjaldedigtning*, B i (1912), 34, 220 ff.; *Guðrúnarqviða*, i and ii: ed. G. Neckel and H. Kuhn, *Edda* (1962), pp. 202, 224 ff. Mozarabic *kharjas*: ed. K. Heger, op. cit., esp. nos. 4, 5, 9, 15, 16, 23, 27. Irish laments: ed. G. Murphy, *Early Irish Lyrics* (1956), pp. 50, 74, 86 ff.; W. Stokes, *Irische Texte*, ii (1884), 145; K. Meyer, 'Über die älteste Irische Dichtung II', *Abh. der kgl. Preuss. Akad. der Wiss.* 1913, Abh. 10, esp. pp. 4 (on the dating), 16–17. Welsh: Sir Ifor Williams, *Lectures on Early Welsh Poetry* (1944), pp. 40–8; Gwyn Williams, *An Introduction to Welsh Poetry* (1953), pp. 32–7; id., *The Burning Tree* (1956), pp. 30 ff. Latin *planctus*: *CC* no. 40; *MLREL* ii. 357–60; *Poetae*, iii. 131, 732 ff. (completed by B. Bischoff, *Medium Aevum Vivum* (1960), pp. 64–5); *AH* vii. 253 ff.; M. de Marco, 'Un "Planctus" sulla morte di Ettore', *Aevum* (1959), 119–23; *CB* no. 100; *MARS* iv. 389 ff.; Orpheus: ed. M. Delbouille, *Mélanges Paul Thomas* (1930), p. 174; Oedipus: ed. S. Gaselee, *An Anthology of Medieval Latin* (1925), pp. 79–82.

nonna fletibus. Then there are (ii) dirges, represented in Latin from the eighth century with Paulinus of Aquileia's song on the death of Duke Eric of Friuli, and abundantly from then on;[1] in the vernacular by Egill's deeply individual elegy for his sons, *Sonatorrek*,[2] and earlier, at least through allusions, by the dirges in *Beowulf*; earlier still, there are Irish dirges of the sixth and seventh centuries mourning the deaths of heroic kings and princes.

There is (iii) a Germanic tradition of complaints of exile and voyaging, often enriching the literal sense of these with a wider range of evocative meanings (the Anglo-Saxon *Wanderer* and *Seafarer*, stanzas of the scaldic poet Sigvatr Þórðarson); so too, in ninth-century Latin, we have Gottschalk's song of exile *Ut quid iubes*, and the anonymous lament of the swan, *Clangam filii*. Again, the vernaculars know (iv) fictional narrative *planctus*: Deor's lament in Anglo-Saxon and Guðrún in Norse; in Irish, Deirdre's for Noisi, and Créide's for Dínertach; in Welsh a group of laments (now dated *c.* 850) is attributed to the sixth-century chieftain Llywarch Hen. In Latin the melody-title *Prosa de planctu pueri capti* may point to the existence of a fictional lament in the ninth century; in the eleventh a lament for Hector is preserved; and in the later twelfth—that is, after Abelard—a larger range of *planctus* with ancient themes: two laments of Dido, one of Tharsia, one of Orpheus, and one of Oedipus.

Lyrical *planctus* with biblical themes (v) are attested for the first time, to my knowledge, in Notker's 'lament of Rachel' (see below, p. 140), and are relatively rare before Abelard. There is an eleventh-century Irish lyrical 'lament of Eve'. The elaborate laments of the Virgin, however, both Latin and vernacular, that come to be embodied in passion plays do not seem to be traceable before the second half of the twelfth century. So, too, a man's *complainte d'amour* (vi),

---

[1] *V.* C. Cohen, 'Les Éléments constitutifs de quelques *planctus* des Xe et XIe siècles', *CCM* i (1958), 83–6.

[2] Cf. the remarkable discussion of individuality in this poem by Georg Misch, *Geschichte der Autobiographie*, ii. i (1955), 131–77.

though not unknown earlier, is characteristically a twelfth- and thirteenth-century phenomenon. It is then that it becomes a definite 'type', stylized and often conventionalized.

Even so swift an indication of these ranges of *planctus* will make it apparent how far Abelard's cycle stands apart from anything else in the genre. In two important ways, regarding form and content, his *planctus* are related to the older tradition. It is striking how often in the earliest Latin evidence the lyrical *planctus* seems to go with a sequence form: this can be seen not only from extant examples but from the melody-titles of lost sequences that were specifically designated *planctus*. Abelard, too, takes the sequence as the formal point of departure for his laments. Two (the second and fifth) are in strict 'classical' sequence form; the rest develop the 'archaic' type of sequence, though with an unprecedented breadth of formal inventiveness.[1] They take up a sophisticated poetic and musical form which, as far as the extant records can show us, had been virtually extinct for two centuries, and yet from Abelard onwards—even if not directly through his influence[2]—flourishes

---

[1] Cf. H. Spanke, 'Über das Fortleben der Sequenzenform in den romanischen Sprachen', *ZfrP* li (1931), 309 ff.

[2] The extent of influence of Abelard's *planctus* is hard to estimate. Until 1957, when a second manuscript of the *Planctus David super Saul et Ionatha* was brought to light (see below, p. 114 n. 1), the six *planctus* were known only from the one manuscript, Roma Vat. Reg. lat. 288. While this alone would suggest that their influence was negligible, certain other considerations may point in a different direction:

1. The *Lai des pucelles*, which shares the melody of Abelard's *Planctus virginum Israel*, is more likely to derive from the *planctus* than to be its source. (Cf. G. Vecchi, *Pietro Abelardo, I 'Planctus'*, p. 25.)

2. The Florentine version of the song *Parce continuis* seems to echo Abelard's *Planctus David super Saul et Ionatha* (cf. *MLREL*, 2nd ed., I. x–xi, II. 351–2).

3. There are two thirteenth-century *planctus*—the dramatic one of Samson (see below, p. 132) and one of Jacob (ed. J. Leclercq, *Hispania Sacra*, ii (1949), 115–16)—which according to Josef Szövérffy are influenced by Abelard's Samson and Jacob laments (cf. *Die Annalen der lateinischen Hymnendichtung*, ii. 73). This seems to me possible, though not certain: there are no decisive verbal parallels in either case.

4. Can the exceptional vogue, after Abelard, of forms based on the 'archaic' sequence—*lai lyrique*, *estampie*, *Leich*—have anything to do with the influence

again not only in Latin but in French and German, and gives rise to further extensive variations in all three languages. The presumptions here seem to me in favour of continuity—that a range of 'archaic' sequences, vernacular and Latin, and some of them almost certainly *planctus*, existed in the tenth and eleventh centuries, which were not written down, or of which copies have not survived. Yet I shall try to show in detail how, even assuming such a lost tradition, one can still point to certain aspects of Abelard's achievement as both individual and deliberately experimental.

Again, already from the ninth century (in Notker's *Rachel*, and possibly also in the Anglo-Saxon *Seafarer*) one has the sense that the *planctus*, in which essentially the poet creates a dramatic *persona*, could become a vantage-point for dramatic development, i.e. extension into dialogue without narrative interruptions. While the *planctus* of Abelard's cycle themselves contain little dialogue,[1] the sense of the dramatic potential in the genre is stronger here than ever before: the poet both uncovers his characters' extremes of emotion with a dialectician's accuracy, and allows them to reveal nuances of thought, impulse, and motive in a way that perhaps only a poet who was also a major innovator in the realm of ethical analysis could have achieved.

The lament for Samson contains a psychological and dramatic insight that has almost nothing in common with earlier interpretations of Samson. Here this insight is revealed indirectly, by a chorus, not (as in four of the other *planctus*) by the protagonist in soliloquy. But the way the chorus is used also involves a further indirection, a deliberate use of enigma by the poet. It offers a juxtaposition of partial views, almost of

of his *planctus*? This possibility cannot be dismissed out of hand. It is conceivable that the *planctus* may have become part of the repertoire of a number of skilled clerical performers—who did not necessarily sing to an exclusively clerical audience—without their being at all frequently set down in writing or notation.

---

[1] Dialogue occurs only in the third song, the *Planctus virginum Israel*, and even there with narrative transitions.

caricatures, designed each to be criticized and questioned by
the audience, and by that means to bring an understanding that
goes beyond anything the chorus itself affirms. This 'critical'
use of the enigmatic is the essence of Abelard's experiment—
an experiment that has perhaps more affinities to techniques and
achievements in twentieth-century drama than to anything
in the medieval *planctus* or in the poetry of Abelard's day.[1]

In the fifth chapter the poetry and the play of Hildegard of
Bingen raise two problems in their most acute form: that of
a wholly individual use of imagery, and that of the individual
creation of a new genre. It is not that Hildegard's images as
such are all wholly original or wholly private: rather, well-
known biblical images, and at times established philosophical
and scientific ones, play their part in a symbolic fabric which
is so much her own that they can no longer be 'read' in the
expected ways; they enter into combinations previously unknown, in conjunction with other images and expressions that
are far more private. Often these images too, born from Hildegard's extensive visions, become in the poetic context a law to
themselves, their meaning now determined by their function
in the poem and almost unrelated to their explicit meaning
in the prose record of the visions. And again this seemingly
inward-looking poetess was able to objectify some of her
imaginings in a new formation: a morality-play that is not only
the first of its kind, but perhaps unique in the means it uses—
both intensely lyrical and filled with dramatic unpredictability,
with suspense. Once more nothing in earlier literature—in the
tradition of the *Psychomachia*, in Hrotsvitha's Terentian variations, or even in the contemporary *Ludus de Antichristo*—
could begin to account for the qualities of the *Ordo Virtutum*.

Such, in outline, is the range of problems exemplified by the
works I have chosen for closer consideration. They are problems of the untypical; often they involve the question of traditions that may or may not be legitimately surmised. I
should like to try with each illustration to define more closely

[1] See discussion below, pp. 142–5.

the nature of the untypical elements, and to adumbrate the areas of *missing* knowledge that would be necessary for a fully satisfying account to be given. For to do more than that—to explain the untypical, or to reconstruct poetic and dramatic traditions whose traces are quite lost (or perhaps never existed) —would seem 'to dere a date'.

II

RUODLIEB: THE EMERGENCE OF ROMANCE

To define its genre and intent, and to explain its literary and cultural context, the poem *Ruodlieb* has been showered with more suggestions than the Sleeping Beauty with presents at her birth. The author's style has been explained in terms of his knowledge of a whole gamut of Latin poetry, classical and medieval (Braun), and again, in terms of his almost total ignorance of Latin poetry except Vergil (Brunhölzl). Various aspects of the poem's fable have been explained in terms of folk-tale (Seiler); in terms of Greek and Byzantine romances (Burdach) and Christian legends of saints (Gamer); in terms of a proto-*chanson de geste*, that has to be reconstructed from a fifteenth-century tale in prose (Singer); in terms of a type of Germanic saga, whose existence in Germany around the year 1000 has to be inferred from literary developments in Iceland around 1200 (Naumann); in terms of an earlier (hypothetical) German 'Ruodlieblied' (Schneider); for one episode, even, an Arabic anecdote has been adduced (Löwenthal). The spirit of the poem has been treated in terms of a reflection of political realities, whether in the reign of Henry II (Giesebrecht and others) or of Henry III (Hauck); in terms of the entertainment provided by mime-players and mountebanks (Winterfeld, Singer); in terms of an ideal inspired by Cluniac monasticism (Braun).[1]

[1] Werner Braun, *Studien zum Ruodlieb* (1962), especially pp. 96–106; Franz Brunhölzl, 'Zum Ruodlieb', *Deutsche Vjs.* xxxix (1965), 506–22; Friedrich Seiler (ed.), *Ruodlieb* (1882), pp. 45–74; Konrad Burdach, *Vorspiel*, i. i (1925), 153–7; Helena M. Gamer, 'The Ruodlieb and Tradition', *Arv* xi (1955), 65–103, especially pp. 99–100; Samuel Singer, *Germanisch-romanisches Mittelalter* (1935), pp. 206–31; Hans Naumann, 'Die altnordischen Varianten des Ruodlieb-Romans', FS Felix Genzmer, *Edda, Skalden, Saga* (1948), pp. 307–24; Hermann Schneider, *Germanische Heldensage*, i (1928), p. 263; Fritz Löwenthal

None of these suggestions, even when they have been, with more or less assent, accepted, has been found fully satisfying. Scholars still speak of *Ruodlieb* as enigmatic, *ein Rätsel*. Is this not partly because they have always tried, with great historical ingenuity, to explain everything about this poem in terms of something else? Is it not equally important, perhaps even more fundamental, to see what can be explained on the poem's own terms, what can be illuminated simply by close critical attention to the artistry of *Ruodlieb* itself?

For *Ruodlieb* is a poetic experiment. Its author, I am convinced, was trying to create a new kind of poem. Even if we could be certain about the milieu in and for which he wrote, about everything he had and had not read, even if we could trace every story that he knew, this would still not have accounted for the greater part of his achievement.

This is particularly striking in the case of experimental poets. The author of *Beowulf*, like the author of *Ruodlieb*, may well have read Vergil; and with *Beowulf*, unlike *Ruodlieb*, we can also gain a good knowledge of the 'data', Christian and pagan, historical and legendary, that the poet had—or might have had —at his command. But for his use of this material no parallels have ever been found, and in all probability it was a wholly individual and experimental conception. For the plays of Hrotsvitha our knowledge of sources appears to be complete; we know exactly where and when she wrote; she herself writes about why. Yet the particular imaginative form that her plays took was surely unpredictable then, and remains unaccountable even now.

In southern Germany, in the middle of the eleventh century, a Latin poet wrote the first medieval verse romance. Usually when one says 'the first' in such a context one immediately qualifies, if challenged, to 'the first surviving', or 'the first

'Bemerkungen zum Ruodlieb', ZfdA lxiv (1927), 128–34; Wilhelm von Giesebrecht, *Geschichte der deutschen Kaiserzeit*, ii (5th ed., 1885), 625; Karl Hauck, 'Heinrich III. und der Ruodlieb', PBB lxx (1948), 372–419; Paul von Winterfeld, *Deutsche Dichter des lateinischen Mittelalters* (2nd ed., 1917), pp. 491–503.

recorded instance'. Here, too, this may be necessary.[1] Still it
seems to me certain that in *Ruodlieb* we can observe a unique
moment of poetic creation. A cultivated, sensitive man, who
has received the normal Latin education, secular and sacred,
of his day, familiar with the milieu of the German imperial
court and (at least by hearsay) with some aspects of the Byzantine world and the Saracen, decides to hold up a mirror to his
own time. He is passionately interested in every aspect of the
world around him. He is no respecter of persons: kings and
peasants concern him equally as human beings. He is a strange
blend of idealist and realist. Occasionally his vision lights up
and becomes a picture of perfect human behaviour and (he believes consequently) perfect human happiness. But most of the
time he is also aware of people's faults, missing none, yet still
observing sympathetically and humorously. His basic purpose
may be called (as it often has been) didactic and Christian—
but only if we have in mind a sense of these terms that would
apply equally to the artistry of a poet such as Chaucer. Like
Chaucer, the *Ruodlieb* poet was aiming above all at a certain
human comprehensiveness. How was he to achieve it? We can
watch him experimenting: he takes deliberately many-sided
contemporary story-material, and attempts to weld it and transform it into a greater poetic whole. A picaresque adventure
story, a mirror of chivalry and kingship, a folk-tale exem-
plifying proverbial saws, a *fabliau*, which this poet takes
into a dimension as deep and serious as Chaucer's *Merchant's
Tale*, a love-story as gay as that of Benedick and Beatrice, a
light *novellino* of deception that would be at home in the
Decameron, and at the last a fairy-tale of dreams and dwarfs
and treasure-hoards—such were his ingredients. All these were
among the imaginative realities of his own world, and it was

---

[1] I am excluding from the present discussion works such as *Waltharius*, the
Gesta Apollonii, and the reconstructed *Hague Fragment*. While in various ways
these could be relevant and illuminating in the study of *Ruodlieb*, none of them
shows *Ruodlieb*'s essential affinity with a later world, the world of *König Rother*
or *Erec et Enide*, which effectively sets it apart from earlier experiments with
fictional poetic narrative in medieval Latin.

these that he longed to transmute and unify into a poem of epic stature. Not another Troy or Thebes, but the whole teeming imaginative world that belonged to him and his own generation. Thus, even if other medieval romances conceived on a large scale existed before *Ruodlieb*, I doubt if any other would have attempted quite so far-reaching a synthesis. The surviving evidence from the twelfth century onwards suggests nothing of comparable versatility. It is here especially that, whatever else may have existed in his time, I would see the experimental quality in this poet's work.

Perhaps he was over-ambitious—the work as far as we can tell remained unfinished, like Chaucer's *Canterbury Tales*. Even in what survives we can spot a number of loose strands, episodes that the poet was not yet sure where to insert,[1] and inconsistencies.[2] He seems to have felt a particular difficulty in fusing the folkloristic and proverbial elements with the rest of his conception—was he to try to make them humanly plausible, or treat them ironically, or simply to diminish their importance in the whole? We see him attempting all three. And was he happy with the pattern he had chosen to bring about the denouement of his plot? Or did he leave the final stage unfinished because, as with Chaucer in the *Squire's Tale*, the straight use of *féerie* began to seem unsatisfying to one whose powers of realism had grown with every stage of his work?

Such questions are intriguing, but perhaps unanswerable. In what follows I shall leave them aside and make some observations chiefly on two aspects of the *Ruodlieb* poet's art, the aspects in which I think he shows his powers of expression and his powers of narrative most distinctively. One is his creating of personality through dialogue, individualizing his characters by their tone and manner of speech. The other is his gift of

---

[1] e.g. Ruodlieb's feat of fishing with 'buglossa' pills, which is told in fragment II and more fully in X.

[2] e.g. Ruodlieb is commanded to open one of his 'loaves' on returning home, and the other not before his own wedding (v. 548 ff.); instead, he opens both on the day of his homecoming (XIII. 49 ff.), and there is no suggestion of disobedience in the episode.

shaping a narrative pattern symbolically, that is, of using a
wealth of realistic detail not just for its own sake but to enhance
and illuminate the dramatic action. Time and again the words
of dialogue, and the poet's acute observations and descriptions,
mean more than they say. This is what I mean by their symbolic power. They are more than excellent recording, they
have powers of evocation and innuendo that find their reson-
ance in the narrative and give it a richness of texture unparalleled in Medieval Latin storytelling.

A young knight, Ruodlieb, whose nobility was an inward
as well as an outward thing, decides to leave home because in
his own land malicious lords have blocked his advancement
at every turn. Our first glimpse of him is as he gallops away
from his village, leaving his old mother and a weeping crowd
of peasants behind him:

> Detersis lacrimis qui tunc, lotis faciebus,
> Consolaturi dominam subeunt cito cuncti,
> Que, simulando spem, premit altum corde dolorem:
> Consolatur eos, male dum se cernit habere.[1]

These four lines (to give only one brief illustration from a

---

[1] I. 56–9 (58 is adapted from Vergil, *Aen.* I. 209):
Then, wiping away their tears, dewy-eyed,
they all run up to comfort the lady of the castle;
she, feigning hope, suppresses her grief deep in her heart—
it is she who comforts them, when she sees them taking it badly.
King Arthur's court shows just such a well-bred dissemblance of grief at the
departure of Gawain (cf. *Sir Gawain and the Green Knight*, 539–42). So too
in the English poem the tact with which the identity and origin of a stranger
should be elicited is noted (901 ff.), as in *Ruodlieb* (see below, pp. 39–41).
My quotations from *Ruodlieb* are based on the facsimile edition of the
manuscripts (München Clm 19486 and, for fragments XI and XIII, Sankt
Florian 22), produced by Gordon B. Ford, Jr. (Pyramid Press, Kentucky,
1965), with reference to the chief printed texts, especially those of Friedrich
Seiler (1882) and Edwin H. Zeydel (1959). The fragments are given the now
generally accepted numbering (proposed by Ludwig Laistner, *AfdA* ix (1883),
70–106). I have written 'ę' as 'e' throughout; punctuation is my own. When
in illegible lines I have adopted the readings or conjectures of various editors
of the poem, I have noted this explicitly. The translations are my own, and are
intended as an extension of the literary discussion, to indicate my interpretations of textual nuances and of disputed passages.

scene in which no detail is capricious)[1] say a lot by way of
human observation, but their imaginative power is not limited
to recording a touching gesture. The gesture of Ruodlieb's
mother is suggestive of a whole ideal of *gentilezza*—an ideal
in which reticence, self-control, and considerateness all play a
part, and which cannot help having an aristocratic stamp: the
peasants are effusive in their grief and spontaneous in their desire to comfort the lady of the manor, but the lines evoke not
only the friendship and kindness that subsists between them
and their châtelaine, but also the distance. Hers is the 'deep
grief', too intimate for public expression, theirs the cruder
'feeling sorry' that is so precisely conveyed by the colloquial
ring of *se habere male*—'taking it badly'.

Ruodlieb's journey brings him to the realm of the Greater
King (Rex Maior), which seems to be a region surrounded by
the Saracens in southern Italy.[2] His introduction at court there

---

[1] There are a number of changes of focus within the scene (I. 17–59)—
summary of action, static image, 'flashback', static image, continuation of
action, then (48 ff.) a full 'rehearsal' of the scene from the beginning. In my
view it is through the conjunction of these varied emphases that the poet makes
the scene both visually and emotionally memorable. Brunhölzl (art. cit.,
p. 516), however, sees the scene as 'ein rechtes Durcheinander'; I think he
ignores the possibility of artistic purpose in the alternations of focus, and he
seems unaware that this technique of alternation has received extensive literary
discussion in the context of *chansons de geste* (cf. recently Eugène Vinaver,
'From Epic to Romance', *Bulletin of the John Rylands Library*, xlvi (1963–4),
476–503).

[2] Rex Maior's kingdom is said to be 'apud Afros' (XVI. 5; cf. XIII. 42, 47).
In the fragmentary condition of the text it is not easy to estimate what importance the *Ruodlieb* poet might have given to this location. It is not quite accurate to say, as several scholars have done (cf. E. H. Zeydel, ed. cit., p. 151),
that 'Saracens were sometimes called "Africani"'. The passage in Liutprand
(*Antap.* II. 44–5) on which this assertion is based says something rather different: that those Saracens who had come to southern Italy (at the request of
Byzantium, to crush a rebellion) and who had then entrenched themselves
there were in fact from Africa. Liutprand calls them 'Africani' not as a
synonym for 'Saracens' but to indicate their place of origin. As Ruodlieb seems
to reach the kingdom 'apud Afros' entirely by a land journey, it seems
likeliest that the poet had in mind a principality in southern Italy which was
still surrounded by Saracens from Africa. This would go well with the passage

is treated with fine dramatic subtlety. On his way he meets one of the king's hunters, who greets him (I. 74). Ruodlieb returns the greeting, with grave dignity (*grandiloquus, seriosus*). Then the hunter becomes inquisitive, asks several personal questions at once—*quis et unde sit, ire velit quo*—and Ruodlieb disdains to answer. The hunter ponders the implication of this silence: 'I think he must be poor in worldly power, but rich in *virtù*.' The leap of thought is not made explicit, rather we are invited to follow through the hunter's thought ourselves—a man who travels on so modest a scale, and yet is clearly not used to, or prepared to accept, being questioned bluntly, must have a high standard of courtesy both for himself and others. So the hunter waits for what he considers an appropriate time (*satis*) before

about border-dwellers and intermarriage (II. 52 ff.), and with the chess episode at the court of Rex Minor (for which Löwenthal, art. cit., p. 131, noted an interesting Arabic analogue): the most recent article on 'The Earliest Evidence of Chess in Western Literature', by Helena Gamer (*Speculum*, xxix (1954), 734 ff.), suggests 'an Arabic transmission [of the game] by way of Italy and not Spain, or not only Spain'; St. Peter Damian, writing in 1061/2, condemns the passion for chess among the Italian clergy. Rex Minor's gift of a range of exotic animals, including the white bears, which are Syrian in origin (*v.* S. Singer, op. cit., p. 224—several scholars since have claimed them to be polar bears, but the description of their gentleness and their dancing with women puts this out of the question), also suggests a traditional kind of lavishness practised by Saracen rulers. While the meeting of the two hosts (v. 29 ff.) might be read to imply that Rex Minor also is a Christian, with clergy in his retinue, this is by no means a necessary inference, and the later passage (v. 210-14) in which the function of monks is explained to Rex Minor rather suggests the contrary. If this clarification of the setting is correct, then the humaneness of Rex Maior (and by implication of the poet himself), his total lack of intolerance on grounds of race or creed, is particularly striking.

Perhaps a decade before *Ruodlieb* was written, the young Norwegian hero Harald harðráði, like Ruodlieb, left his native land because of feuds, and during his travels joined the great Byzantine general George Maniakes, fighting for him against the Saracens at the conquest of Sicily in 1040 (cf. E. R. A. Sewter, *Michael Psellus, Fourteen Byzantine Rulers*, Penguin Classics 1966, p. 385). It is interesting to note that before reaching Italy Harald, according to the earliest (poetic) Norse sources, fought with Saracens in 'Serkland' (Saracen-land)—a term used for any region occupied by Arabs and here probably referring to Lydia—but that in the later prose of *Heimskringla* 'Serkland' becomes 'Affríká' (cf. *Heimskringla*, iii (Íslenzk Fornrit, xxviii, 1951), 74 ff.; S. Blöndal, *Væringjasaga* (Reykjavík, 1954), ch. 5, especially pp. 116 ff.).

speaking again, and this time he begins with a courteous preamble, he couches his thoughts about Ruodlieb in hypothetical terms ('If you should have left home because of a great feud . . .'), in a delicate parenthesis ('I too am a foreigner here') he reassures Ruodlieb and makes the first suggestion of having something in common with him which could become a basis of friendship (I. 84 ff.). Then he seems to change the subject entirely, to praise of the king at whose court he is staying. Yet this change of subject is only apparent: the evocation of life at Rex Maior's court, the love of good things, the gaiety, the generosity which is always tactful, exercised not so much to reward the courtiers as to honour them (*plus quam mercedis, honoris*)—all this has an implicit double purpose: to persuade Ruodlieb that he would find a congenial life there and, inseparably from this, to show him how highly the hunter is judging him, how he knows that Ruodlieb is just the kind of person for whom a life of such grace and aristocratic gaiety would be appropriate. By describing this way of life the hunter is indirectly making amends to Ruodlieb for the superficial judgement, based on mere outward appearances, that was implied by his first brusque questioning. And having done this, he feels he can go on to a direct invitation to friendship, though even this begins very tentatively, and therefore with a slightly formal stiffness: 'If it should please you to make a pledge of friendship . . .' (I. 108). Ruodlieb's reply and acceptance in turn contain a line that suggests more than it says, that gives us a further glimpse into his character:

'Namque meas causas, ut sunt, tu coniciebas'.

'As for my troubles, indeed, you guessed them for what they are.'

Behind the colloquial simplicity we can perceive the sensitive thought: *causas* can mean both Ruodlieb's situation (*choses*)—exile and poverty—and his grounds for complaint in his own land. By the parenthetic *ut sunt* Ruodlieb both vouches for the genuineness of his *causas* and shows his modesty: it is an affirmation, and at the same time a half-ironic disclaimer (as if to imply, 'I know I'm not as important as all that').

The king, when they arrive, at once questions the hunter—but this, we are told explicitly (I. 131), is the familiarity of friendship, not of social inequality. With the stranger he is far more circumspect. He does not interrogate Ruodlieb, but by a deliberate, gentle pretence (asking the hunter 'Did you find a bear or a boar in the woods today?' when he had evidently returned empty-handed) he gives the hunter the most favourable chance to introduce his new friend. Then Ruodlieb offers the king a gift, which the hunter as expert assures him is 'modest, but not to be discounted' (*parva, nec abicienda*): his hunting-dog, 'which had a collar of gold around its neck'. This again is no trivial, ornamental detail, nor was it fortuitous that a hundred lines earlier (I. 45) this dog had been called 'better than any other'. The gift is like the giver—not great, but the best of its kind. It can stand as a symbol for the giver. And the gold collar suggests that the gift, like the giver, comes from a more lavish, more exalted world, of which the signs are not wholly lost even in exile.

At the foreign court Ruodlieb distinguishes himself as hunter, warrior, and diplomat. His new lord has a battle to defend his borders against a lesser king (Rex Minor). But we are in a more humane world than that of heroic poetry or of most of the later chivalric romances. It is not that the poet ignores the violence of battle, but that he looks beyond it to the human issues involved. He thinks of the civilians—

And though they see that their homes are burning,
they were not sad, since they still enjoyed their freedom (III. 25–6)—

and above all he thinks of the question of honour and dishonour between peoples (*honor* is a key-word repeated many times from III. 3 till the end of the peace-settlement in v). The fighting and deaths in battle are seen only briefly, through the eyes of a comic messenger, as pompous, obtuse, and sly in turn as Shakespeare's Dogberry. The peace negotiations, on the other hand, are presented very fully: first at the court of Rex Minor, where Ruodlieb has been sent as ambassador, then in Ruodlieb's report of his mission to his lord—two scenes that in their rich detail complement each other dramatically without ever being repetitious—and at last in the meeting between the two kings.

To illustrate again the poet's power to characterize through speech, let us consider more closely some aspects of the scene between Ruodlieb and Rex Maior. Ruodlieb begins by praising the king's mercy—the language is simple but dignified, by no means fulsome (IV. 81 ff.). But soon it becomes clear that Ruodlieb in his account of what happened on his embassy is idealizing the behaviour of the lesser king and his court almost beyond recognition. The poet is deliberately inviting us to compare the negotiations he has shown us with this heightened diplomatic report on them. What is the king's reaction? He is delighted with the gist of what he has heard, and that things have gone honourably (IV. 174). He smiles a little, and shows no arrogance. He praises God for the success of the peace-talks, and does not say anything either to exalt himself or to crush Ruodlieb. In fact he changes the subject, asks Ruodlieb about the more specific arrangements, and authorizes these. But then he cannot resist trying to probe into what had led up to the final, improbably submissive, attitude of the lesser king: had Ruodlieb perhaps contributed to making him feel small? Suddenly his tone becomes informal and conversational:

> 'Dum fueras at ibi, quid agendum, dic, habuisti?' (IV. 184)
> 'But while you were there, tell me, what did you have to do?'

Ruodlieb answers by telling of events at the enemy court of which we have heard nothing so far, and which he had clearly thought it more prudent not to mention in the official report. The negotiations had been conducted over a series of games of chess. Ruodlieb was easily able to defeat the various courtiers and the lesser king himself at the game, but their chief purpose in playing with him had not been to win. It was rather to test Ruodlieb, to 'learn the unknown moves he will make' (IV. 207), to trick him in the course of play into giving away more about his mission than he ought, and, when this did not succeed, to try to embarrass him by being over-generous to the point of condescension, suggesting high stakes for each game, refusing to accept any money from Ruodlieb but forcing him to accept his winnings (IV. 220 ff.):

> 'At once they wanted to give me what they staked.
> At first I refused, indeed I thought it unworthy
> for me to make money like that, or for them to be fleeced
>   by me.
> I said "I am not accustomed to growing rich by gaming."
> They said "While you're with us, live as we do;
> when you get home, there you can live as you please."
> When I'd shown enough reluctance, I accepted—
> Fortune gave me the advantage, honourably.'
> The king said 'I'm sure you will always be fond of chess,
> if that's the way you can get your shoes so well mended.
> But now, accept my thanks—you are serving me well.'

How revealing is this brief dialogue! In the games of chess Ruodlieb had not been quite as diplomatic as he should: he had snubbed the other court by a haughty remark (which was wrong, even though they were trying to discountenance him), and now he tries to gloss this fact over by the comment 'When I had resisted enought, I accepted.' Outwardly, he means, his behaviour had been irreproachable—*sat lorifregi*[1]—he intends the cynicism as a little joke to share with the king. Yet even as he says it Ruodlieb has the suspicion that the king, with his high standards of honour and his strong views about receiving gifts,[2] will not be amused—the next line reveals Ruodlieb's defensiveness and uncertainty: it is as if to say 'After all, it was luck, wasn't it? There's nothing dishonourable about having luck, is there?' But for once the greater king, usually so gentle, is provoked into a flash of cruelty: his ironic reply—

> 'I'm sure you will always be fond of chess,
> if that's the way you can get your shoes so well mended'—

[1] The hapax legomenon *lorifregi* ('I broke the reins, I resisted') has a German marginal gloss *Zugilprechoto*.

[2] Later, before the defeated king can present his gifts, Rex Maior lectures his own knights and orders them to accept nothing, 'so that it does not look as if you need his riches' (v. 158).

reminds Ruodlieb that he had arrived at the court with next to nothing, it warns him not to presume too far. But with the very next line the king relents, and restores the young man's confidence: 'But now I must thank you—you are doing well.'

The use of the present tense (*causas quod agis bene nostras*) here, instead of a perfect, has recently been cited as an instance of the poet's lack of grammar and poor command of Latin.[1] I suggest that the present is used deliberately, that the dramatic context requires not merely a commendation for something done in the past but a reassurance at that particular moment, which links the commendation of past achievement with spontaneous and warm encouragement in the present.

There is a great meeting between the two kings and their armies at the site where the battle had been fought and where the peace-treaty is now concluded. The greater king is determined to exercise 'the noblest revenge—forgiveness'. The defeated side have prepared lavish gifts of compensation—the poet gives an inventory—five hundred gold talents, silver, a hundred cloaks, a hundred breastplates and helmets, thirty caparisoned mules, thirty wild asses, thirty camels, a pair of leopards and a pair of lions; and suddenly comes an item that is not just listed but described with sheer delight:

> Also there were two bears, twin brothers,
> snow-white all over, with black legs and paws.
> They lifted a dish like a man, and walked erect.
> When mime-players touch the strings and their fingers play,
> the bears dance, keeping time with the music;
> sometimes they leap and turn somersaults,
> they sit and carry each other on their backs,
> they embrace and wrestle and throw each other down.
> When the music swells and people start to dance,
> the bears run up and join the women
> who sing with gentle voice, delightfully;
> putting their paws in the women's lovely hands,

---

[1] Brunhölzl, art. cit., p. 513.

they walk upright, step by step, and make little murmurs,
to the astonishment of those who pass nearby—
and they don't grow angry, even if they are teased.[1]

It is a beautiful vignette (observed or imagined?), but I think
it is also more. Why, in the long list of gifts establishing peace,
is this one singled out?[2] Is it not because, more than all the
others, this gift can be seen to symbolize the establishment of

[1] v. 84–98:

> Et pariles ursi, qui fratres sunt uterini,
> Omnino nivei, gambis pedibusque nigelli,
> Qui vas tollebant ut homo, bipedesque gerebant.
> Mimi quando fides digitis tangunt modulantes,
> Illi saltabant, neumas pedibus variabant;
> Interdum saliunt seseque superiaciebant,
> Alterutrum dorso se portabant residendo,
> Amplexando se luctando deiciunt se.
> Cum plebs altisonam fecit girando choream,
> Accurrunt et se mulieribus applicuere
> Que gracili voce cecinerunt deliciose,
> Inser]tisque suis harum manibus speciosis,
> Erecti calcant pedetemptim, murmure trinsant,
> Ut mirarentur ibi circum qui graderentur:
> Non irascantur, quodcunque mali paterentur.

87 MS. *digitis* corr. from *manibus*.   96 *murmure trinsant*: Winterfeld
and Langosch translate this as 'brummen', Zeydel and Ford (*The Ruodlieb*,
1965) as 'growl'. But the very rare *trissare, trinsare* is used elsewhere (if we
exclude the variants*trissitare*and *trinsire*—cf. Forcellini-Corradini, s.v., and Du
Cange, s.v.) only of the twittering of swallows. The poetic context stresses
the bears' gentleness with the women, and precludes a loud or frightening
noise. A 'growl' is a bear's predictable noise, and would have frightened, but
scarcely astonished, those who walked nearby: what astonishes them is the
little murmuring, twittering noises that these bears make. The people are also
astonished by something else (98): that the bears do not grow angry 'whatever
hurt they suffer' (i.e. from someone in the crowd teasing them). Yet the four
translators have taken this line to refer to the crowd, not the bears. Grammatically this is not impossible, but it gives an awkward syntax and a gro-
tesquely inappropriate sense: that people in festivity should not have minded
suffering injuries from mauling bears seems wholly unlikely.

[2] The only other gift described in any detail, immediately after the bears, is a
lynx, which gives the poet a pretext for his lighthearted 'do-it-yourself'instructions for making gems from the animal's urine. This seems to be little more
than an entertaining digression, which could have been delightfully mimed
by a skilful reciter.

the peace itself, the peace that restores the harmony of a dance and makes those—humans like animals—who are naturally fierce, gentle? These bears are civilized according to a human ideal; in the harmony of music they show their accord, they leap for joy, carry each other, and embrace; even their struggles are only a game. When the people are joyful and festive, they too can be chivalrous, considerate, and soft-spoken, and can even take an injury with good grace. Significantly, the greater king accepts the bears (as well as two little birds for his daughter), though he refuses all the other costly gifts.

As the armies return, Ruodlieb is met by a messenger: the lords of his native land have sent a letter inviting him to return —his chief enemies have meanwhile died or else been stigmatized as criminals. The letter is friendly though somewhat solemn in tone; but Ruodlieb's mother has added a postscript in which the diction changes, the tone becomes intimate and in a few lines reveals all the nature of the writer, the intensity of her love for Ruodlieb and the prudence and sensitivity that have made her resist possessiveness:

> 'Mi fili care, misere matris memorare,
> Quam, sicut nosti, discedens deseruisti
> Inconsolatam . . .
> Sed tamen utcumque decernebam tolerare,
> Secure miseram dum posses ducere vitam . . .'[1]

After elaborate ceremonies of leavetaking, Ruodlieb sets out for home, richly rewarded by his king, who has given him silver bowls filled with jewellery, disguised as loaves of bread (perhaps in deference to an ancient German custom of giving

---

[1] v. 251–8:

> 'My dear son, remember your poor mother,
> whom, as you know, you abandoned, comfortless,
> when you departed . . .
> Yet I resolved to bear it—I don't know how—
> as long as your ill-fated life was safe . . .'

251–3 almost illegible; I follow Seiler's text. 258 MS. *Secure miseram* corr. from *Secure vitam*.

'Abschiedsbrot' to a traveller).[1] Some of the jewels that are given to Ruodlieb are described so precisely and vividly that scholars have been tempted to identify them with particular surviving pieces, notably with some from the Mainz treasure, which were probably commissioned for the coronation of Empress Gisela in 1024. Yet to attempt such a historical identification seems to me mistaken: it brushes aside the differences, which are considerable, between the real jewels and the poet's images, and it ignores the fact that these are masterpieces of imagination in their own right. The eagle-brooches of Empress Gisela, for instance, are pieces that have been hammered on a gold plate, of which the background segments were then cut away;[2] the brooch that the poet describes, by contrast, is a solid moulded piece—twice he stresses that it was not hammered (v. 341, 343). It is several times as large as the larger of the real brooches, it is a sumptuous ornament for the breast, not for fastening a cloak, and its eagle is surmounted not by three circlets but by a crystal ball

> in which three little birds are seen to move
> as if alive, about to flutter and fly.

It seems likely, as Löwenthal suggested, that this effect could have been achieved in Byzantine jewellery of the time through the use of secret springs (one thinks at once of the gold singing-birds in the Emperor's palace at Byzantium mentioned by Liutprand a century earlier).[3] It is possible that the *Ruodlieb* poet had seen such a brooch, perhaps at the German imperial court. But whether he had seen it or imagined it, what is certain is that he is evoking a far more spectacular work of art than even Gisela's brooches, and that he is making it into an imaginative

---

[1] Thus Karl Hauck, 'Rituelle Speisegemeinschaft im 10. und 11. Jahrhundert', *Studium Generale*, iii (1950), 619.

[2] *V.* Otto von Falke, *Der Mainzer Goldschmuck der Kaiserin Gisela* (1913), pp. 12 ff. The larger eagle-brooch is 10 cm. high, 9·3 cm. broad, the smaller 7 cm. high, 7·3 cm. broad. They were used as 'Mantelschliessen' (p. 15).

[3] Löwenthal, art. cit., pp. 129–30; Liutprand, *Antap.* vi. 5.

reality. He achieves this, here as in his other descriptions of inanimate things, by never allowing description to become mere cataloguing, by always integrating it with a human perspective. It is the way in which he conveys the effect of the brooch on a human sensibility that in the last resort makes the object itself memorable. So too with the live birds and animals that appear in so many scenes of the poem: it is the part they play in revealing human beings more fully that raises their presence above the merely quaint and anecdotal.

Before the bowls of jewellery, the greater king had also given Ruodlieb another parting 'gift': a set of gnomic counsels, such as are common in ancient Germanic poetry, here a strange mixture of homely and cynical advice, of proverbial pagan and Christian lore, that the poet may at one time have intended as a framework to guide the rest of his narrative, but soon found somewhat intractable and then largely ignored.

The first three of the king's maxims, however, are exemplified in the Rufus episodes that follow (v. 585–VIII). In the *fabliau* of the redhead, the old farmer, and his young wife, the vivacity of dialogue and the dramatic quality of the visual elements (whether or not these can be directly related to a mime tradition) have been widely acknowledged since Reich and Winterfeld,[1] and I shall not dwell on them here. What has not been emphasized is the dramatic unity underlying the comic and the serious halves of this *fabliau*: it is not a ribald tale followed by an *exemplum* of Christian repentance, but a single story, in which sexual deception is seen in a new light when the three characters—cuckold, wife, and lover—are suddenly brought face to face with death, as the redhead by accident gives the old man a fatal blow, and he and the wife are arraigned for murder. But in the characters themselves there is continuity: the old man is ugly (watching the lovers through a crevice *ceu fur*—as if *he* were the thief), and also pathetic, especially in his

---

    Winterfeld, loc. cit. (p. 34, n. 1); the same book contains Hermann Reich's notes 'Der Mimus als Quelle des Rudlieb und der humoristischen Dichtung des Mittelalters', pp. 114–22.

irony ('Satque fatigastis hunc, nunc pausare sinatis!' VII. 129), which, while intended to be masterful, shows him in all his helplessness. He is just as pathetic and helpless in dying as he had been with his wife—'he has no strength but to groan, time and again, "I believe"'—as impotent in saying his last Creed as in his marriage. The woman, in her wonderfully dramatic speech in court, insisting on her guilt, still shows the same impulsive and unbridled qualities in her self-accusation and desire for punishment as she had shown in her sensuality (the provocative whisper 'Si decies possis, fac . . . vel quotiens vis') and in tormenting her husband by refusing to have supper served.[1] Rufus himself remains as cynical and false when confronted with death as he had been when planning the seduction. It is not till some of the greatest of Chaucer's tales, notably those of the Merchant and the Pardoner, that the common stock of diverting stories of deception is again exploited in so penetrating and serious a fashion.

The robustness of the Rufus story has perhaps tended to overshadow the subtlety of its counterpiece, the shepherd's tale of the young man with an old wife. It begins with a proverbial phrase, used as a kind of epigraph (VI. 32):

> Agna vetus cupide vas lingit, salis amore.[2]
> An old ewe licks a dish longingly, for love of salt.

This answers Ruodlieb's question, why should a rich widow want to marry a young man who has nothing? The poet treats the older woman's physical desire frankly, but not mockingly: the shepherd's words are a blunt, homely recognition of sex, not a sneer. This becomes clearer from the poet's complex use of the word *sal*, which recurs thematically throughout the story. The woman, while she had lived *dirissime* with her insanely stingy old husband, had been longing for some salt in her life—the word suggests not only physical stimulation but humour, taste, elegance, anything that gives life flavour or makes it worth living. The young man, who had come to

---

[1] VIII. 35 ff.; VII. 86, 123–4.

[2] Largely illegible; I follow Langosch and Zeydel's reading.

their farm from elsewhere, ragged and begging for bread, and had begun to ingratiate himself in the house by waiting on the husband at table, meaningfully puts the salt in front of him, 'that in case anything were not well enough seasoned he should season it' (VI. 52). Nothing in that house had a good savour—the kitchen, as the shepherd intimates, was the sort where cat and dog were likely to piss on the dirty dishes—but at last, with deference, the young man suggests that he could run the house better: he would cook food salted so that it had a delightful taste (VI. 70 ff.); the bread (by metonymy the life) of that household was dark and bitter (*fuscus, amarus*)—he would bake loaves made of refined flour, seasoned with celery-seeds, and sprinkled with salt (VI. 83–4). This epitomizes the rudiments of a courteous way of life that the servant-lad tries, by gently ironic hints, to teach his rich master (at least in appearance—it was hopeless to teach him an inner *virtù*): 'You won't lose much wealth by this. . . . When the servants are being fed, don't walk away, try to give an impression of good grace, then the whole house will be eager to do your bidding.' After the old farmer's death the widow finds fulfilment—both of her physical love and of a maternal feeling for the young man, and also in realizing that ideal of generosity, towards the poor and towards honoured guests, from which she had been prevented for so long. This ideal is inseparably courtly and Christian, and is presented by the poet in a remarkable passage that is inseparably realistic and symbolic: the realism does not preclude the symbolism, any more than the earthly beauty precludes the heavenly, but rather makes it possible:

> He cut the bread and served it to the poor,
> and the meat, which came to them in six dishes.
> When they had gone home, happy and satisfied,
> the host said (to Ruodlieb): 'If Christ sends me any guest,
> it is an Easter-festival for me and mine,
> as it is tonight, when you will make us happy.
> I feel the joy you bring is sent by God.'
> He passes his guest the shoulder and shin of meat,

and Ruodlieb, cutting it into many smaller slices,
shares it out ritually among the servants.
Then he himself is brought boiled and roast meat in plenty,
and, in a walnut goblet of finest shape,
an excellent spiced wine, or mead—
a goblet in which four rivers are carved in gold,
and, deep within it, the right hand of God.[1]

Previously Ruodlieb, to express the joy that reigned at Rex Maior's court, had said to the King 'With you I felt it was Easter every day' (v. 305). Now we see this same ideal of festivity reflected in the lowlier house of the widow and the young man: the dinner is not only an event of the most gracious joy and decorum for masters and servants alike, it has a sacramental quality ('Inasmuch as ye have done it unto one of the least of these my brethren, ye have done it unto me'), which does not discountenance the human joy but deepens it. A number of analogies to such a meal spring to mind: Baucis and Philemon's reception of the disguised divine guests in Ovid,[2] as well as episodes in the life of Christ. It is perhaps

---

[1] VII. 1–15:

> Panes ille secat et in illos distribuebat,
> Carnes de senis discis quod et accidit illis.
> His consolatis letis ad doma reversis,
> Hospes item dixit: 'Cum Christus quem mihi mittit,
> Tunc est pascha meum mihi velque meis cel[e]bra[ndum,
> Sicut in hac nocte, dum letificabimur [a te.
> Est mihi quod venit de te deus ut mihi mittat.'
> Cui mox de scapula partem mittit, quoque s[ura,
> In plures offas quam concidendo minutas
> Pro sacramentis pueros partitur in omnes.
> Post hec sat cocti domino, sat ponitur assi,
> Potus at in patera summi tuberis nucerina
> Precipui vini piperati, sive medonis—
> In qua bis bina sunt aurea flumina sculpta,
> Dextra dei fundo patere confixa stat imo . . .

[2] *Metam.* VIII. 631 ff. While there are no close verbal parallels, the wooden wine-goblet in *Ruodlieb* may well have been linked in the poet's mind with Ovid's *fabricataque fago pocula*. Again, an episode described by Bede (*Hist. Eccl.* III. 6) affords a certain parallel: at dinner on Easter day, King Oswald orders the royal dish to be taken to the poor outside his hall and divided among them.

significant in a Christian sense ('The last shall be first') that the
poor are given food first of all, then the servants, and finally
the aristocratic guest, who himself helps to serve the servants.[1]
The phrase *pro sacramentis* unites the pagan and Christian senses
of the term: the ceremonial serving of the food is both a solemn
human pledge and a token of divine grace.[2] The goblet
holds both a human festive drink and the rivers of
Paradise.

In the later part of his homeward journey Ruodlieb meets a
young nephew of his who is having an unhappy love-affair with
a courtesan. Ruodlieb, to distract him from this, persuades
his nephew to accompany him. Then, at one of the castles
nearer home where they stop, the nephew falls in love again,
this time happily. The poet's language conveys the very sensation of love at first sight: he shows us the girl in the castle,
as she comes down the stairs to dinner, as if through the eyes
of the enraptured young man:

> As she walked she shed light like a sparkling moon.
> How graceful she was! No one could tell
> whether she flew or swam, or in what way she moved.
> She was always like a bird, raised aloft in beauty.[3]

Description of feminine beauty in the rhetorical tradition
tended to be static set pieces. Often they were pedantically
methodical, describing hair, forehead, eyes, nose, lips, and the
rest in inexorable order.[4] The *Ruodlieb* poet knew such cata-

---

[1] So, too, Wolfram's Parzival shares out the food with his own hands at
Pelrapeire (*Parzival*, 201, 8 ff.).

[2] This 'rituelle Speisegemeinschaft', as Karl Hauck showed (art. cit., p. 47
n. 1), has both pagan Germanic and Christian roots.

[3] x. 55–8:

> Que dum procedit, ceu lucida luna reluxit,
> Quam sollers esset!—nemo discernere posset
> An volet an naret, an se quocumque moveret:
> Semper ut avis erat, vel se form]osa levabat.

In 58 I adopt Zeydel's attractive conjecture. For āvis, cf. Seiler's examples of
lengthening in the stem-syllable (ed. cit., p. 157).

[4] Cf. my *Medieval Latin and the Rise of European Love-Lyric* (2nd ed.,
Oxford, 1968), i. 193 ff., ii. 450–2.

logues—in fact he plays his own brilliant variation on one later, when Ruodlieb's mother has a frightening vision of what she will be like when she is really old:

> A woman, like the moon in her flower of youth,
> like a little old monkey in age:
> the brow furrowed that was smooth before,
> the eyes, once dove-like and now darkened . . .
> the tongue moving like an egg full of flour,
> the chin drooping in a crooked curve,
> the lips, once full of laughter and allurement,
> gaping like a cave to frighten people. . .[1]

This is his virtuoso piece, his *Belle Heaulmière*. But in the earlier passage, catching sight of the young girl, the poet attempts something even more remarkable: the first medieval 'portrait in motion' that I know,[2] a symbolic portrait, one in which all that is literal and external is ignored so that a few brush-strokes may suggest the essence.

The scenes in the castle are rich in observation and sensibility. It is an impoverished castle, in which the girl lives with her widowed mother; here no great banquets or festivities are organized, and yet gaieties do break out spontaneously:

> Meanwhile the knight, together with his nephew,
> go with the lady to where the harpers play.
> When he heard how badly the tunes were being played

---

[1] xv. 3 ff.:

> Femina, que lune par est in flore iuv[ente,
> Par vetule simie fit post etate senecte:
> Rugis sulcata frons, que fuit antea pl[ana,
> Ante columbini sibi stant oculi te[nebrosi . . .
> Et verbum profert plenum ceu pollinis o[vum;
> Utque recurvatum resupinum stat sibi m[entum,
> Os et risibile, quod plures allicit in se,
> Stat semper patulum, populum terrere vel [antrum . . .

[2] There are perhaps distant echoes of Vergil's description of the *bellatrix* Camilla (*Aen.* VII. 808 ff.), though the transformation into the new context is complete.

by even the best of the artists among them,
he said to the lady 'If there'd been another harp here . . . .'[1]

Ruodlieb does not want to assert himself, but very tactfully, in a half-finished sentence, he intervenes. The pluperfect subjunctive (*Ibi si plus harpa fuisset*) emphasizes his extreme tentativeness, the courtesy that makes him reluctant to interfere. So too his hostess, in answering, reveals herself: her words cannot help betraying the sexual longing that she still feels for her dead husband:

'There is a harp', she said, 'there will never be a finer one,
on which, while he lived, my lord used to play.
At the sound of it my mind grows sick with love.
No one has touched it since his life ended.
But you, if you wish, may play on it.'

The professional minstrels are put to shame by Ruodlieb's playing. Then the girl, with her mother's support, asks Ruodlieb for a dance-tune, so that she may dance with his nephew:

The young man has risen, and she comes to face him.
He dances like a falcon, she like a swallow:
on coming together, they passed each other swiftly,
he seeming to swoop, but she to float.

[1] XI. 25 ff.:
> Interea miles, consanguineus simul eius
> Cum domina vadunt harpatores ubi ludunt.
> Miles ut audivit male quam rithmum modulavit
> Inter eos summus illius artis alumnus,
> Ad dominam dixit 'Ibi si plus harpa fuisset—';
> 'Est' ait 'hic harpa, melior qua non erit ulla,
> In qua, dum vixit, meus heros simphoniavit,
> Cuius clangore mea mens languescit amore;
> Quam nemo tetigit is postquam vivere finit,
> In qua, si vultis, rithmos modulare valetis.' . . .
> Surrexit iuvenis, quo contra surgit herilis.
> Ille velut falcho se girat, et hec ut hirundo,
> Ast ubi conveniunt, citius se preteriebant;
> Is se movisse, sed cernitur illa natasse . . .
> Tunc signum dederant, ibi multi quod doluerunt,
> Deponendo manus, finitus sit quia rithmus.
> Insimul et resident et in alterutrum nimis ardent . . .

XI. 34 largely illegible; I follow Seiler.

I believe that these are similes for the movements of an elegant courtly dance, and that it is over-literal to interpret the passage as describing a folkloristic dance in which the dancers impersonate birds.[1] In the context, the images of falcon and swallow are rich in symbolic associations: not only do they convey his strength and her gracefulness, but they foreshadow the whole courtship, or chase, and the many alternations between uncertain conflict and momentary accord that the two will experience before they are at last blissfully married.

Then, dropping their hands, they gave a sign
that the dance was over, which many people regretted.
And they sat down together, inflamed with love for each
other . . .

The dancing had been in an open place, and a crowd had formed. All at once the young couple were as shy as any pair might be today who remain, absorbed, on a ballroom floor and suddenly notice that everyone else is watching them, not dancing. And this shared shyness before the outer world helps to bring them together: now they want to be alone, and her mother, with gentle complicity, 'makes it easy for them to talk as they wish' (xi. 61). But her daughter is quick-witted as well as romantic: humorously she proposes to catch the young man out:

The young mistress asks him to play with her at dice,
that the loser's ring be given to whoever wins three times.[2]

[1] First suggested by Winterfeld, op. cit., pp. 497–500, and again recently by Hauck, art. cit. (p. 47, n. 1), p. 617.

[2] xi. 62–72:
> Hunc dominella rogat quo secum tessere ludat,
> Annulus ut victi donetur ter superanti.
> Tunc is 'Qui ludum quem ludamus modo primum
> Acquirat,' dixit 'digitalis uterque suus sit.'
> H[ec] ea laudavit, ludens et eum superavit,
> Gratis perdente iuvene, gratis sibi dante;
> Que nimium leta se sic habuisse trop[hea
> Ludendo proprium cito perdebat digita[lem,
> Quem trahit a digito, iaciebat eique rotand[o;
> In cuius medio nodus fuerat cavus intro—
> Hunc nisi laxaret, digito non inposuisset.

He agrees, but changes the conditions slightly: one win is enough, not three. Why does he say this? Is it simply eagerness, because he senses that to win or lose a ring, even in jest, is to deepen his involvement with her? Or is it rather that, like Congreve's Mirabell, after Millamant has laid down her rules of marriage for him, he feels he owes it to himself as a man to make up some rule as well?—

> She agrees to this, she plays with him, and beats him—
> he is glad to lose to her, and glad to give.
> She, full of joy at having won such winnings,
> played him again, and quickly lost her ring.
> She pulled it from her finger and tossed it over.
> In a cavity in that ring a catch was fastened—
> he could not have worn it without loosening it.

Her little gesture is significant: she does not hand him the ring, she tosses it across the table, impetuous and teasing. Nor are the next two lines a superfluous detail: her ring does not fit him, yet if he wishes he can adjust it so that it fits—this is a perfect symbolic epitome of the wedding-scene that will follow later, at Ruodlieb's home.

The last moments in the castle are a wonderful dramatic juxtaposition. Ruodlieb asks the widowed châtelaine for news of his own mother, and her answer reveals so much: not only how unaware Ruodlieb had been in his ten years of exile of the extent of his mother's attachment to him, but also how different the two widows are—the one to whom her son has become everything, the other who still has physical longings for her husband, who classes herself along with her daughter as a young woman, over against Ruodlieb's mother, and who thus can face the prospect of soon losing her daughter without a sense of tragedy:

> 'Ah, what did you say? That you thought she had married again—
> when without you life itself had no sweetness for her?
> Weeping for you she has nearly lost her sight.

She was godmother to this daughter of mine,
and since then has thought of us both as her daughters . . .'[1]

Beside this is set the joyful ardour of the young lovers:

Now they do not conceal how deep they are in love:
if her mother let them, they would make love that night;
and she would even allow it, if reputation allowed—
the girl can hardly be convinced she must wait.

But the girl also knows about her fiancé's past, and she is determined not to be taken advantage of once they are married. So at the wedding-ceremony, wittily and bravely, she bargains for equality in marriage. There must be no double standard of morality. She makes this point in two ways: first, when asked if she will have him, by wryly poking fun at the clichés of *amour courtois*, of the lover who is his lady's subject and does nothing but serve and obey her, clichés that many a lover (even then, in the earlier eleventh century) must have used during courtship—and conveniently forgotten once the wedding was over:

'How could I refuse the slave I won by gambling,
whom I beat at dice and from whom I won a pledge
that, win or lose, he would marry none but me?
Let him serve me steadfastly—I wish it—night and day:
the better he does it, the more I'll cherish him!'

[1] XII. 7–11, 29–32:
'Ah, quid dixisti? quod eam nupsisse putasti—
Cui fuerat sine te non ipsum vivere dulce?
Nam flendo visum post te iam perdidit ipsum.
Illa meam natam de fonte levaverat istam,
Et pro natabus propriis nos post habet ambas . . .'
Nec iam celarunt se quin ardenter amarent:
Mater si sineret, vel in ipsa nocte coirent;
Illa tamen sineret, sibi si non dedecus esset—
Ut prestoletur tunc virgo vix superatur.
XII. 11 *habet* corr. out of another word, of which only *-rat* is legible. Again in XII. 7 Brunhölzl (art. cit., p. 513) censures the choice of tense (*quod eam nupsisse putasti* instead of *putas*). But it seems to me that the present would here sound stilted, that the full shock-effect of the half-begun question depends on the colloquial use of both *quod* and *putasti*.

Her fiancé begins to reply sententiously, protesting his loyalty, but he cannot finish the sentence without teasing her in turn:

> 'As the ring encircles the whole finger, all around,
> so do I bind you with firm and lasting faith,
> which you too must keep, or—off with your head!'[1]

Now she has got him to the very point she wanted: she makes his reply the basis of her second and serious argument, answering him 'shrewdly enough, and rightly' (*satis astute . . . et apte*)—this is one of the very rare moments in *Ruodlieb* where the poet comments in person, setting his own attitude beyond a doubt—

> 'It's only fair that both be judged by the same standard.
> Why should I be more faithful to you, tell me,
> than you to me? Tell me, could you justify it
> if Adam had a wench as well as Eve,
> though God made but one rib into a woman?' . . .
> The young man said: 'Beloved, it's as you say.
> If ever I deceive you, let me lose all I give you—
> and *you* shall have the right to cut off *my* head!'

---

[1] xiv. 52–6, 66–8:
> Post ait 'An servum nolim ludo superatum,
> Tessere quem vici sub talis fenore pacti—
> Seu vincat seu succumbat, soli mihi nubat?
> S]erviat obnixe, volo, quo mihi nocte dieque:
> Quod quanto melius facit, est tanto mihi karus!' . . .
> 'Anulus ut digitum circumcapit undique totum,
> Sic tibi stringo fidem firmam vel perpetualem;
> Hanc servare mihi debes—aut decapitari!'

As was pointed out by Herbert Meyer, to whose remarkable reconstruction of the ceremonial and legal aspects of this wedding I refer the reader, because the 'threat' of decapitation is made mutual in this scene, 'gerade daraus ergibt sich, daß dieses Tötungsrecht überhaupt nichts mit der eheherrlichen Stellung des Mannes zu tun haben kann' ('Die Eheschliessung im "Ruodlieb" und das Eheschwert', *Zeitschrift der Savigny Stiftung für Rechtsgeschichte*, lii (1932), 280). But it is worth adding that the 'aut decapitari' cannot therefore be serious in tone: it is a mock-serious reference to an older and more barbarous convention, as a bridegroom today might refer to being 'loved, honoured, *and obeyed*' by his wife.

Laughing gently, she turned to him again:
'This then shall be our marriage-bargain—no deceit.'
Her lover said 'Amen', and covered her with kisses.[1]

A marriage based on such mutual frankness and trust,
achieved by a girl who is like no one so much as some of
Shakespeare's young women—Beatrice, Rosalind, or Viola, the
innocent, spirited, humorous and passionate ones—it seems to
cut across all our preconceptions about medieval heroines and
medieval attitudes to marriage. It has the ring not of literary
models but of dramatic truth. And for this astonishing poet
this girl and her marriage are also unmistakably an ideal: once
more he intervenes in person, to say 'What anxiety (could
there be) for me as to how they will harmonize?'[2]—What
can disrupt a love-match in which the lovers have kept nothing
from each other?

One further detail about the wedding deserves mention: as
a wedding-present Ruodlieb gives his nephew a new coat. For,
one evening while they had stayed at the bride's castle, lodging
in the same room, he had noticed the young man's 'badly
washed underwear, and his coat of marten fur dark with age

---

[1] xiv. 69–87:

> Que satis astute iuveni respondit, et apte:
> 'Iudicium parile decet ut patiatur uterque.
> Cur servare fidem tibi debeo, dic, meliorem
> Quam mihi tu debes? Dic, si defendere possis,
> Si licuisset Ade mecham superaddat ut Eve,
> Unam cum costam faceret deus in mulierem?' . . .
> Cui dixit iuvenis: 'Fiat, dilecta, velut vis.
> Umquam si faciam, tibi que dedero bona perdam,
> Istius capitis abscidendique potens sis!'
> Que modicum ridens, ad eum seseque revertens,
> Inquit 'Ea lege modo iungamur, sine fraude.'
> Huius 'Amen' dixit procus, et sibi basia fixit.

[2] This, I believe, is the emphasis in the line *Qualiter inter se concordent, quid
mihi cure?* (xiv. 99). The older translations construe *quid mihi cure* as an expression of the poet's indifference ('why should I care?') to the fate of the lovers,
rather than his lack of anxiety for them. Zeydel (ed. cit., p. 152) even speaks
of the line as 'probably a jest', as did Burdach (op. cit., p. 157) before him. But
I would find this interpretation hard to reconcile with the poet's previous,
approving intervention only thirty lines earlier (xiv. 69).

and sweat' (x. 129–30): clearly the mistress with whom he had
lived had not looked after him so well in these respects! So the
new coat is, we might say, more than a wedding-present: it
is an augury of the young man's *Vita Nuova*.

The last completed part of the poem offers a Boccaccian
contrast to the courtship and marriage of Ruodlieb's nephew:
Ruodlieb himself becomes engaged—at his mother's insistence;
his fiancée deceives him; and he succeeds in getting his own
back. By his juxtaposition of the two episodes the poet neatly
pricks the bubble of some of the maxims of the Greater King:

> If you should wish to marry a well-born wife
> (in order to beget children that you will cherish),
> then choose a woman who is presentable—
> but certainly not unless your mother advises.
> When you have found her, show her every honour:
> treat her kindly—but still remain the master,
> lest she presume to have dispute with you.
> (There cannot be greater disgrace for men
> than to be overruled where they should rule!)
> And though she agree with you in everything,
> you must never tell her all you have in mind . . . (v. 484–94)

The engagement that flouts almost every point of this royal
wisdom ends in bliss, the one that conforms to it ends in a
fiasco. Rex Maior may be in most respects a splendid king—in
his practical advice he may also at times be a stuffed owl. The
many scholars who have seen Rex Maior as a wholly idealized
figure, the embodiment of all Christian wisdom and chivalric
virtue, should take note: this poet is too good a dramatist to
show even his finest characters quite uncritically. Ruodlieb,
likewise, is not meant to be perfect: he is basically sensitive and
courteous, but allied to his shrewdness is a streak of cruelty
(cf. vi. 7) and of vulgarity (cf. iv. 226); a touch of both is seen
again in the trick he plays on his fiancée (whose infidelity a
perfect Christian would no doubt have forgiven).[1] He sends

---

[1] Cf. for instance the way that Saint Gongolf pardons his wife's adultery
in Hrotsvitha's delightful *Gongolfus* (especially ll. 429–30).

a messenger to her with a sealed box containing (so the messenger imagines) an engagement-gift. The girl receives him, and again the characterization through dialogue is brilliant. She at once engages the envoy in a slightly risqué, cynical badinage: she asks him about the girls in his native land:

> 'Cuius sint fame? Formose sint, an honeste?'
> 'What might their reputation be? Are they beautiful, or virtuous?'[1]

He is both amused and a little embarrassed. He wards off her question with what seem extravagant protestations, the words at first coming out in an excited stammer:

> Subridens ille, 'Scio, quod, minime, rogitas me!
> Nil minus intromisi me, quam tale notare
> Quid facerent domine—morem talem sino scurr[e!'
> He replied with a smile, 'I say, what, I haven't any idea!
> It's never crossed my mind to be concerned
> with what the ladies might do—that sort of thing's for a playboy!'[2]

What is the reason for these disclaimers? Here again I believe we can see poetic design: three times in this scene the messenger is called Ruodlieb's *contribulis* (XVII. 43, 60, 79), a term that is used elsewhere in the poem only of his nephew. Is not this messenger, with whom we later see Ruodlieb to be on the most familiar terms of friendship, the nephew himself, and are not his asseverations given a special piquancy if we are meant to remember how newly won was his respectability? He asks the young woman for a message for her fiancé. Her

---

[1] XVII. 4. The line is best construed, in my view, as a direct question, governed by *rogitabat*.

[2] The first line, literally, 'I don't know at all what you are asking me'. Brunhölzl (art. cit., p. 514) does not envisage the possibility that the word-order might have a dramatic purpose: 'wer einfache Gedanken wie "Ich weiss nicht, wonach du mich fragst" mit "scio quod minime rogitas me" (XVII. 5) auszudrücken sucht, *nur um dem Versmaß genüge zu tun*, dem fehlt offensichtlich das Empfinden dafür, was die Sprache noch verträgt' (italics mine).

reply is famous: it is the earliest love-greeting that contains some German words:

> She said: 'Now send him from me, with loyal heart,
> as much of love as there is now of leaves,
> as many loving words as there are joys of birds,
> as many honours as the grass and flowers.'[1]

The hyperboles of affection—'as many kisses as the Libyan sands'—and the *adynata* of constancy—'sooner will the sea bear leaves and algae grow on mountain-tops'—are very ancient and widespread poetic formulae.[2] The poet in the Harley lyrics greeting his beloved 'ase fele syþe ant oft as dewes dropes beþ weete', or Burns vowing to love 'till a' the seas gang dry', show later variants in a long tradition, a tradition in which the *Ruodlieb* verses also have their place. It is as such a *Liebesgruss* that they are printed in numerous anthologies of German poetry. But in its context has not this greeting a dramatic, even more than a poetic, function? This lady is disloyal, her protestations are hollow. Is it not a superb dramatic stroke, then, that every image by which she swears her love and honourableness turns out to be an image of transience as well as of joy? 'As much of love as there is now of leaves'—but how much love when the leaves and birds, the grass and flowers, are gone in winter? I do not mean that the lady herself is thinking of this, only that even in protesting constancy she cannot help choosing just those images which reveal her inconstant nature. So, too, in Shakespeare: where Troilus conjures up images of truth—'As true as steel, as plantage to the moon, | As sun to day . . .', Cressida, in the very moment of swearing her truth, can call

[1] XVII. 11–14:
> Dixit 'Dic illi nunc de me, corde fideli,
> Tantundem *liebes* veniat quantum modo *loub[es*,
> Et volucrum *wunna* quot sint, tot dic sibi *m[inna*,
> Graminis et florum quantum sit, dic et honor[um.'

[2] Catullus VII; Ovid, *Metam.* XIV. 37 ff. Cf. H. Walther, 'Quot-Tot. Mittelalterliche Liebesgrüsse und Verwandtes', *ZfdA* lxv (1928), 257–88; F. R. Schröder, 'Adynata', in FS Felix Genzmer (cit., p. 33, n. 1), pp. 108 ff.; E. Dutoit, *Le Thème de l'adynaton dans la poésie antique* (Paris, 1936).

to mind nothing but images of falsehood—'as false | As air, as
water, wind, or sandy earth. . . .'¹

The lady breaks the seal, glances into the box, and finds, not
an engagement-gift, but a pair of her own garters, that she had
lost during one of her rendezvous with the *clerc* who was her
lover. She calls back the messenger and changes her greeting:
'If he were the last man left on earth, and he gave me the whole
world as my dowry, I would not marry him!'

These illustrations and analyses of some aspects of the *Ruod-*
lieb poet's art, while they cannot hope to convey the richness of
the work, may at least permit one or two inferences of a more
general kind. We can see from them something of the amazing
range of what this poet's language could convey. Out of the
Latin that was the spoken *lingua franca* of a sophisticated set of
people—of the lawyers and doctors, diplomats and civil servants, scholars and chaplains attached to the imperial court,
and of the higher nobility, in so far as they too shared the Latin
clerical education—this poet created a poetic diction of flexible,
mercurial power. To adapt such a spoken language, which is
naturally unclassical and almost devoid of ancient echoes, to
poetic purposes, demanded an individuality of technique as
startling in its own way as the individuality of this poet's vision
of the *comédie humaine*. Thus it is not legitimate to conclude
from the rareness of his reminiscences from Roman poetry that
this poet was not well read: on the contrary, if we consider his
Mors . . . Cur mihi sera venis? (xv. 58–9) as a direct citation of
Propertius (II. 13, 50)—it seems unlikely to be mere coincidence
—his reading must have been exceptional.² Brunhölzl's suggestion that this poet would have liked to imitate classical
diction but could not³ has, quite simply, no foundation in the

¹ *Troilus and Cressida*, Act III, scene 2.
² Of Propertius' poetry there survives only one manuscript of *c.* 1200, and
two of *c.* 1300. The only other echoes of Propertius in medieval poetry that
I know are in *Iam dulcis amica venito* (cf. op. cit., p. 52, n. 4, i. 271 n.), in the
Archpoet's *Confessio* (st. 16), and in Albert of Stade's *Troilus* (cf. H. Krefeld
and H. Watenphul, *Die Gedichte des Archipoeta* (1958), p. 145).
³ Art. cit., p. 512: 'der Autor des Ruodlieb hat von lateinischer Dichtung

text. To speak as he does of this poet's 'unlateinische Ausdrucks-weise'[1] is to set up arbitrarily a particular norm of Latin as if this were valid for every age and every artistic purpose. To speak of *Ruodlieb*'s Latin as 'so wenig lebendig'[2] is to have failed to enter its own vivacity and mode of life. Brunhölzl concludes his comments on the 'weaknesses' (read 'unclassical aspects') of this poet's language and technique:

> Die Schwächen sind so häufig, daß sie den Charakter des ganzen Werkes mitbestimmen; sie betreffen so wesentliche Dinge der literarischen Kunst, daß man sich fragen muß, was denn vom literarischen Kunstwerk außer dem Versuch, ein solches zu schaffen, überhaupt vorhanden sei. Das Genie allein tut's nicht, die reiche Fülle kraftvoll geschauter und erlebter Bilder und Vorstellungen ohne die bändigende Zucht der Form ergibt kein Kunstwerk. . . .[3]

But form at its best is something intrinsic, it is controlled and guided by the poet's own conception of his intentions, not by a set of extrinsic rules. If in the passages here discussed I have to some extent deduced the poet's artistic aims correctly, to that extent it will be clear that his use of language did not thwart those aims but realized them; in so far as we can still perceive those aims in their subtlety and originality, surely this poet's powers of expression have *not* let him down.

If the *Ruodlieb* poet's imaginative approach to his story-matter and his unusual powers of expression are admitted, has this not certain implications for the historical and philological study of the poem? Should we still be surprised if no historical or literary sources and analogues are found which seem to account fully for any aspect of *Ruodlieb*, or even which seem wholly relevant to it? Is it perhaps naïve to expect an artist with such a cast of mind to have had thematic or stylistic 'models' in the more obvious ways that the authors, for instance, of *Waltharius* or *Ecbasis Captivi* had? *Ruodlieb*, it seems to me, shows so

über Vergil hinaus nicht viel und dies Wenige nicht gut genug gekannt, um *bei Bedarf* ein formales Muster gegenwärtig zu haben' (italics mine).

---

[1] Art. cit., p. 513.   [2] Ibid.   [3] Art. cit., p. 521.

pointed and rich a use of so much unusual perceptual detail, that the poet could not have learnt this from any of the works that have hitherto been suggested as his possible models or sources. As a model for narrative art of this particular quality little less than the *Odyssey* itself would come in question—and this of course is a hypothesis one cannot entertain!

III

SEMIRAMIS · THE RECREATION OF MYTH

          Fama puellaris tauri corrumpitur extis—
          Surdescant tenere torquentes fila puelle
          Ne pudor ad frontes possit transire nitentes!
          Est per concubitus iniuria facta deabus:
          In terris meretrix numquam crudelius arsit
          Quam lupa Semiramis, moechum que traxit ab herbis—
          Temporibus Nini bos est inventus adulter.
          Si regina bovem durum quesivit in ervo,
          Cur non regalem portavit vacca coronam?
          Fiat vacca Nini, fiat regina *iu*venci.   10
          Prodiit a Babilon talis confusio stupri.
          In terris quod plus potuit sordescere scortum?
          Purpureas vestes faciunt palearia viles,
          Semiramis virides discit mugire per herbas,
          In tenera luna taurinis saltibus usa.
          Femina que Babilon cepit se sub bove stravit!
          In multis urbem contrivit, sola pudorem.
          Cur non auxit ei genius palearia largus?
          Quadrupes est moechus Nino pereunte repertus.
A⟨UGUR⟩ Augur odoriferus, dictus per fata Tolumpnus,[1]   20
          Invoco palloris numen de limine mortis
          Ut nunc terribilis reddatur imago sororis.
          Semiramis, translata redi de vallibus Orci!
S⟨EMIRAMIS⟩ Audio. Non possum, quia sum religata deorsum.
        A Omnia sum passus quibus aspera mors celebratur.
          Dum voco te, lugenda soror, sine mente volutor.
        S Cur te consumis, frater, sub peste dolendi?
          Antistes fati solvat sua vota Plutoni.

---

10 uiuenti MS.   14 dicit MS.   18 Here, as in 13, the pl. of *palearium*
would also be possible, though less likely   22 torribilis MS. (corr. *horribilis*?)
[1] Unconventional spellings are retained from the manuscript.

A Sentio monstra meis manibus sine lumine solis—
  Crescit in orbe seges Lerne ratione sororum. 30
S Hora resurgendi nondum datur ore Plutonis.
A Archadie non sum quem Luna fefellit aruspex
  Qui numquam solis potuit fuscare sororem.
S Nox est ista precum: non est vigilando silendum.
A Sint exaudibiles centum mihi milia Manes,
  Ut post cras possim vultum lustrare sororis!
S Orfeus Euridicem quesivit carmine dulcem.
A Non diffido. Dii, memores estote Molosi,
  Solis in abscessu cito turpiter excerebrati:
  Sicut vos decuit, latrantis flamma refulsit. 40
  Si flox, Vulcanus, canis hic absorbuit artus,
  Qui sunt inferius, qui mittunt somnia vana,
  Omnes consurgant! Umbram sine carne reducant.
  Non precor ossa—Ceres Nature dente voravit—
  Sed voco vos orare gravem, nigra castra, Plutonem,
  Si color ille niger diffunditur undique vester,
  Exorare tetrum, quia noscitis ignibus ipsum!
  Impetrat exorans redeuntem corporis umbram.
  Non peto Semiramis—putruerunt—menbra sororis.
  Sol est sub terra, lune pallescit amictus, 50
  Auster propitiam non sufflat Apollinis aram,
  Noctis in adventu flatum Septentrio misit.
  Obsecro, Semiramis que sunt reticenda loquatur.
  Semotis somnis, pollex est sepius unctus,
  Nunc scio vervenam vobis calcare repertam.
  Te peto per tenebras, bovis es quae passa ruinas!
  Ut credas verbis, dentes agitabo draconis,
  More Phitonisse tibi murmura spargo Sibille.
S Humanum non est perfecte posse cavere:
  Materiam luteam cur arguis ante Dianam? 60
A Si cum noctividis tantum vigilare mererer,
  Que scrutantur opes saciando ventre palustres,
  Omine felici cordi merore carerem.
S Me procedentem frustra sub nube videbis:

45 voto MS.   47 tetrem, os sitis MS.   52 fletum MS.   54 Sinotis
est somnus (somniis?) MS.   55 Nescio, calcabo MS. *Calcabŏ* might be
supported by 57 *agitabŏ*, 75 *Apparebŏ*   59 Inserted at foot of fol. 30ᵛ

Dum tociens quereris, leti mage supprimor undis.
A Pernoctant clare volucres in honore Minerve;
  Pervigil in tenebris meditor mala scandala stirpis.
S Quid resides tumulis, lacrimis suffusus amaris?
  Pre textu fati minor est effusio voti:
  Pallida sum damnabilibus revocanda Molosis.   70
A Iam non sum frater: soror est (cur vivo?) cadaver.
  Artor ab insidiis, terrorem colligo bustis.
  Quot combustorum resident hic nescio Manes.
S Tres aras itera. Post cras laxabor ab urna:
  Apparebo tuis oculis quasi libera mortis.
A Tres simul igne canes argumentosius uram,
  Ut bis sex horis rumpantur vincula mortis,
  Quo despecti⟨bi⟩lem possim relevare sororem.
S A canibus galli non sint sub cede remoti,
  Qui furvis plumis imitentur tempora noctis.   80
  Non sit in orgiis alicuius guttula mellis.
A Cur oculi bini sint tota nocte patentes?
  Sunt aures patule, sed per responsa beate,
  Nam consolatur solis ex auribus augur.
S Si pilus ex asina fuerit delatus ab aura
  Ut cadat in cineres inimica sorte caninos,
  Perdet vim totam sciomantia vivificandi.
A Obsecro te, Pallas, asinas interfice cunctas,
  Ne cadat in nostris hodie confusio votis.
  Abiectis asinis maneat sine pestibus orbis!   90
S Grana salis remove—non sit sapor ullus in ore.
  Insulsus prono cibus est gratissimus Orco.
  In precibus nihil ambiguum proferre memento.
A Me facit insanum pecoris commixtio totum—
  Quae revocent dulcem mihi desunt cuncta soporem.
  Dum dormit dapifer, mihi prestet Apollo papaver.
S Quid prodest curvare genu sub Apollinis ara?
  An ego Poeonias modo sum revocanda per herbas
  Que pre cornuto sponsale cubile reliqui?
A A falso verum sapiens discernit apertum: 100
  Augurium pulsat nostrum secreta deorum.

66 Pernotant clere MS.   78 possint MS.   82 sunt MS.
93 proferro MS.   99 Quem precor nuto MS.

Numquam precincxit lumbos cornutus adulter.
S Planctus fit vocum, ploratus fit lacrimarum;
   Inter utrumque moves tectos fuligine Manes,
   Instrumenta pudicicie dum plangis abesse.
A Ei mihi, captivam predixerat uppupa famam:
   Cum fabricaretur cornutus de bove moechus,
   Nongentis stadiis fueram sub sole remotus!
S Festina claras simul obscurare lucernas—
   Ebullit cursu furiosi pectoris ignis.   110
   Emendabo meam tibi cum surrexero famam.
A Voces cornicis resonabant stupra sororis.
   Corvinis rostris quis contulit acta sororis?
   Iam mare transivit mala corruptela iuvenci.
S Auguris expressit conceptio suspiciosa
   Quicquid inauditum superaddunt fata malorum.
   Quid furis, Echate, fraterno tristis ab ore?
A Incipit obscuri nunc obse*quu*tio voti.
   Si detestabilis mea sit conquestio vobis,
   Nec canis excidium, nec gallus sentiet ictum.   120
   Surge, soror, fratri! Moritur iam preco diei:
   Manibus in spaciis non precon*ando* diurnis,
   Ambiguum ceco munus non cedimus Orco—
   Que damus inferno nunquam fient in aperto.
   Restibus astricti non possint rudere stulti.
   Extinguam lumen, pandat mihi threnara carmen,
   Lucis splendores nos excecavimus omnes.
   O regina, vale, ceco mandamus ab igne.
   Quid facis in tumulo? Nihil infortunius antro,
   Valde molestatur qui tali sede tenetur.   130
   Suscipe paulatim, Mamuhel, mea murmura sensim:
   Ut tibi complaceam, vite contraria dicam.
   Inventor vani, Pluto, phantasmatis, audi:
   Dum sex degluttis, speciem dimitte sororis!
   Cur me falsilocus non consolaris Apollo?
A⟨POLLO⟩ In Libia fueram. Tibi mox prestabo figuram.

104 fuligigine MS.   110 Cursu ebullit MS.   118 obseruatio, *r* expunged
MS.   122 preconabo MS.   124 nŏnquam MS.   132 contrariam,
m expunged MS.   133 Erased after *Pluto*: rae   136 In MS. this A is
written differently from the rest, presumably to indicate Apollo, not Augur,

Floxus, ab Egipto miseram revocare memento!
⟨A⟩ Excessi de mente mea per federa vestra.
Esto mee vocis, Diana, capabilis ut scis,
Si te glorificent qui non sunt verba loquuti,   140
Cui plaudunt pueri mammarum lacte refecti!
Signum nocturnis dedit incantatio monstris.
O mediatores, dum quero sororis amores,
Parturit horribilem presentia vestra stuporem.
Est rudis in *n*ostris insania nata cerebris.
Semiramis iamiam videam sollempniter umbram:
Fallen*t*i fu*n*us celebrabitur octo diebus.
Postulo, prestolor, quinis in sensibus uror.
Possibile*m* peto rem—per vos iam cerno sororem!
Pugna fuit tenebris de libertate sororis—   150
Nunc adamantinum, Beetmohth, depone furorem!
Audio dispersos noctis properare colonos,
Maxima spirituum facit adventacio motum.
Iam videt umbrifere fratrem plasmatio forme!
Quondam regalis vultus fuit iste sororis—
Hec est illustris species notissima matris.
Da, regina, manum. Soror, os mihi porrige flendum.
S Ne tangas artus! Non sum palpabile corpus.
A Sunt obscura nimis propera spectacula noctis.
Investigo tuas sedes ubi rapta quiescas—   160
Sed ne respicias post posteriora relictas:
Euridices oculos frustra post dorsa retorsit.
S Quid conturbaris, rabie potatus Orestis,
Plenus adulterio si lusit Iuppiter orto?
Fermentate, malis que pars tibi cum furiosis?
Si deus illusor hinnivit sicut amator
In bovis effigie, pius est sub fronde repertus.
Qui de stellifero solio sua fulgura mittit
Iupiter appetiit, sed me de*v*otio traxit.
Per celi tonitrum presumptio pulchra deorum   170
Arrisit leviter, sed pressit amore potenter.

as speaker. This line ends with a question-mark (possibly the scribe's faulty
repetition of his correctly placed one at the end of 135).   138 A *om.* MS.
145 monstris, *n* expunged MS.   147 Fallendi fumus MS.   149 Possibile MS.   169 denotio MS.

Si deus illusit, non est da⟨m⟩pnatio facti—
Divino scortatori proscriptio non est;
Inculpabiliter talis mihi risit adulter!
Cum Iove, si vellet, me quis peccare negaret?
Quis prohibente deo castus remeavit ab orto?
Me stuprante pio, iuste peccavimus ambo—
Lascivis penitus lex est ablata deabus.
Tollat merorem mea testificatio tristem;
Amplexu duram retrahor Plutonis ad urnam.   180
Non est, crede, iugis concessus sermo sepultis.

180 Amplexū MS.

A woman's honour was stained by the loins of a bull—let tender
girls at their spinning stop their ears, lest shame should show itself
on their candid brows! By these couplings goddesses were wronged.
Never did any courtesan on earth burn more fiercely than wanton
Semiramis, taking her paramour from the fields: it was a bull was
found to be adulterer in Ninus' reign. If a queen sought out a rude bull
among the vetch, why did a heifer not wear the royal crown?
Let a heifer be Ninus' bride, if the queen becomes a bull's! Such
lewd disorder spread from Babylon. What prostitute in the whole
world could have been more debased? His dewlaps make her purple
robes seem worthless, in the green grass Semiramis learns to low,
under a young moon delights in the bull's mounting. The woman
who took Babylon has submitted to the bull. One of many, she
crushed the city, alone she has crushed her modesty. Why did not
an accommodating god grant her a dewlap too? To Ninus' undoing,
a beast was found his rival.

AUGUR. I, the incense-bearing augur, called Tolumnius by the
Fates, invoke the god of pale Fear from the threshold of death, that
the dread image of my sister may be brought back. Semiramis, come
over, return from the valleys of Orcus!

SEMIRAMIS. I hear—I cannot come. I am bound down.

A. I have gone through all the rites by which harsh death is
honoured. While I call you, my poor sister, my mind reels sense-
lessly.

S. Why waste yourself, brother, in a plague of grieving? Let the
high-priest of Fate address his prayers to Pluto.

A. Without the sun's light I perceive monsters with my hands:

Lerna's brood springs up on the earth, through the (fateful) sisters' decree.

S. The hour of my rising is not yet granted by Pluto's lips.

A. I am not like the Arcadian augur whom the moon deceived, who could never darken the sister of the sun.

S. This is a night of prayer—one must not be silent keeping the vigil.

A. May a hundred thousand shades listen to me, that after to-morrow I may behold my sister's face.

S. Orpheus sought sweet Eurydice by song.

A. I'll not despair. You gods, remember the Molossian hound, its brains swiftly dashed out in unsightly death when the sun was down: the fire of the (sacrificed) dog blazed forth, as was fitting for you. If Vulcan the flame has devoured the hound's limbs, let all who are below, who send forth idle dreams, arise, let them bring back a bodiless shade! I do not ask for the bones—goddess Earth has devoured these with Nature's tooth—but I call upon you to beseech grave Pluto, you dark dwellings, if your blackness is diffused on every side, to implore the dread one, for amid the fires you know him: he who implores can obtain the return of a body's shade. I do not seek the limbs of my sister Semiramis—they have decayed. The sun is below the earth, the moon's cloak grows pale. No south wind blows upon Apollo's gracious altar; as the night comes, the north wind has sent forth his blast. I beseech that Semiramis may tell her secrets. Sleep has been banished, repeatedly my thumb has been anointed; now I can tread for you the vervain I have found. I seek you through the darkness, you who have undergone the bull's assaults. That you may believe my words, I'll shake the dragon's teeth—like a sorceress I'll scatter Sibylline murmurs for you.

S. Human beings cannot take the perfect care they should. Why do you speak vile matter in Diana's presence?

A. If it were my right to keep watch with the night-owls that scan the rich marshlands to feed their bellies, with joyous omen my heart would be void of grief.

S. Your sight of me, as I come forth, will be vain and clouded. While you complain so much, I am submerged more deeply in death's waves.

A. The famed birds stay awake at night in honour of Minerva; I, ever vigilant in the dark, ponder my family's infamous transgressions.

S. Why do you stay among the tombs, suffused with bitter tears?

Before the fabric of Fate, the outpouring of prayer is too weak. Pallid, I must be summoned back through the hounds to be sacrificed.

A. I am a brother no more—my sister a corpse, why do I live? I am hemmed in by snares, I gain only terror from the tombs. I do not know how many shades of the burnt dwell here.

S. Set up three altars once more. After tomorrow I shall be released from the urn; I shall appear before your eyes as if free from death.

A. I shall now, to more effect, burn three dogs together in the fire, so that for twelve hours the chains of death may be broken, that I may bring my abject sister back. .

S. Let cocks not be far from the dogs, at the slaughter, imitating the hours of the night with their dark plumage. In the ritual feast let there be no single drop of honey.

A. Why should my two eyes be open the whole night? My ears are open, but blessed by the replies they hear: an augur is solaced only by what he hears.

S. If an ass's hair should be carried by the wind, and, by an unlucky chance, fall amid the dogs' ashes, the magic of resurrecting will lose all its strength.

A. I beseech you, Pallas, destroy all asses, lest confusion fall upon our offerings today. May the earth remain without further plagues when asses are banished!

S. Remove any grains of salt—let there be no savour in your mouth. Unsalted food is most pleasing to Orcus below. Remember to utter no ambiguous words in your prayers.

A. The mixing of the animals makes me wholly distraught—I lack all that could restore sweet sleep to me. While the attendant sleeps, may Apollo grant me the poppy.

S. What use to bend your knee before Apollo's altar? Or am I now to be brought back through Paeonian herbs, I who left my bridal chamber because of the horned one?

A. A wise man can tell overt truth from falsehood; my augury knocks at the door of the gods' secrets: never has the horned adulterer girded his loins.

S. Sounds of lamentation are uttered, tears are being wept; between complaint and tears you are moving the shades covered by darkness—and all the while you weep that no signs of shame are here.

A. Ah me, the hoopoe had foretold that your good name would be enslaved: when out of a bull a horned adulterer was made, I was taken down nine hundred stades below the sunlight!

S. Hasten at once to darken the bright torches—the fire is seething as swiftly as your demented heart. I shall better my fame in your eyes when I arise.

A. The raven's cries echoed my sister's violation. Who brought my sister's deeds to ravens' beaks? Already word of the bull's foul defilement has crossed the ocean.

S. The augur's suspicious imagination has wrung from him all the unheard-of ills that the Fates can lavish. Why do you rage, Hecate, distressed at my brother's words?

A. Now the duty of my dark sacrifice begins. If my lament is hateful to you (shades), the dog will not feel death, the cock not feel the blow. Rise, sister, meet your brother! Now the day's herald is dying: we do not invoke the shades in the hours of day, we do not offer blind Orcus an ambiguous gift; what we give to hell shall never see the day's light. May the foolish creatures (the dogs and cocks), muzzled in ropes, not succeed in crying out! I shall put out the light—let the dirge-singer give me her song, we have darkened all the bright gleams of the light. O queen, by this sightless fire I give you greeting. What do you do in a tomb? Nothing is more wretched than that cavern, one who is confined in such a dwelling is deeply wronged. Receive my prayers, Mamuhel, one by one: to please you I shall utter words that run contrary to life. Hear me, Pluto, author of vain phantasms! As you engulf six (other lives), release my sister's shade! Why do you not comfort me, false-tongued Apollo?

APOLLO. I had been in Libya—I shall soon grant you her shape. Floxus, remember to summon the hapless woman out of Egypt!

AUGUR. I was beside myself, because of your promise. Be receptive of my voice, Diana, as you know how to be, if those who cannot speak glorify you, who are proclaimed even by suckling infants! My incantation has given a signal to the monsters of the night. Oh mediators, while I seek to know of my sister's loves, your presence brings about horrified numbness in me: a harsh dementia has been born in my brain. Let me now solemnly behold Semiramis' shade: the adulteress's exequies shall have eight days' celebration. I beseech, I wait, I burn in my five senses. The thing I ask is possible—through you I now see my sister! There was conflict in the darkness about freeing her: now, Behemoth, cast off your adamant rage! I hear the scattered habitants of the night hastening, a stir is caused by the huge advance of spirits. Now the creation of shadowy form can see her brother! Once this was my royal sister's face—it is she, most renowned likeness of an illustrious mother. Queen, give me your hand. Sister, bring near your tragic lips.

S. Do not touch my limbs! I am not a palpable body.

A. The fleeting visions of the night are all too dark. I am scanning your dwelling, where, snatched from the world, you must rest. But do not look back at what you have left behind (on earth)—Eurydice cast her eyes back once more, but in vain.

S. Why are you deranged, drunk with Orestes' madness, because Jupiter, filled with adulterous desire, played in my garden? Rank-witted man, how have you fallen into this mad disease? If the god in love, dissembling, lowed in a bull's shape, in the arbour I found him full of grace. Jupiter, who sends his lightnings from his starry throne, was filled with desire—but it was devotion drew me to him. Across heaven's thunder the beautiful divine audacity smiled at me gently, yet pressed hard upon me with love. If the god played, this does not condemn his deed—there is no judgement against a divine seducer, such an adulterer smiled at me without blame. Who, even if he wished, could deny me the right to sin with Jove? Who has come back chaste from the garden, if the god willed otherwise? When the blessed one ravished me, we both sinned guiltlessly. When goddesses yield to voluptuousness, law is wholly overcome. Let my testimony remove your dire grief—in Pluto's embrace I am being drawn back to my harsh urn. Believe me, the dead are not granted speech for ever.

The poem printed and translated above is preserved uniquely in a northern French manuscript of the late eleventh century.[1] The text, which has not previously been edited, is uncertain in many places; philologically, much remains to be done. Yet enough of the text is clear for us to perceive the outlines of a poem remarkable in its conception, a poem so unlike any other which we know from the eleventh century that it challenges interpretation and discussion. In the explorations that follow,

---

[1] Paris, B.N. lat. 8121A, fols. 30^r–32^v.

which must of necessity be incomplete and often speculative, I shall concentrate on problems of four kinds: (i) literary context; (ii) meaning and dramatic structure; (iii) the possible sources; (iv) the poet's use of myth and the nature of his individuality. The last of these is the most tentative, but also, in terms of the present discussion, the most important.

I

To what extent do the contents of the codex itself indicate a literary context for the poem *Semiramis*? The manuscript, in its present state, begins with two pieces in leonine couplets by Warner of Rouen. The longer (498 verses) is a fantastic invective against an Irish *clerc*, Moriuht, who had come to Rouen;[1] the shorter (162 verses) is a 'flyting', a contention in dialogue between Warner and a runaway monk from the Mont Saint-Michel.[2] Both are dedicated to the Archbishop of Rouen Robert I (989–1037), great-uncle of William the Conqueror. There follows the pseudo-Plautine comedy *Querolus* (probably composed at the beginning of the fifth century);[3] then an eleventh-century misogynistic satire on Jezabel,[4] in leonine hexameters (*c.* 135 verses), after which, with the rubric 'Explicit liber primus. Incipit secundus', follows *Semiramis*.[5] To these five literary works must be added a sixth, now lost: a fourteenth-century hand, indicating the contents of the manuscripts on its final leaf (fol. 34ᵛ), shows that it once also contained the 'Vita et actus Tirii Apolonii'.[6]

---

[1] MS. fols. 2ʳ–9ʳ; ed. H. Omont, *Annuaire-Bulletin de la Société de l'Histoire de France* (1894), pp. 197–210.

[2] MS. fols. 9ʳ–11ᵛ; ed. L. Musset, 'Le Satiriste Garnier de Rouen et son milieu', *Revue du Moyen Age Latin*, x (1954), 237–66. Warner's poems can be dated between 996 and 1026 (ibid., pp. 243–5).

[3] MS. fols. 11ᵛ–27ʳ; most recently ed. W. Emrich, (Berlin, 1965).

[4] MS. fols. 28ʳ–30ʳ; see discussion below.

[5] I have supplied this title (and the titles *Jezabel* and *Moriuht*) for convenience.

[6] Presumably, that is, the fifth- or sixth-century Latin *Historia Apollonii* (ed. A. Riese, Teubner 2nd ed., 1893). Preceding this, according to the fourteenth-century scribe, was a kind of encyclopaedic gazetteer: 'Provinciale

It is possible that these works were assembled in one collection because of certain affinities of form, tone, or theme. It is
just such a principle of compilation that Kenneth Sisam was
able to suggest for the renowned *Beowulf* manuscript (copied
c. 1000), showing that 'the Beowulf codex, even allowing for
Judith, is a collection in verse and prose of marvellous stories'.[1]
Here we might tentatively make the following observations.
The Apollonius story contains motifs akin to those in *Semiramis*:
sexual perversion in the incest-story of the opening (1–4); the
restoring of Arcestrate, thought to be dead, by means that are
tantamount to a 'sciomantia vivificandi' (26–7); at the end of
the story (50), Apollonius pretends to summon his daughter
Tharsia up from the underworld, and she, sustaining the
fiction, says to her evil foster-mother 'saluto te ego ab inferis
revocata'.[2] Like *Semiramis*, *Apollonius* is set in a fabulous ancient
world. Warner's poem against Moriuht contains, as we shall
see, the themes both of sexual perversion and of magic. His
'flyting' contains neither, but is linked with the pieces that
follow by its dialogue form and satirical intent. Magic again
provides a central motif in the *Querolus*: the parasite Man-
drogerus pretends to be a magus and to exorcize ill fortune
from Querolus' house by a magic rite in the *sacrarium*. (This
rite, however, is not itself presented in the play.) Sexual de-
pravity is the theme of the poem *Jezabel*, which once more is
in dialogue form. But this poem also raises a problem that goes
beyond questions of thematic or formal affinities: the rubric

provinciarum, civitatum, montium, fluminum.' The last page but one of the
extant manuscript contains rules for making organ-pipes: 'Primam fistulam
quam longam latamve libuerit facies. Eius latitudinis fiant omnes. . . .' (This
is a work distinct from, and considerably shorter than, the one listed in
Thorndike–Kibre (1963), col. 1097: 'Primam fistulam quam longam et latam
libuerit facies. Partire longitudinem . . .', from B.N. lat. 7377C, s. XI/XII
fols. 44^r–47^r.) These two didactic prose pieces at the beginning and end of
the manuscript are of course unrelated to the thematic grouping of imaginative
writing that I suggest for the rest of the codex.

[1] *Studies in the History of Old English Literature* (1953), pp. 65 ff.

[2] This detail occurs only in the β version (according to Riese's classification
of the manuscripts), ed. cit., p. 112.

I have cited gives the impression that the poem *Semiramis* is a continuation of *Jezabel*. I am convinced that this is a copyist's error and cannot be correct. I believe not only that these are two wholly distinct poems, but that they are most unlikely to be by the same author. A brief analysis will make my reasons for this clear.

After seven extremely problematic lines, of which only one may be part of the poem itself,[1] the piece consists entirely of an 'interview' of Jezabel, conducted in a series of half-line exchanges:

> Unde venis, Iezabel? — De fedo carcere Babel.
> Unde redis, mulier? — De curvo fornice Thofe*th*.
> Dat sponsus tibi mel? — Mihi contemptibilis est fex.   10
> Unde peruncta putes? — De forti smigma*te* Iahel.
> Quid tibi cum Nazareth? — Multum, quia *vis* mea floret.
> Unde nates tumuere tue? — De sumine porce.
> Continuat risus que vis? — Meretricius usus.

9 thofech MS. (cf. Jer. vii. 31–2, xix. 6 ff.)   11 smigmata MS. Is the 'medicine' death? (cf. Jud. iv. 18 ff., v. 24 ff.)   12 ros mea MS. The reply must turn on the common interpretation of the name 'Nazareth' as 'florida'.

1   Nomen Abie sonat Iaezabel quia corruit—ah, ah!
> Sors est fallendi solis concessa poetis.
> Musca parit camum, simul transfertur ad imum.
> Alati formantur equi sculptoris in arte.
> Laus est . . . sub mobilitate trochei.   5
> Pistorum digiti cornu fecere rudenti,
> Sub vatum lingua cornuta creabitur ursa.

Line 1 presents difficulties both of metre and meaning. If the reading ABIE is correct, the allusion would seem to be to the death of Abia (*III Reg.* xiv)— though this biblical episode does not mention Jezabel. I have speculated whether the readings ABIE and AH AH may be corruptions of the names Abdias and Ahab (cf. *III Reg.* xviii ff.), yet this does not seem to allow a satisfactory reconstruction of the line. Lines 2, 4, 6, and 7 appear to belong together as *sententiae*, 3 and 5 to be independent proverbial verses, 5 being fragmentary. With 8 the 'interview' of Jezabel begins. While lines 2–7 are clearly unrelated to the poem that follows, I am inclined to think this also of 1: if not, it would be the only verse in the poem without dialogue, and the only verse but one without leonine rhyme. It is likely that 1–7 were a series of *probationes pennae* that preceded the poem in the copyist's original, and that the occurrence of Jezabel's name in the first of these led him to incorporate all seven lines into the poem.

Quid queris primum? — Per centum lustra, Priapum.   15
Quid petis assidue? — Quo possim pressa subesse.
Quid minus exoptas? — Personas corpore castas.
Quid magis exhorres? — Divinas, ut puto, leges.
Quis deus est in corde tuo? — Qui regnat in horto . . .

Sometimes Jezabel's replies are to statements rather than
questions:

Non redeunt ludi. — Stricti sunt ergo tenendi.
Me finis torret. — Me delectatio mulcet.
Aufertur species. — Hilares caro servat amores.
Tristis sors mundi. — Gravis intermissio ludi.   40
Curvamur senio. — Trux circumflector amando.
Ardeo spe vite.—Flamesco libidinis igne.[1]

37 ergo sunt MS.

Her ripostes vary in coarseness, but otherwise are totally
predictable: they are designed only to display, and thereby
satirize, Jezabel's shamelessness. To achieve this the author uses
poetically the crudest means: the technique never varies, the
interview continues inexorably for 134 such lines (if we exclude
1–7). It is lightened only by an occasional gleam of wit, seen
at its best in the succinct, allusive closing line:

Suspendam vestes.—Caudam Iunonis ut ales.

[1] From where do you come, Jezabel? — From the foul prison of Babel.
From where, woman, are you returning? — From the arched vault of Tophet.
Is it sweet, what your husband gives you? — To me it's contemptible excre-
ment. What is the ointment of which you reek? — The strong medicine of
Jael. What does Nazareth mean to you? — A lot, for (?) my vigour still
flourishes. What has made your buttocks swell so? — Eating belly of pork.
What has the power to keep you laughing? — The prostitute's ways. What
do you look for most? — For the next hundred *lustra*, Priapus. What do you
seek so eagerly? — How I can lie pressed in the act. What do you desire
least? — Those who are chaste in body. What do you find most repulsive? —
In my view, divine laws. Who is the god who reigns in your heart? — Priapus,
god of the garden . . . Love's sports do not return. — So we must cling to them
fast. The (thought of the) end consumes me. — The (thought of) delight
soothes me. Beauty passes away. — But the flesh preserves joyful loves. Sad
is the lot of the world. — Sad only the end of the game. We are bent by old
age. — I am bent in wild loving. I burn with the hope of life. — I am aflame
with lust's fire.

Jezabel's interlocutor resolves to hang up his garments for display, like the man who has escaped from Pyrrha's snares (Horace, *Carm.* I. 5, 15–16, *suspendisse . . . vestimenta*), while Jezabel declares she will display her tail, for men to marvel at like the peacock's tail.[1] But this is a rare, isolated instance of intellectual adroitness in a piece that essentially belongs among the more primitive and monotonous in the voluminous genre of *Frauenfeindliche Dichtungen* in the Middle Ages.[2]

Semiramis is evidently not a continuation of this piece; at the same time, it is possible to see how at least three superficial resemblances—the theme of lasciviousness, the dialogue form (however different in the two poems), and the use of leonine hexameters—could have led a somewhat foolish copyist to think so. Again, it is possible that the 'Explicit liber primus. Incipit secundus' rubric was not meant to signal a continuation at all, but that a collector had planned a 'Legend of Bad Women', a compilation drawing on diverse poetic materials, which were to be ordered in a whole series of 'libri'. Finally, we cannot rule out the possibility that the rubric was inserted quite unthinkingly by a scribe who found a blank line between two poems.

Could *Jezabel* and *Semiramis* be by the same poet? While it cannot be categorically denied, the differences of style and of imaginative conception in the two poems are formidable and make it unlikely. Again, it is worth noting that the two differ strikingly in their technique of leonine hexameters: among the 181 lines of *Semiramis*, no fewer than 30 (i.e. virtually a sixth) show no trace of leonine rhyme or assonance. This would be a quite exceptional proportion for a poem composed much after the year 1000.[3] A further ten lines in *Semiramis* do not rhyme

---

[1] Cf. Ovid, *Amores*, II. 6, 55: *ales Iunonia*.

[2] Cf. A. Wulff, *Die frauenfeindlichen Dichtungen in den romanischen Literaturen des Mittelalters* (1914).

[3] *Ruodlieb*, for instance, composed *c.* 1050, has only fourteen wholly rhymeless lines among the surviving 2306 (this latter figure includes the fragmentary lines, of which occasional ones might also have been rhymeless). The *Ecbasis Captivi*, if written in the years 1043–6, as is now generally held, would also be exceptional for its time in the number of unrhymed verses among the

with the word at the penthemimer. In *Jezabel*, of the 134 lines that certainly belong to the poem, only one has no leonine rhyme, and in all but two the rhyme is with the word at the penthemimer.[1]

More probable is a direct relation between *Semiramis* and the first of Warner of Rouen's poems, *Moriuht*. After the opening dedication to Archbishop Robert, this poem is a spirited, often scabrous, satire against Warner's Irish enemy (who, it seems, was his literary rival in the school at Rouen). Moriuht is a goat in his lustfulness (this is the poem's dominant metaphor), he is bald and repulsive, and absurdly vain of his literary gifts. He and his wife Glicerium (the name of Terence's 'lady of Andros' is doubtless chosen with mocking intent) are captured by Vikings and sold separately as slaves at Corbridge. Having vaunted his literary talents, Moriuht is bought by some nuns, but they find him more useful for his sexual than his literary prowess. Then the townsfolk, catching him in the act with a nun, drive him out. He escapes in a small boat but, despite his heathen rites of propitiation (*Sacrificat ventis, immolat atque diis*), is again caught by the Vikings. This time he is taken to a Saxon port, where he is bought by a widow, who pays for him with a false coin. Again Moriuht finds desire gratified—not only by

leonines (due partly at least to the poet's extensive adaptation of verses from classical poetry). It is noteworthy that this proportion of unrhymed verses long prevented Strecker from accepting a date later than the tenth century for the *Ecbasis*.

  [1] The contrast is suggestive, though indeed not by itself a decisive argument for difference of authorship, as can be seen by comparing Warner of Rouen's two satires. The second is extremely regular in its hexameters as well as its pentameters (even in l. 17, which as cited by Musset is one foot short, the rhyme was probably at the penthemimer), while the first contains many hexameters where leonine rhyme is lacking or irregular. Some of these may be due simply to the bad condition in which the text is preserved, others (particularly in the last third, where the level of the verse drops technically as well as imaginatively) to the poet's haste to finish, others to his inexperience at the time of writing this piece. But any general attempt to date leonine verse earlier or later according to the consistency and accuracy with which the rhymes are employed must be used with great caution and admit numerous exceptions (as Strecker saw in his valuable 'Studien zu den karolingischen Dichtern V', *Neues Archiv*, xliv (1922), 213–51).

his owner but by 'many boys, nuns, widows and wives'. Again
he is chased out of the region, with blows, like an animal. It
is at this point that he turns to magic arts:

> Vindicta cesus, Germanis belua factus,
> Currit ad invisum Beelzebub auxilium.
> Accipiens vita functa tenera exta puelle,
> Prospicit in fibris gausape Glicerii;
> Et dum sacra suo proferret verba labello,
> Distortis oculis et manibus tremulis,
> Fertur ab adverso: 'Vivit tua cara puella,
> Et magis intento i Rotomago cito;
> Illic amissos plorans tua cara furores,
> Expectat caprum pulchra capella suum.
> Ambulat ad portum, Moriuht ut cernat amatum,
> Conlustrans cunctas undique naviculas;
> Te non invento, vult se coniungere Dano,
> Dicens quod dominus mortuus est Moriuht.'[1]

Struck by vengeance, treated as a beast by the Germans, Moriuht
has recourse to Beelzebub's fiendish aid. Taking up the tender inner
organs of a girl newly dead,[2] in the entrails he descries Glicerium's
dress. And while with his lips he utters the infamous words, with
his eyes rolling and with trembling hands, the fiend says: 'The girl
you love is alive; what's more, I charge you, go quickly to Rouen:
there your dear one, mourning the frenzied love-sports she has lost,
your pretty little she-goat is waiting for her buck. She walks to the
harbour to look for her loved Moriuht, scanning all the boats far
and wide. Not having found you, she means to marry a Viking,
saying her lord Moriuht is dead.'

Moriuht directs a prayer to Venus: he will sacrifice a dove
to her if she protects his wife till he arrives. Swiftly he sets out
on foot towards Rouen. There follows a coarsely mocking
description of Moriuht's body, with touches of ribald fantasy—
a stork or hoopoe (*uppupa*) could build its nest in his forest of
pubic hair. In Rouen, Moriuht throws himself on the mercy

---

[1] MS. fol. 4ᵛ (Omont, p. 202, ll. 189–202; 191 *functae* Omont).
[2] I do not think the Latin implies 'un sacrifice humain', as Musset (p. 252)
claims.

of the *comitissa*—probably, as Musset suggests, Duchess Gonnor, widow of Richard I (†996) and mother of the Archbishop. She encourages him in his quest, offering to pay Glicerium's ransom. When Moriuht has again sacrificed to and placated the gods, the supernatural voice directs him to a nearby harbour where he finds Glicerium. She is living wretchedly as a slave in a poor man's house. At their reunion the poet unleashes a new invective against Moriuht for his lasciviousness.

Moriuht ransoms Glicerium, and carries her back to Rouen on his shoulders. A further ransom paid by the Duchess frees their little daughter also, about whom we now hear for the first time. Then Moriuht boasts of his immense poetic talents, and Warner makes fun of him once more: his quantities are all topsy-turvy, his verse ridiculous. The lampoon turns into sexual accusations against Moriuht and Glicerium (*Vidi ceventes, Hercule, vos mutuo*), and a final mocking challenge to Moriuht, lest he find a bull should supplant him in perversely pleasuring his wife:

> Nam, Moriuht, vigila, recubans ne forte capella
> 　Iuxta te lenem dicat adesse bovem,
> Qui lingendo nates capre subcedat amice . . .[1]

The poet concludes with a final commendation of his satire to both Archbishop Robert and the Duchess.

The elements of pagan cult and of magic, the theme of sexual perversion, treated with extravagant hyperbole, and especially the final taunts about the bull as a sexual rival, would seem to indicate that there may be a direct relation between the poems *Moriuht* and *Semiramis*.[2] Moreover, the leonine rhyming in *Moriuht*, at least in the hexameters, is comparably irregular. The possibility that Warner of Rouen might also have written *Semiramis* cannot be dismissed out of hand; nevertheless on literary grounds I have come to think it unlikely.

---

[1] MS. fol. 9ʳ (Omont, p. 210, ll. 485–7); 487 subcădat MS.

[2] Possibly a minor detail such as the occurrence of the rare *uppupa* in both of Warner's poems (I. 234, II. 100) as well as in *Semiramis* (106) may also be relevant. The three contexts, however, are dissimilar.

Semiramis, as the detailed discussion will show, has a stylistic originality and imaginative richness, a seriousness of conception and a freedom from both monotony and vulgarity that set it far from *Moriuht*, whatever incidental details the two poems share. In the crudity of its sexual language and sexual mockery, as in the lengthy labouring of its satire, *Moriuht* is far more akin to *Jezabel*; the question of the possible relation between these two poems, however, cannot be broached here. If these conclusions can be accepted at least tentatively, it would seem that Warner, who composed *Moriuht* before 1026, and quite possibly in the first decade of the eleventh century,[1] knew the slightly older poem *Semiramis*[2] and occasionally echoed it. This is probably also why *Semiramis* was copied, together with Warner's own poems, in the source from which the Paris manuscript derives.

Another approach to the problem of the literary context of *Semiramis* can be made by way of its quasi-dramatic form. In medieval Latin, poems in dialogue form had been common since the time of Charlemagne. These were of various kinds: the eclogue is used as a vehicle for panegyric (Modoin, Walafrid Strabo), for a dirge (Ratpert, Agius of Korvei), or for local history (Purchard of Reichenau). Panegyric as well as didactic verse could be cast in the form of interchanges between the poet and his Muse (Sedulius Scottus, Mico of Saint-Riquier). Somewhat isolated stands a touching fragmentary dialogue, in epanaleptic couplets, between a runaway Irish monk and the saints Zeno and Columba to whom he appeals for help. Then again there are the poetic contentions and debates where often, as in the older bucolic tradition, the speakers reply to each other in alternate strophes of equal length (as Semiramis and her brother do for a large part of our poem). These debates could be used for pure entertainment (the Winter–Spring debate attributed to Alcuin, Sedulius's contention between rose and lily),

---

[1] L. Musset, art. cit., p. 245.

[2] For *Semiramis* I suggest a provisional date *c.* 1000: I can see no compelling reasons for moving it far back into the tenth century.

Semiramis · *The Recreation of Myth* 85

or again, for a Christian didactic purpose (the *Ecloga Theoduli*, or the remarkable older fragment on the harrowing of hell, a debate between Infernus and Satan). From an early period also we have two 'flytings', preserved only fragmentarily in ninth-century manuscripts, in which human (or once perhaps animal) speakers rail at each other. The high point of the 'flyting' genre is of course the renowned dialogue between Terence and his 'Delusor', where the exuberant dramatic inspiration is evident, and where the stage directions leave no doubt that dramatic performance was intended.[1]

Terentius et Delusor challenges us to reassess the extent to which the various kinds of Carolingian dialogue-poems can be seen as dramatic. All of them, presumably, were read aloud in company, not just in private. I can see no reason to doubt that when they were thus read the different parts were allotted to different readers. In such 'reading-groups', then—to assume no more—the exchanges of verse-dialogue were a living experience. A slightly later, more complex work such as the *Ecbasis Captivi*, with its much larger range of speakers, has recently been thought by two German scholars to have arisen as an Easter entertainment, 'as a kind of play, or school-declamation aided by mime'[2]—a most attractive hypothesis. In the tenth (or perhaps early eleventh) century a Latin poet composed a verse narrative of Apollonius in leonine hexameters, which he designed to be declaimed or chanted by two performers in alternation. Only a fragment survives[3]—the whole, if it was ever completed, would have been immense. The Apollonius story itself, as I have indicated, has several affinities with *Semiramis*; here the use of leonines, and a certain delight in language that is *pathétique*, suggest further similarities. Yet the differences are also important: *Semiramis* is an intense and

---

[1] *Poetae*, i. 385; ii. 370; iii. 45, 372; v. 263; iii. 225, 298; iii. 688; i. 270; iii. 230; *Ecloga Theoduli*: ed. J. Osternacher (1902); *Infernus and Satan*: *Poetae*, iv. 636; 'Flytings': *Poetae*, iv. 1082, 1086, 1088.

[2] H. R. Jauss, *Untersuchungen zur mittelalterlichen Tierdichtung* (1959), p. 92, paraphrasing W. Ross.

[3] *Gesta Apollonii*, *Poetae*, ii. 484.

compact poem, the *Gesta* a sprawling one; *Semiramis* is poten-
tially dramatic in a way the *Gesta* are not. The *Gesta* are a narrative in which different portions of the story have been allotted
to the performers, but the distribution has nothing to do with
whether the narrator or a character is speaking—it seems in
fact to be arbitrary. In *Semiramis*, after an opening prologue,
or 'chorus', the poem works entirely through its dialogue. The
speeches contain strongly visual elements, and it is at once
evident how excitingly a declamation of this dialogue could
have been enhanced by 'stage-business'. Clearly we cannot leap
from what could have been to what was. Yet as we are still so
far from having found a literary context in which *Semiramis*
can truly be said to belong, one other suggestion is worth entertaining, however tentatively. Between 1057 and 1064 Meinhard
of Bamberg, in a much-discussed letter, wrote of his Bishop
Gunther to a friend:

> What indeed is our lord bishop doing? What is his host of
> helmeted hares about? What battles, what encounters are they per-
> forming? What triumphs are they celebrating now? Great heavens,
> what a swarm there, not of men but of flies! What bombastic and
> empty sounds! There there is no seriousness, no discipline. And oh
> that wretched and deplorable bishop's life, oh what behaviour! Never
> does he think about Augustine, never about Gregory, he always
> manages to wear (the costume of) Attila, always of Theodoric,
> and other things of that kind. He does not handle books but
> lances, he looks not at the forms of the letters but at the points of
> swords.[1]

The passage bristles with difficulties of interpretation, but it

---

[1] Quid vero agit domnus noster? quid suus ille exercitus galeatorum
leporum? que bella, quas acies tractant? quos triumphos celebrant? Dii boni,
quanta ibi colluvio non virorum, sed muscarum! quam magnifici et vani
strepitus! Nulla ibi gravitas, nulla disciplina. Et o miseram et miserandam
episcopi vitam, o mores! Numquam ille Augustinum, numquam ille Gre-
gorium recolit, semper ille Attalam, semper Amalungum et cetera id genus
portare tractat. Versat ille non libros, sed lanceas, miratur ille non litterarum
apices, sed mucronum acies. (*Briefsammlungen der Zeit Heinrichs IV*, ed. C.
Erdmann–N. Fickermann, *MGH*, 1950, p. 121; cf. also C. Erdmann, 'Fabulae
Curiales', *ZfdA* lxxiii (1936), 87–98, and *ZfdA* lxxiv (1937), 116.)

seems to me, as to Karl Hauck,[1] that Meinhard is reproaching the Bishop for not only countenancing, but himself taking prominent parts in, performances with heathen themes. It is not certain that these performances included dialogue as well as mime—though the *magnifici et vani strepitus* may well suggest fulminating speeches rather than simply war-cries or clashes of armour. At all events, the convincingly realistic presentation of pagan legendary material here seems beyond reasonable doubt. Here the material was drawn from Germanic, not antique, heathendom, and was of a less-sophisticated kind than *Semiramis*. Perhaps indeed it was more in the nature of a charade, a kind of Germanic 'Nine Worthies' spectacle. But it shows that an eleventh-century episcopal court was at least on occasion a place where a legend that had nothing in common with Augustine or Gregory could be not only read but enacted.

II

Semiramis begins with a prologue condemning the heroine for her lasciviousness. It is the only passage in the work that is not assigned to be spoken by a character. It anticipates the thoughts of Semiramis' brother the augur, but that it should originally have been intended for him seems improbable, as his opening words (20) give the impression of introducing the first character, and a sign in the manuscript margin confirms this. There are no precise parallels to such an opening in either the hexameter summaries or the prologues of Terence's plays. Hrotsvitha in her plays seems to use her prose summaries as a kind of prologue, though here too there is a difference: the prologue in *Semiramis* does not summarize what will happen, nor does it tell a background 'objectively'; rather, the condemnation has a dramatic function within the whole. It expresses the common view of Semiramis' conduct—the *materia lutea* on every man's lips—that drives her brother mad with shame and

---

[1] *Germanisch-romanische Monatsschrift*, xxxiii (1951–2) 14.

provokes him to call up her shade; and it is this salacious condemnation by the world that will be explicitly contradicted by
Semiramis' disdainful revelation at the close.

Two slightly later works may provide an analogue for such
a prologue: the play of the *Sponsus*, in the second half of the
eleventh century, opens similarly with a verse prologue that
is not assigned to a character yet is unmistakably a part of the
play; it has been given in the past to an otherwise not mentioned Chorus (Karl Young), or to Ecclesia (L. P. Thomas), or,
as the most recent editor suggests, can be given to 'questo o
quel personaggio a seconda delle necessità del momento'.[1] In
the twelfth-century 'comoedia' *Baucis et Traso*, a verse prologue
supplies the narrative background and leads into the dramatic
action; but in an important respect this piece is less dramatic
than *Semiramis*: there the dialogue throughout is linked by
transitions of the 'she said' type, which occur within the verse,
not in the manner of stage-directions.[2] If we envisage *Semiramis*
as a declamation for at least three speakers (by whatever
mimetic elements it may or may not have been enhanced), it
seems simplest to assume that this opening was assigned to a
fourth speaker who acts as prologue and then takes no further
part.

The augur then introduces himself. He claims he has been
called Tolumpnus (i.e. Tolumnius) by the Fates—his name is
that of the Rutulian augur who (*Aen.* XII. 258 ff.) interprets
the eagle seizing a swan as a heaven-sent sign for his people to
attack the Trojans, and who himself launches the first spear
against them. The poet has chosen the name, as far as I can
tell, simply as a well-known augur's name. That it was given
to Semiramis' brother *per fata* suggests the augur's special rela-
tionship to the forces of fate, as again when Semiramis shortly
afterwards calls him 'fate's high-priest'. He seems to be a com-

---

[1] D'Arco Silvio Avalle, *Il 'Sponsus'* (1965), p. 68.

[2] *La 'Comédie' latine en France au XIIᵉ siècle* (1931), ii. 70 ff. In the *Babio*
(ed. Faral, p. 2), where the dialogue dispenses with such transitions, the opening,
which occurs only in one manuscript, is not a prologue but a preface to the
reader (*legentibus*), 'ut manifestius intelligatur quod isti versus volunt dicere'.

bination of shaman and necromancer. In the first part of the poem he calls back Semiramis' soul from the other world and converses with it, but this shamanistic performance is not enough for him: his goal is to conjure up a corporeal phantom of Semiramis, and with the help of her soul that he has evoked and of a necromantic ritual,[1] as well as of the direct intervention of Apollo (if I interpret a difficult passage aright), he finally succeeds in this. He is also a sanctimonious man, querulous, given to striking tragic poses. He is effectively characterized by his manner of speech: his language is bombastic and diffuse whereas Semiramis in her replies is pithy, ironic, and succinct. From their first interchanges onwards we sense that she is wholly sure of herself, and impatient with her grandiloquent brother.

Already with his opening invocation Semiramis hears her brother and answers him. The augur claims to have done all that is necessary to summon her back from the world of death, and at the same time is in anguish at what he imagines his sister's disgrace. She by her question (27) suggests to him that his grief is inappropriate, and tells him that, if his wish is to be granted, he must address himself not to her but to the god of the underworld. While he tells of his hallucinatory experience of the infernal monsters, she reminds him once more that only Pluto can sanction her return in phantom guise.

The augur's next couplet (32-3) is not immediately clear. It contains verbal echoes of the passage in *Georgic* III (391-3) where Pan seduces Luna, changing into a white ram that lures her into the woods so that she follows him: *Pan deus Arcadiae captam te, Luna, fefellit.* . . . But difficulties remain: Pan is not an *haruspex*; in the Vergilian passage it is he who tricks Luna, whereas in the medieval allusion Luna tricks her man; Vergil affirms what the medieval poet denies, that the lover *was* able to 'darken' Luna, though he adds *si credere dignum est*. It is noteworthy that Servius (*ad loc.*), claiming Vergil has altered the

---

[1] On the details of ancient necromancy, cf. Th. Hopfner, 'Nekromantie', *RE* xvi. 2218-33; F. Cumont, *Lux Perpetua* (1949), pp. 97-108.

legend, attributes the whole escapade not to Pan but to
Endymion:

> Mutat fabulam: nam non Pan, sed Endymion amasse dicitur
> Lunam: qui spretus pavit pecora candidissima, et sic eam in suos
> illexit amplexus.

Endymion in some respects fits the medieval poetic context
better: he is, if not an *haruspex*, at least widely known as the
first meteorologist[1] (an activity central to the divination of
haruspices); and he did not possess Luna, because in at least one
version of the legend she lulled him into an endless sleep, so
that she might kiss him as he slept (cf. Cicero, *Tusc.* I. 38, 92)—
this presumably would count as 'tricking' him. The medieval
poet's obscure allusion would seem to result from a conflation
of the Virgilian passage with Servius' note on it,[2] and a recollec-
tion of another, independent detail about Luna and Endymion.
Such an explanation sounds awkward and over-complex, but
I can think of no better. The dramatic impact of the augur's
words seems to be that of an impatient rejoinder to his sister's
instructions: 'I am no incompetent, moonstruck augur—I know
well enough how to perform the necromantic rite successfully.'
In the context of magic, to be able to darken the moon, that
is, bring about a lunar eclipse, is a basic prerequisite for the
sorcerer.[3]

Once more Semiramis reminds her brother that he must
pray, and as he begins bombastically to invoke 'a hundred
thousand shades' she reminds him that Orpheus won over
Pluto not by such grandiose conjurations but by the magic of
his song. The augur is undeterred. In fact he claims that he has

---

[1] Pliny, *Nat. Hist.* II. 43; Fulgentius, *Myth.* II. 19; Mythogr. Vat. I. 229,
III. 7, 3.

[2] One must reckon with the possibility that the Servian comment found
its way into later glosses and may have reached the poet through these rather
than through Servius direct. On the other hand, with the word *sciomantia*
(see below, p. 95) the presumption seems to me in favour of a direct use of
Servius, especially in that the word (as Dr. Otto Prinz has kindly informed me)
is completely unrecorded in the materials of the *Mittellateinisches Wörterbuch*.

[3] Cf. Georg Luck, *Hexen und Zauberei in der römischen Dichtung* (1962), p. 8.

already performed a sacrifice sufficient for the necromantic
return of the phantom to take place: he had sacrificed a dog
at the appropriate hour, at nightfall, and the burning had taken
place without mishap. The burning of dogs occurs in both
Roman and Germanic magic.[1] Now, the augur imagines, the
effect of the sacrifice should follow, the other inhabitants of
the underworld should persuade Pluto to release one of their
number for a brief time. For the night is appropriately dark,
and the right wind is blowing—from the north, not from the
south. The specific associations that these two winds have for
the poet remain uncertain. Hrabanus Maurus, for instance, in
his encyclopaedia claims that each of the winds can have good
or bad connotations: thus the south wind brings pestilence
with it, which the cold north wind can drive away; but again
the south wind can have blessed associations (*Significat Auster
aliquando calorem fidei . . . gratiam spiritus sancti*), while the north
wind—here strictly Aquilo, not Septentrio—has satanic and
pagan ones (*Significat autem vel diabolum vel homines infideles*),
which might be the most fitting in the context of an invocation
to the underworld. Either the purifying or the satanic aspect
of the north wind could have been in the poet's mind, just as
the absence of the south wind could suggest a freedom from
pestilence or the absence of the Christian deity.[2]

   In the following lines the augur claims the sacred powers that
fit him for the task that is to come. He has often dipped his
thumb in holy oil, he knows that next he has to crush *verbena*
(does he tread on fronds in the performance of his rite, or perhaps pound in a mortar vervain[3] he has specially gathered—

[1] Roman: the *sacrum canarium* (Ovid, *Fasti*, IV. 935 ff.; Pliny, *Nat. Hist.*
XVIII. 14); Germanic: Adam of Bremen, *Gesta*, IV. 27.
   [2] Cf. Hrabanus Maurus, *De universo*, IX. 25 (*P.L.* III, 281–2); also Hans
Liebeschütz's chapter 'Windkräfte und Sternenkräfte', *Das allegorische Weltbild
der heiligen Hildegard von Bingen* (1930), pp. 72–86.
   [3] Servius (*in Aen.* XII. 120) gives *verbena* the general sense of *herba sacra*. But
it is specifically vervain that is important for magic purposes, as can be gauged
from the exceptional number of its occurrences in A. Delatte's researches on
the rituals of gathering magic plants in antiquity (cf. his *Herbarius*, 3rd ed.,
1961, Acad. royale de Belgique LIV. 4, Index, p. 222, s.v. *verveine*). So too the

repertam—for a libation?). The use of oil for both ritual and magic purposes is well-nigh universal;[1] *verbenae*, too, are common in Roman poetry in contexts of conjuration, sacrifice, and magic.[2] The power evoked in the next two lines (57–8), however, is a most unusual one, and can only, I believe, have come to the poet from one ancient source. Servius is our unique authority for the notion that in the temple of Apollo at Delphi there was a tripod containing the teeth of the dragon Python whom Apollo had killed (*quod in eodem templo tripus est cum ossibus et dentibus Pythii serpentis—in Aen.* III. 360). At the same time, three Greek sources, which the Latin poet is unlikely to have known, relate that the cauldron of the tripod contained lots (not teeth), and that these lots were shaken—or shook spontaneously—whenever the oracle was consulted.[3] Presumably these lots were marked with signs indicating different destinies, and when they were shaken the first to leap out of the cauldron signified the god's will.[4] Even without this Greek testimony, however, it was almost inevitable that a Latin poet who through Servius had acquired the notion of dragon's teeth in the tripod at Apollo's shrine, and whose own dramatic action demanded a context of 'Sibylline murmurs', should link his augur's claim to oracular powers with the use

paeonia (l. 98) is one of the magic herbs most frequently discussed in the treatise (cf. ibid., p. 219, s.v. *pivoine*). For the problematic line 55, M.-Th. d'Alverny suggested to me the attractive possibility of emending to 'vervenam . . . *circare* repertam', i.e. when the plant is found the man who wants to use it for magic must turn around it three times.

[1] It is difficult to distinguish which of the many associations of oil in the religious sphere the poet has in mind. Anointing is a sign of sacred, priestly or royal office in Graeco-Roman, Jewish, and Christian religion alike (cf. Cabrol–Leclerq, s.v. *Huile*, VI. 2, 2777 ff.). It may be relevant to note that in Greece anointing took place before consulting an oracle (Cabrol–Leclerq, loc. cit.), and that there is a specific branch of magic, onychomancy, in which the sorcerer's thumb is anointed with a mixture of oil and soot, from which the phantoms that are summoned take shape (Bächtold-Stäubli, s.v. *Öl*, VI. 1234).

[2] Cf. e.g. Vergil, *Ecl.* VIII. 65; Horace, *Carm.* I. 19, 14; Ovid, *Metam.* VII. 242.

[3] Texts (Nonnos, Eudokia, the Suda) cited and discussed by P. Amandry, *La mantique apollinienne à Delphes* (1950), pp. 29–30, 256–9.

[4] Cf. Amandry, p. 30.

of these *dentes draconis.* The allusion from Servius does not of course imply that the action in our poem is conceived as taking place at Delphi: the augur claims to be able to imitate the Pythia, he does not say he is one of her attendant priests. The décor, like so many details of the poem, is a fabulous confection: it is a graveyard (cf. 72–3), in which there seems to be a shrine consecrated both to Apollo and Diana (cf. 51, 60, 97, 138 ff.).

The augur, so confident in his necromantic powers, is laconically interrupted by his sister's voice: he has not done all he should to make the conjuration effective, he has offended Diana by the way he has spoken. This can only refer to his phrase *bovis es que passa ruinas* (57), which alluded in an unworthy way to what—as Semiramis will finally reveal—was her sacred union with the highest god.

The augur renews his complaints (61–3, 66–7): he is sleepless, but his is not the wakefulness of a sacred office, as with Minerva's owls (the rare expression *cum noctividis* is from Martianus Capella, VI. 571); it is only a restless torment caused, as he reproachfully reminds Semiramis, by his sister's shame. Semiramis' voice breaks in to warn him that his complaints are jeopardizing the chance of her return in bodily shape.[1] To achieve this he must not only pray but perform another sacrifice. After a renewed outburst of self-pity from the augur, her voice instructs him in the preparations for the new ritual. This time there are to be three altars, and not only three dogs but three cocks are to be burnt. They must be black, for it is black cocks that are demonic and are sacrificed to the powers of the underworld.[2] The only context I know in which dogs and cocks are sacrificed together is in the Germanic New Year's feast described by Thietmar of Merseburg as taking place at Leire in Zealand in the early tenth century:

Every nine years in January, after the time in which we celebrate

---

[1] I take the *bis sex horis* (77) to mean, for the space of a single night.
[2] Cf. Jacob Grimm, *Deutsche Mythologie* (4th ed., 1876), ii. 843–4. For the sacrifice of a cock in necromancy, cf. Th. Hopfner, art. cit., col. 2227.

the birth of Christ, they all came together and there immolated to their gods ninety-nine human beings and as many horses, together with dogs and cocks (instead of sacrificing hawks), certainly thinking, as I said before, that these would aid them before the powers of the underworld, and would placate them for the crimes the people had committed.[1]

Thietmar's text implies that there was a special cultic reason for sacrificing cocks and not hawks on this occasion (were cocks more fitting *apud inferos*?), and may also imply that dogs and cocks were immolated in equal numbers (presumably ninety-nine of each).

After enjoining the addition of black cocks to the rite, Semiramis warns of the need to avoid honey in the accompanying ritual banquet. The reason for this, it would seem, is that honey is used in magic for warding off the powers of the underworld and the ghosts of the dead, whereas here the object is to attract them. An Egyptian magic incantation (*c.* 1580 B.C.) speaks of 'honey which is sweet for mankind, but terrible for phantoms'; in the *Iliad* (XIX. 39) Thetis uses nectar and ambrosia to protect Hector's corpse from decay.[2] If honey is used, the world of the dead will not at this moment be able to impinge on the world of the living, and the augur's goal will remain unachieved.

Amid renewed complaints from the augur, sleepless and distraught, the voice of Semiramis prescribes further what must

---

[1] Est unus in his partibus locus, caput istius regni, Lederun nomine, in pago, qui Selon dicitur, ubi post VIIII annos mense Ianuario, post hoc tempus, quo nos theophaniam Domini celebramus, omnes conveniunt, et ibi diis suimet LXXXX et VIIII homines et totidem equos, cum canibus et gallis pro accipitribus oblatis, immolant, pro certo, ut predixi, putantes hos eisdem erga inferos servituros et commissa crimina apud eosdem placaturos (*Chronicon*, I. 17).

[2] These instances, and many others, cited by Bächtold-Stäubli, s.v. *Honig*, sect. 8: 'Honig als dämonenvertreibendes und antiseptisches Mittel.' None the less, the proscription of honey here is strange, as honey is often required as an offering during necromancy (cf. Th. Hopfner, art. cit.; F. Cumont, loc. cit.). So too, though Semiramis here warns against asses coming near, an ass's skin could also be used for necromancy (Hopfner, col. 2230).

be avoided during the *sciomantia*[1] of bringing back her shade: asses, salt, and ambiguous phrases in the invocations. Only the last seems self-explanatory. The danger from asses may stem from the notion, already current in Roman times, that an ass's head can drive away the powers of darkness.[2] Once more the poet contrasts Semiramis and her brother by their tones of voice: her matter-of-fact caution to keep the ass far hence provokes his comically unbalanced outburst 'Destroy all asses!' Salt, again, is widely and anciently used in cult in order to banish demons. Already an Accadian imprecation calls upon salt to undo the spells wrought on the suppliant by evil powers.[3] In early Christian tradition the Gelasian blessing of salt expressly alludes to thereby banishing Satan; in popular superstition, devils and witches hate salt so much that they never eat it; nymphs, too, eat only unsalted food.[4]

The augur, still neurotic and querulous, implores sleep from Apollo. He alludes to a *dapifer* who is sleeping: this may refer to an attendant who had waited on him during the ritual banquet (*in orgiis*), or just possibly the sense may be 'while even the (meanest) servant sleeps . . .', so that the presence of another

[1] I have found this word, which is not in the dictionaries, only in Servius, who explains (*in Aen.* VI. 149):
est et alia opportunitas descendendi ad inferos, id est Proserpinae sacra peragendi. duo autem horum sacrorum genera fuisse dicuntur: unum necromantiae, quod Lucanus exsequitur, et aliud sciomantiae, quod in Homero, quem Vergilius sequitur, lectum est. sed secundum Lucanum in necromantia ad levandum cadaver sanguis est necessarius, ut (VI. 667) *pectora tunc primum ferventi sanguine supplet*, in sciomantia vero, quia umbrae tantum est evocatio, sufficit solus interitus: unde Misenus in fluctibus occisus esse inducitur. (Cf. also *in Aen.* VI. 107.)

[2] Bächtold-Stäubli, s.v. *Esel*, ii. 1012. I note that an ass's *hair* is used in a love-charm in a bilingual Greek and demotic papyrus, ed. and transl. H. I. Bell, A. D. Nock, and H. Thompson, *PBA* xvii (1931), 245.

[3] A. Falkenstein and W. von Soden, *Sumerische und Akkadische Hymnen und Gebete* (1953), p. 354.

[4] Bächtold-Stäubli, s.v. *Salz* (esp. vii. 900). Even in the present-day Roman liturgy, in the 'Ordo ad faciendam aquam benedictam', the salt is exorcized, so that 'effugiat atque discedat a loco, in quo aspersum fueris, *omnis phantasia* et nequitia, vel versutia diabolicae fraudis, omnisque spiritus immundus'.

human being during the dialogue is not necessarily implied.[1] Does the banquet presuppose other participants? The poet does not make this clear.

Semiramis treats the augur's prayer to Apollo with mocking irony: if I am as disgraced and wanton as you suppose, she says in effect, is a prayer to Apollo appropriate? Or can I be brought back to the upper world through Paeonian herbs, at Diana's intercession, as if I were another Hippolytus? (The thought alludes wittily to *Aen.* VII. 769, where Hippolytus is *Paeoniis revocatum herbis et amore Dianae*). The augur admits that the truth, as he sees it, is more complex: it is not only Semiramis who is lascivious, but Jove himself who has never held back his lusts.[2]

Semiramis observes her brother's misguided tears with detachment, and he begins a fresh outburst (105): the hoopoe had foretold his own disgrace through her adultery, and to him this was like death. The hoopoe is popularly regarded as a demonic bird, and can be an augury of evils such as war and famine. Further, it can cause terrible dreams and nightmares (this last only if one has been anointed with its blood).[3]

Now Semiramis grows more impatient: in his hysteria the augur is neglecting the torches, which are shining too brightly for a magic that calls upon the dark powers.[4] She hints at the revelation she will give that will make his sorrows groundless.

---

[1] The *threnara* too is problematic—see below p. 97, n. 2.

[2] For the interpretation of the expression *praecingere lumbos* (which in its biblical contexts normally suggests readiness and the summoning of one's strength rather than sexual self-restraint), cf. Alan of Lille, *Dist. Theol.* s.v. *Cingulum* (*P.L.* 210, 740B): '*Cingulum*, proprie, castitas . . . et de hac dicitur in Luca: *Sint lumbi praecincti*.' It is not possible to follow D. W. Robertson Jr. (*A Preface to Chaucer*, p. 451) in reading a sexual meaning into Job xxxviii. 3, *Accinge sicut vir lumbos tuos*: the context shows that God is there demanding Job's attentiveness, not continence.

[3] Bächtold-Stäubli ix. 566 (citing Isidore, *Etym.* XII. 7, 66, and Albertus Magnus, *De animalibus*, XXIII. 143). Albertus adds significantly: 'Upupam etiam et upupae membra et praecipue cerebrum et linguam et cor, multum quaerunt incantatores.'

[4] On the need for darkness during necromancy, cf. Th. Hopfner, art. cit., col. 2227.

Still the augur persists, lamenting how widely the story of her shame has spread: the allusion to crow (*cornix*) or raven (*corvinis rostris*) would here seem to refer only to the bird's proverbial garrulity, rather than to any connection with death or with magic.[1] This time Semiramis ignores her brother: speaking of him in the third person—her shade being still in the underworld—she addresses Hecate, trying to placate the goddess for her brother's impious speeches.

The next transition in the dialogue is more than usually abrupt, as if a new scene were beginning. The augur now finally performs his conjuration, making a somewhat diffuse speech. During it we must imagine him dispatching the dogs and cocks; he hopes that meanwhile they will give no sound— this would be an ill-fated sign. Repeatedly he stresses that the darkness which the rite requires has come; the torches are out; only the sacrificial fire gleams. A woman mourner (if I interpret *threnara* aright) is called upon to sing a ritual lament.[2] The augur addresses Semiramis as if to win her by persuasion to emerge from her tomb. Then his prayers, now palpably 'black' magic, *vite contraria*, go out to the demon Mamuhel[3] as well as to Pluto: he is to grant the appearance of Semiramis' phantom in exchange for the lives of the six creatures that are sacrificed.

---

[1] The poet probably had in mind Ovid, *Metam.* II. 534 ff., which makes a similar conflation between raven (*corve loquax*, 535) and crow (*garrula . . . cornix*, 547–8).

[2] I have not found *threnara* in Latin or Greek dictionaries, though there are numerous other *thren-* formations. The *Patristic Greek Lexicon* adduces an instance of θρηνήτρια with the sense 'female professional mourner', from St. John Chrysostom (*P.G.* 64, 856D), where the Latin version has *lamentatrices*. The emendations 'pandant mihi Taenara carmen' would be attractive; yet I find it hard to believe that by a double accident we have in the manuscript both a hapax that would fit the context extremely well and the correct adjustment of plural to singular verb that it would entail.

[3] Mamuhel: I have not found this demon's name elsewhere, though the Greek magical texts published by Armand Delatte, *Anecdota Atheniensia*, i (1927), invoke demons called Μαμουράς and Μανουήλ (cf. Table alphabétique, p. 699). There is also a Marbuel (Bächtold-Stäubli, v. 1597), a demon named in magic books as one of the seven great princes of hell, who makes hidden treasures and suchlike accessible.

The conjuration affects the augur with mounting excitement; but still no result follows. Then, in a cry of demented despair, he rails at his own god, Apollo, for not helping him.

This brings on Apollo as *deus ex machina*.[1] The two lines he is given to speak seem bald and poorly contrived on the page, yet if the work was performed dramatically the brief apparition could have been made visually a high point in the action. Apollo orders an attendant spirit, Floxus,[2] to bring back the bodily shape (*figura*) of the heroine.[3]

Apollo disappears, and at once the augur realizes that he had spoken blasphemously. He asks for strength from Diana, the other deity of the shrine. But again his mind turns obsessively to the 'monsters of the night': he still imagines that it is his own necromancy, and not Apollo's command, that will release the shade of Semiramis. Though it is not indicated explicitly, the contrast between Apollo's brisk command and the augur's next speech, with its talk of raging demons, is such that the poet may well have conceived the speech as embodying the character's

[1] My interpretation of the passage, that Apollo intervenes and speaks at this point, is based on several assumptions. The augur has been speaking since 118, where the manuscript has in the margin the normal A that indicates his speeches. At 136 (directly, that is, after the augur's impassioned question to Apollo) the margin has a different A that occurs nowhere else in the poem. The lines 136–7 remain difficult, but suggest some meaning if Apollo is speaking; they would be quite incomprehensible to me if spoken by the augur. On the other hand 138, the recognition of blasphemy, seems to demand the augur as speaker once more. That he now turns to address Diana rather than Apollo, and that Diana gives no reply, remains puzzling—unless perhaps one assumes a lacuna at this point.

[2] Floxus: the name presumably from φλόξ (cf. *flox Vulcanus*, 41)—an appropriate spirit-servant for the god of light. But a demon named Florus or Floron appears in a magic book *De umbris idearum*, attributed to Solomon, which is cited by Cecco d'Ascoli († 1327) in his commentary on Sacrobosco's *Sphaera mundi* (cf. A. Delatte, *La Catoptromancie grecque et ses dérivés* (1932), pp. 44–7).

[3] As Babylon was frequently identified with Cairo in the Middle Ages (cf. Du Cange, s.v. Babilonia), Semiramis, queen of Babylon, is here brought back 'ab Egipto'. It is not incongruous that it should be the god of light, rather than any of the chthonic powers, who brings Semiramis back: Hopfner (art. cit., col. 2220) points out that the sun-god is invoked often enough in necromancy: archaically he too, through his nightly journey below the earth, was thought to have a chthonic aspect.

own *insania*. Behemoth, whom the augur imagines as opposing
the release of his sister, though originally the fabulous creature
described in Job (XL. 15 ff.), was taken in the early Middle Ages
to be a name for the powers of hell.[1] At last, as the phantom
emerges, the augur's hysteria ceases and he greets his sister with
dignity (though in a tone that, as she soon indicates, she finds
too tragic by half). The phantom gives so perfect a semblance
of her presence that he attempts to embrace her, till she dis-
illusions him. The moment would seem to owe something to
Aeneas' vain attempts to embrace the phantom of Anchises
(*Aen.* VI. 695 ff.).

The augur looks past her, peering into the world of spirits
from which she has emerged. But sanctimoniously he tells her
she must not look at the upper world: for in a moment she will
be gone again, like Eurydice when Orpheus lost her a second
time. That Eurydice looked back towards Orpheus as she dis-
appeared is not explicitly stated, as far as I know, in any version
of the story known to the Latin Middle Ages, though it is
implied in Vergil's *Georgic* (IV. 498), where she bids Orpheus
farewell *invalidasque tibi tendens, heu non tua, palmas*.

This final, palpably superfluous, piece of advice releases in
Semiramis all the irritation she had felt while her brother was
so tragically lamenting her alleged guilt. How dare he, a mere
mortal, condemn her who has become divine?[2] Now in her

---

[1] Cf. St. Jerome, *in Job* XL (*P.L.* 26, 782C): 'Behemoth namque doctores
Ecclesiae, qui Hebraeas litteras contigerunt, in Latinum *quasi plures* interpretati
sunt. Proinde inimicus diabolus cum toto corpore satellitum suorum hoc loco
a Deo describitur.' In the same passage (782B), Jerome speaks of Behemoth's
'immanissimus furor'.

[2] In the context it seems to me certain that Semiramis is including herself
in the reference to *lascivis . . . deabus* (179). The line is a part of her speech of
self-justification, and within this it would be hard to see what other function
or meaning it could have. That she also admits a moment later that her shade
is being drawn back to its urn does not, I think, contradict this: it suggests
simply that the phantom (which arises from the tomb) remains below, while
the soul has risen and taken its place *cum deabus*. I believe that the sudden
reassessment that Semiramis's final speech demands of all that has preceded
is an essential part of the poet's design: the whole poem hinges on the two
contrasted views of her—the tragic or degrading one of the opening, and the

corporeal shape she is able to reveal unequivocally what the
disembodied voice had only hinted at: it was a god in bull's
shape who possessed her, and it is madness for human beings
to judge such a sacred union by their own narrower laws. The
phantom, as she disappears, coldly tells the augur to stop
grieving, and her curtain-line seems to contrast her own speech
scornfully with his heated loquacity. Only the ignorant living
can waste so many words; she accepts with dignity the silence
of the dead. Semiramis' speech also raises the deeper question
of its dramatic function in the whole: does the poet wish or
require us to accept her claims unquestioningly? Is this speech
not only a striking denouement but, poetically, the revelation
of the full truth? This question presupposes an inquiry into the
poet's use of myth, and we shall return to it there.

III

The poet of *Semiramis* was well read in ancient authors. We
have already noted reminiscences of the *Aeneid*, a possible
reflection from the *Metamorphoses*, a rare detail and a rare word
borrowed from Servius, another from Martianus Capella. But
he is no straightforward imitator of ancient poetry, his language
never becomes copy or mosaic; he has used his sources sensi-
tively and eclectically, and has concealed his art in this almost
as much as the *Ruodlieb* poet has.

Legends about Semiramis were widespread in the Middle
Ages.[1] The chapters relating to her in Orosius (I. 4) and
holy, 'divine' one of the close. Thus while it might seem possible to attenuate
l. 179 to mean something like 'If goddesses are allowed to yield to wantonness, it cannot be so wicked for a woman to sin with a god', this would blunt
the effect of the peripety, while not altering the basic tension between the two
judgements of the heroine sufficiently to make a radically different interpretation possible.

The strong positive element in Semiramis' final speech is striking: contrast
for instance the attitude displayed in Pasiphae's self-defence in the remarkable
fragment of Euripides' *Cretans*: 'If I had given my body to a man, selling my
love for secret hire, how justly were I then exposed for a wanton! As it is,
God visited me with madness: so though I suffer, my sin was not freely
willed.' (Transl. D. L. Page, *Greek Literary Papyri*, i (1941), 75.)

[1] Cf. the valuable survey of Irene Samuel, 'Semiramis in the Middle Ages:
the History of a Legend', *Mediaevalia et Humanistica*, ii (1943), 32–44.

Justinus (1. 1–2), and the allusions to her in Jerome and Augustine, were particularly influential. She became a byword for lasciviousness. None the less, the poet of *Semiramis* has disregarded all those legends about his heroine that were common medieval currency—that she wore trousers, killed her lovers, committed incest with her son, and was at last murdered by him, as well as her reputedly great achievements in building and in warfare. None of these are relevant to his treatment of Semiramis. Only two small details handed down from antiquity seem to pertain specially to the Semiramis of his dialogue:[1] the first is Pliny's reference (*Hist. Nat.* VIII. 155) to her sexual passion for a horse:

Equum adamatum a Samiramide usque in coitum Iuba auctor est.

This passion is implied also by Hyginus (*Fab.* 243), who affirms simply that *Semiramis in Babylonia, equo amisso, in pyram se coniecit.*

The second is a detail preserved in a Greek tradition, which I am not even certain that the medieval Latin poet could have known directly: the Greek apologist Athenagoras (second century) records that Semiramis was divinized. In chapter 30 of his *Legatio pro Christianis* Athenagoras asks sarcastically:

If Derceto's daughter Semiramis, a lascivious and blood-guilty woman, was thought to be the Syrian goddess, and because of Derceto the Syrians worship doves and worship Semiramis (for the myth according to Ktesias is that the woman was changed into a dove, which is impossible)—what wonder then that others, through their sovereignty or tyranny, have been called gods by those subject to them?[2]

Semiramis' unnatural passion for an animal, and her divinization, are focal points in the Latin poet's fable. Here the animal

---

[1] These two details are ignored in the mainstream of medieval tradition about Semiramis, and are not even mentioned by Dr. Samuel in her article.

[2] *P.G.* 6, 957D–960A; cf. also Diodorus, *Bibl.* II. 14, 3; Lucian, *De Syria dea,* 14 and 39 (discussed below, p. 111).

becomes a bull: the poet develops his fable at least partly by
adapting to Semiramis the well-known poetic versions of
Europa's passion for the bull that is Jove. There are certain
obvious narrative similarities with Ovid's account (*Metam.* II.
848–75, III. I ff.): Europa loves Jupiter in his taurine shape, her
brother Cadmus, like Semiramis' brother, tries to find her,
and he, too, goes to a shrine of Apollo (to consult the oracle).
But there are also differences: unlike Semiramis' brother,
Cadmus receives no news of his sister; his consultation of the
oracle looks forward to his founding of Thebes and has no
intrinsic connection with the Europa episode. In language,
there is no sign of a poetic debt—only one or two parallels so
slight that they may be coincidence.[1]

Horace's *Europa* ode (III. 27) has inspired the *Semiramis* poet
in a more far-reaching way: again not in language or style, nor
indeed in narrative detail, but in a vital point of structure. Like
Horace, the medieval poet shows the fable under two opposed
attitudes: as a woman's disgraceful wantonness, and as a divine
encounter that neither can nor need be justified to mortals.
There is a significant difference in the dramatic unfolding: in
Horace's poem it is the woman herself who is tormented by
shame and the goddess Venus who reveals to her the divine
meaning of the deed; in *Semiramis* the shocked outcry comes
from the opening 'chorus' and from the augur, and it is the

---

[1] *Semiramis*, 14 may echo *Metam.* II. 851 *mugit . . . herbis* and 864 *viridique . . .
in herba* (or indeed III. 86 *virides . . . herbas*, from a different context); *palearia*
are mentioned in *Metam.* II. 854. The *dentes . . . draconis* (*Semiramis*, 57) are
related by their context to Servius' *dentibus Pythoni serpentis* (see discussion
above, p. 92) rather than to the *vipereos dentes* sown by Cadmus (*Metam.* III.
103). While the story of Pasiphae (where the bull is not Jupiter in taurine
shape) is less relevant to *Semiramis* than that of Europa, *Semiramis* 7 (*bos est
inventus adulter*) and 56 (*bovis es que passa ruinas*) may echo Ovid's allusion to
Pasiphae (*Metam.* IX. 740):
            passa bovem est, et erat qui deciperetur adulter.
In the dream-poem that has been preserved among Ovid's *Amores* (III. 5), we
have the theme of the lovers under the image of bull and cow, an augur to
interpret the dream, and the adultery motif (vv. 43–4). Yet there are no echoes
of this poem in *Semiramis*, and the thematic analogies are only apparent, not
real.

heroine who corrects their judgement, fully convinced of the *hieros gamos* she has experienced. But in both the dramatic structure is governed by this contrast of the first, human and fallible, interpretation, against the second, which shows a divine action as playing havoc with human values and laws. The seemingly monstrous emerges as the numinous. The medieval poet was able to assimilate and transform the structure of emotions and ideas, without the least suggestion of pastiche.

The details of the augur's necromancy raise problems of oral as well as written sources. The scene is a composite, and cannot fully be accounted for in terms of one literary model or of several. One scene in Roman poetry that the medieval poet certainly had in mind was the conjuration of Daphnis in Vergil's eighth Eclogue. The augur alludes, like Vergil's enchantress, to *verbenas* (VIII. 65), though this, as we have seen, is a commonplace in Roman descriptions of sacrifice and magic. The triads in the Eclogue (73 ff.)—three threads, three colours, and three knots, and walking three times round the altar—may have suggested the *tres aras* and *tres canes* in *Semiramis*: the augur, too, believes that a triadic sacrifice will be more effective (*argumentosius*) than a single one, he too knows that *numero deus impare gaudet*. Again the image of Daphnis, who is to be possessed by such love-longing as a heifer wearily seeking her bull through the forest-groves (85–6), must have been for the medieval poet rich in associations with his central theme. In Vergil the moment when the flame flickers up and the dog is heard barking (105–7) is very different from *Semiramis*, 40 (*latrantis flamma refulsit*), yet the poet may have recalled these details too, at least half-consciously. The fundamental difference between the two scenes lies of course in their purpose: one is love-magic, the other necromancy. But Vergil, too, has one swift allusion to necromancy: the sorcerer Moeris is able *saepe animas imis excire sepulchris* (98). None of these details is decisive; not one of them suggests an outright imitation. But taken together they suggest that deep in the medieval poet's memory the Vergilian scene lurked as an imaginative reality, vivid enough to prompt the resuscitation of half-remembered details, in unpredictable collocations, within a new dramatic whole.

The poet seems to have had no comparably intimate relation to other magic episodes in Roman poetry.[1] It is probable that he knew the scene of Medea's rejuvenation-magic in the *Metamorphoses* (VII. 180 ff.), with her invocations to Hecate and the powers of the night (*dique omnes noctis adeste*), her control of the winds (*ventos abigoque vocoque*), and her sacrifice (this time a black sheep, with two altars, and again *verbenae*); he may also have known the account of the dog-sacrifice in the *Fasti* (IV. 935 ff.); yet there is no sign that any of these details, rather than comparable ones known perhaps only through the superstition and hearsay of his own time, kindled his imagination. So, too, he shows no evidence of a debt to any of the fuller descriptions of necromancy proper in Roman poetry (Lucan, *Pharsalia*, VI. 438–830; Statius, *Thebais*, IV. 443–645; Seneca, *Oedipus*, 547–658) or prose (Quintilian, *Declamatio*, X; Apuleius, *Metamorphoses*, II. 28 ff.). One detail in the magic—the swarming up[2] of spirits from the underworld at the moment just before the desired phantom emerges (*Semiramis*, 152–3)— may have a biblical source, in Saul's consultation of the *mulier pythonem habens* (*I Reg.* XXVIII):[3] '*Quid vidisti?*' *Et ait mulier ad Saul:* '*Deos vidi ascendentes de terra.*' But the parallel is in the idea only, not in the language.

For the majority of the superstitious features already singled out in the earlier discussion (pp. 90–9)—prescriptions such as the avoidance of honey and salt in the ritual, or the injunction

---

[1] Georg Luck's essay (cited above, p. 90, n. 3) gives an excellent survey and discussion of sorcery in Roman poetry.

[2] In 153 the rare *adventacio* seems to be used with the sense 'accessus' (*Mlat. Wörterbuch*, s.v. 1), or possibly with the sense 'turba congregata' (ibid., s.v. 3).

[3] In *I Par.* x. 13, referring to the same episode, she is called a *pythonissa*, as in *Semiramis* 58 (but cf. also pp. 92–3). Other accounts of necromancy that were known from early Christian tradition include some narrated of Christ himself in the New Testament Apocrypha (cf. Lynn Thorndike, *A History of Magic and Experimental Science*, i. 391), and some narrated of Simon Magus in the pseudo-Clementine *Recognitions* and *Homilies* (cf. Thorndike, ibid. i. 419).

to keep asses away from the sacrifice—it is unlikely that a decisive literary model will ever be found. They belong to the *koinê* of popular magic, and often, as Bächtold-Stäubli has brilliantly shown by way of many entries in his *Handwörterbuch*, such features can persist through millennia with small variation. Even a relatively unusual feature such as the burning of dogs and cocks together in the sacrifice seems to me more likely to belong to such a *koinê* (if indeed it is not the poet's pure invention) than to derive from a written record such as the passage cited from Thietmar of Merseburg, though this affords a certain parallel. Only the augur's promise to shake the dragon's teeth seems to stand out as a trait with an absolutely specific literary inspiration.

Scenes of necromancy are rare in the Latin literature of the poet's own time. In the story of Proterius' daughter, told in somewhat heavy leonine hexameters by Hrotsvitha (i. 6) and in a deft, exhilarating sequence in the *Cambridge Songs* (30a), the magician to whom the seducer appeals for a love-charm bids the young man to take a letter to Satan, by raising it up in the dead of night over a pagan's tomb and praying to the devil. At once demons come and snatch the young man into hell, where Satan promises to help him at the price of abjuring his Christianity. In neither poem is it stated that the dead man appeared as a phantom or mouthpiece for a demon; neither shows any serious acquaintance with necromancy, or adds any fresh 'realistic' touches to the source in the *Vitae Patrum*.[1] More sophisticated is Anselm of Besate's treatment both of love-magic and necromancy in his *Rhetorimachia* (c. 1050). Anselm alleges that his cousin Rotiland employed necromancy in order to retrieve his book of magic: the book had been stolen by the boy whom Rotiland had used in the performing of a love-charm, since he had not been paid adequately:

Quid? Sepultum desepelivit, mortuum diabolica arte suscitavit, mortuum hominem quasi hominem reddidit. Surgit enim, spirat, loquitur et disceptat. Vas illud sacratum quasi simulacrum fecit

[1] *P.L.* 73, 302 ff.

demonum; plasma Christi, preclarum illud opus domini, fecit taber-
naculum mamone sui. Abita tandem oracione ad illum, se quod non
habebat respondit daturum et facilem illius promisit reditum. . . .[1]

Here the phantom of the dead person becomes the vehicle for
the demon to reveal the place where the book is hidden. As
in *Semiramis*, the necromancy is performed for the revealing
of hidden knowledge of what has happened, not in order to
know future events.

The love-magic in Anselm[2] echoes Horace's fifth Epode, and
I believe also Virgil's Daphnis Eclogue, though with significant
differences: the boy is half-buried in the ground, but only to
act as a sympathetic medium for the love-charm, not to be
murdered; the formulae of the spell are akin to those of the
spell for Daphnis, yet the words have changed, for Rotiland
uses different equipment. Several details, such as the magic
signs in the *quaternio*, seem realistic rather than literary, and
may well, as Karl Manitius has argued, reflect authentic prac-
tices in the northern Italy of Anselm's time. The poetic echoes
are no simple adaptations, but harmonize with the realistic
touches to form a rhetorically vivid scene. It is just such a
decoction of half-borrowed literary reminiscence with the
koinê of popular belief in the author's own age, fanned by his
own wayward imagination, that I would see in the necromantic moments in *Semiramis*.

[1] What shall I say? He undid the burial of the buried one, raised the dead
man up by diabolic art, restored him as the semblance of a man. The phantom
rises, breathes, speaks, and disputes. It was as if he made that sacred vessel
into a simulacrum for demons, made Christ's creation, the glorious handi-
work of the Lord, into a dwelling for his fiend. When he addressed him, the
phantom answered that he would give back the book—though he did not
have it—and promised its easy return. (Karl Manitius, 'Magie und Rhetorik
bei Anselm von Besate', *Deutsches Archiv für Erforschung des Mittelalters*, xii
(1956), 56; Manitius' critical edition of the *Rhetorimachia* appeared subsequently
(1958) in the *MGH*. For an admirable discussion of Anselm's magic in a wider
context, cf. also M.-Th. d'Alverny, 'Survivance de la magie antique', *Miscel-
lanea Mediaevalia*, i (1962), 154–78).

[2] *v.* Karl Manitius, art. cit., pp. 54–8.

IV

Kommt der neue Gott gegangen,
Hingegeben sind wir stumm!
　　　　　Zerbinetta, in Hofmannsthal's
　　　　　Ariadne auf Naxos.

The Latin Middle Ages knew Semiramis only as a historical figure, a queen of Babylon who had lived long ago. Why did this poet uniquely transform her into a mythical figure?[1] Why should he attribute to Semiramis wife of Ninus the destiny of the maiden Europa? The question is a twofold one: what stimulated the poet to do so? and, what was his intention in doing so? To the first question, if we confine ourselves to the written sources that an eleventh-century poet could have known, only Pliny's and Hyginus' allusions to Semiramis' passion for her horse suggest the beginnings of an answer. Yet theirs is a context of anecdote, not myth. Is there any possibility that by way of an oral transmission, no longer traceable, a mythical conception of Semiramis, as a woman singled out for sacred union with the highest god, could have reached the medieval poet? I think it cannot be ruled out, and have set out separately (below, pp. 111–13) some of the considerations that may be relevant to this problem.

The question of intention, on the other hand, resolves itself into trying to define more closely this poet's particular will to experiment. No tradition of Semiramis or Europa of which we have any record can account for, or could have determined, the particular embodiment displayed in the Latin poetic dialogue. What is so rare in this poet's exploit is his attempt to

---

[1] It could perhaps be argued that the poet has simply *invented* a story based on the loves of Europa and Pasiphae, and given the name Semiramis to his heroine quite arbitrarily. But this seems to me highly unlikely: the poet's allusions to Ninus and to Babylon show clearly that he had the specific figure of the Babylonian queen in mind; and it would be too great a coincidence to suppose that, among all the antique historical queens of whom a medieval writer knew, he should have attributed a sexual passion for an animal to the one queen of whom this was in fact related in ancient sources.

recreate mythical material on a plane that would be worthy of it. Where the predominant traditions of Semiramis make her no more than a topic for shallow anecdote or a cliché for misogynistic satire, this poet somehow knew that she could be of the substance of myth. And whether he came to this knowledge by way of oral legends, or through an unexpected piece of antiquarian lore, or indeed intuitively, he acted upon it with all the force of his imagination. Alone in his time—as far as any of the written records show us—he sensed the potentialities latent in such a myth, and determined to develop them dramatically. For him it was not enough for a mythical world to be of a Fulgentian or even an Ovidian atmosphere, nor were its marvels to be those of Christian wonder-tales such as Gregory's. His mythical world was to be a murky, mysterious, grandly barbaric one, a world of pagan gods and demons lurking in the shadows of pagan sacrificial fires, where by fantastic rites a shaman can summon spirits of the dead to speak, or a necromancer cause phantoms to rise up. Leaving aside the question of sources for specific details and expressions, the poet could scarcely have envisaged such a world at all if he had never read the ancient poems most familiar in the medieval schools, if he had never met Vergil's Sibyl, Ovid's Medea, Statius' Tiresias. But we have precious little evidence that passages of this kind in the school-texts kindled quite such a blaze in the minds of his contemporaries.

The poet's empathy gave him the impulse to create his own intense evocation of a fabulous ancient world, an evocation remarkable not least for its complete consistency: unlike the Macedon, Troy, or Thebes of the twelfth-century poets, this author's Babylon contains not one specifically Scriptural or Christian allusion.[1] This is the more surprising as nearly every other Christian writer who mentioned Semiramis was specially concerned to relate her to biblical history.[2]

[1] The nearest approach to such consistency in the twelfth century occurs in Joseph of Exeter's *De bello Troiano*.
[2] Cf. Irene Samuel, art. cit.

His powers of writing were not fully equal to his tenebrous vision. There are flat lines and pedantic lines interspersed, certain details of the magic, such as the darkness, become repetitious; the augur's part particularly is uneven: it is often impossible to tell how far his pathos and rant are in character, a poet's conscious dramatic device, and how far they reflect a loosening of poetic control. Certainly the contrasts in speech and manner between the augur and his sister are deliberate, and I do not believe the poet means us to take the augur's extravagances more seriously than Semiramis herself takes them; we, too, must share her recognition of his primness and his fussiness. At the same time, in his impulsive cry of despair to Apollo the augur can be moving, and in the first moment of encounter with the phantom he shows a true dignity:

> Quondam regalis vultus fuit iste sororis—
> Hec est illustris species notissima matris.
> Da, regina, manum. Soror, os mihi porrige flendum.

Another way in which the poet's language and his vision seem imperfectly matched can be seen in some of the briefer exchanges of dialogue (e.g. 29–37), where the transitions of thought are hard to follow. This may be due simply to an excessive love of ellipsis and compression in these exchanges, yet even after attempting to expand them I still feel unable to reconstruct all the links satisfactorily. Again I suspect a deliberate dramatic intention—that the suddenness and unpredictable swiftness of the turns of thought are to help give the scene its aura of mystery—yet cannot see that it has emerged quite as the poet intended.

The most compelling mystery in the poem lies in the nature of the heroine. If it seems natural to see the augur throughout with her eyes, it is also almost inevitable that the meaning of the whole will be understood from the *anagnôrisis* at the close. Semiramis will then be seen as an exemplification of the mythical mortal girl who is sexually united with the disguised god and thereby attains divinity. Her revelation then would be read as a straight refutation of the world's claim that she was wanton and guilty, the augur in believing it would be shown to have been insanely deluded, even blasphemous. And yet, can the strident opening chorus be so totally dismissed? I think its weight must still lie in an intentional parallelism with the closing speech. The two are deliberately symmetrical, each consisting of nineteen hexameters, and I would suggest that beyond the technical symmetry a certain narrative and emotional symmetry-through-contrast is implied. The scene that had been sketched with repulsion—'making the beast with two backs'—is rehearsed once more at the close, evoking all the divine beauty of the garden of love[1] that the heroine experienced.

The conclusion supersedes the prelude, yet cannot wholly exclude the prelude's reverberations. In the 'wantonness', an ambiguity remains. The epigraph from Hofmannsthal may help to clarify the nature of this ambiguity. We can ask, is the Semiramis of this poem a dedicated Ariadne, who knows she has found sacred 'Verwandlung' in her unique union with a god; or is she a Zerbinetta, for whom wantonness and a heady sense of the divineness of love-making are indistinguishable? The poet does not force the decision. The augur and chorus 'misinterpret' Semiramis' behaviour, just as Zerbinetta 'misinterprets' that of Ariadne. Yet in the medieval Latin poet as in Hofmannsthal the meaning of the whole is conditioned by that misinterpretation, by the ironic juxtaposition of two attitudes to the heroine's welcome of the divine lover. The tone of the irony is very different. In *Ariadne* Zerbinetta, seeing the girl who had sworn to die for Theseus' love united to her new lover, the god Bacchus, sings her own lighthearted *rondo* once more, joyfully making fun of Ariadne:

> Kommt der neue Gott gegangen,
> Hingegeben sind wir stumm!

---

[1] The *hortus* (164, 176) has I think primarily the mystic associations of, for example, *Cant.* v. 1, though the Priapic connotations (as in *Jezabel* 19: *Qui regnat in horto*) cannot be excluded.

In *Semiramis*, the shadow of the 'divine' interpretation is an uglier one—not simply of sexual abandon but of bestiality. So the juxtaposition of the two attitudes to Semiramis is harsher than that of the two to Ariadne: we are aware at the end how close the inhuman is to the more-than-human, the monster to the god.

APPENDIX

WERE there any ancient links between Semiramis' and Europa's legend, or between Semiramis and a bull? A number of points, though not conclusive, deserve consideration. In late antiquity Semiramis was widely identified with and worshipped as the Baby-lonian–Assyrian goddess Ishtar.[1] This, as we noted, was a byword to the late second-century Christian polemicist, Athenagoras. But according to the account given in *de Syria dea* by Lucian, Athenagoras' slightly older pagan contemporary, Ishtar was also identified with Europa:

There is likewise in Phoenicia a temple of great size owned by the Sidonians. They call it the temple of Astarte. I hold this Astarte to be no other than the moon-goddess. But according to the story of one of the priests this temple is sacred to Europa, sister of Cadmus. She was the daughter of Agenor, and on her disappearance from Earth the Phoenicians honoured her with a temple and told a sacred legend about her: how that Zeus was enamoured of her for her beauty, and changing his form into that of a bull carried her off into Crete.[2]

Did Europa's story, then, become linked in the Hellenistic world, by way of such a syncretism, not only with Ishtar but specifically

[1] Cf. J. Fontenrose, 'White Goddess and Syrian Goddess', in *Semitic and Oriental Studies, A Volume Presented to William Popper* (1951), pp. 125–48; W. Fauth, 'Dea Syria', *Der kleine Pauly*, i (1964), 1400–3.

[2] *De Syria dea*, 4, transl. H. A. Strong–J. Garstang, *The Syrian Goddess* (1913), pp. 43–4. On the question of possible pre-Greek roots for the Ishtar-Europa identification, cf. most recently W. Bühler, *Europa* (München, 1968), pp. 24–5.

with Semiramis? And could a vestige of such a Hellenistic tradition have reached a medieval western poet, possibly over Byzantium? This is indeed no more than conjecture—but to suppose that a medieval poet forged a link between Semiramis and Europa independently, fully *ex nihilo*, is equally conjecture.

There is another tradition that links Semiramis with a bull. In Jewish legend Semiramis is the wife of Nebuchadnezzar.[1] Nebuchadnezzar, commanded by a voice from heaven, was made to dwell among the beasts and eat grass *quasi bos* (Dan. iv. 29); and in neither Jewish nor Christian exegesis was this taken merely metaphorically: the king of Babylon was thought to have changed into taurine shape.[2] This link between Semiramis and a taurine consort does not, of course, account for the specific fable of the medieval poem. Yet if the Latin poet, planning to write a verse dialogue about Semiramis, knew some version of this Jewish conception of her (as well as knowing the anecdote of her passion for a horse), it would help to explain what might have led his thoughts in the direction of Europa. One other Jewish Semiramis legend is also interesting in this connection: in the *Midrash Tanḥūmā* the false prophets Ahab and Zedekiah tempt Semiramis (*Shemīrath*) to commit adultery with them, *under the pretext that this is a divine command*.[3] In the Midrash version she refuses to yield, and the would-be seducers are brought before Nebuchadnezzar, who has them burnt in the fiery furnace. Ginzberg, however, points out that Origen and Jerome 'give this legend as they heard it from their Jewish teachers. According to their version, the false prophets used to assure the women that they were destined to become the mothers of the Messiah if they yielded to

---

[1] Cf. W. H. Roscher, *Lexikon*, iv. 698. The passage alluded to is translated in full in *Midrash Rabba*, ed. H. Freedman–M. Simon, pp. 248–9 (*Leviticus* [Metzora], xix. 6). Dr. Samuel does not discuss the Jewish Semiramis traditions in her article. Semiramis is not to my knowledge mentioned in connection with Nebuchadnezzar in the Latin exegetical tradition: I have examined the commentaries on Daniel listed in Migne's *Index Commentariorum in Scripturas*, P.L. 219, 108; I have not seen the unpublished commentary by Hrabanus Maurus (MS. Karlsruhe Landesbibl. Aug. perg. 208).

[2] Cf., e.g., L. Ginzberg, *The Legends of the Jews*, iv. 334 (Nebuchadnezzar's body becomes half ox, half lion), vi. 423–4; St. Paterius (*P.L.* 79, 998A); Petrus Archidiaconus (*P.L.* 96, 1350A).

[3] *Midrash Tan*. B. iii. 7 (ed. S. Buber, Wilna, 1885), mentioned by Ginzberg, *Legends*, vi. 426. In other versions (ibid. iv. 336) it is Nebuchadnezzar's daughter who is tempted.

their wishes.'[1] Here the prophets had their way: in Jerome's words the women *inlectae cupidine praebebant corpora sua quasi matres futurae Christi*. Neither Origen nor Jerome mentions Semiramis as being among these women. But can we rule out the possibility that a version, in which Semiramis was not only tempted, but yielded at a seemingly divine behest, existed and remained current in Christendom through oral transmission?[2]—These are only straws in the wind; but they must be observed and assessed before we can pronounce the eleventh-century poet's decision to mythologize Semiramis fortuitous.

[1] Ginzberg, *Legends*, v. 426; Origen, *Epist. ad Africanum*, 8 (*P.G.* II, 64B–65A—this was not translated into Latin in the Middle Ages); Jerome, *in Hier.* xxix (36), 21–3 (Corpus Christianorum lxxiv. 284–5).

[2] To postulate either the Latin poet's knowledge of Hebrew or the existence of lost Latin translations of Jewish legends would be quite unwarranted in the absence of specific evidence.

When this book was already in press, Dr. Paul Gerhard Schmidt kindly pointed out to me that a text of *Semiramis* (and of *Jezabel*) has recently been printed by Bernard Leblond, in an appendix to his *L'Accession des normands de Neustrie à la culture occidentale* (Paris, 1966). Dr. Leblond is concerned with the text chiefly as a historical indication of tenth- and eleventh-century Norman culture: thus he does not attempt to elucidate or discuss the poem, and indeed many lines in his transcription are not intelligible as they stand. He considers *Semiramis* to be merely the second part of the 'Satire contre Jézabel' (p. 185), not a piece in its own right. Thus—apart from one or two corrections of the text, arrived at independently—his approach to the poem and mine do not overlap.

I am most grateful to Dr. Schmidt not only for knowledge of Leblond's book but for several valuable last-minute observations of his own on the text of *Semiramis*.

IV

PETER ABELARD: *PLANCTUS*
AND SATIRE

AMONG Peter Abelard's six *planctus*,[1] three especially are arresting in the individual way they treat biblical characters and
themes. The first, the lament of Dina for herself and Sichem,
explores emotions of which the swift account in Genesis tells
us nothing, and clarifies these in the dramatic transitions of her
monologue.[2] First, there is haughtiness—she, of a great family,
of the illustrious blood of patriarchs, has lost her honour—
followed by an outcry of self-reproach, 'by myself betrayed'.
She cannot at that moment think of Sichem as her lover—he
is one of the other side, 'the unclean people'. Then she realizes
that Sichem's plight was like her own: he too has lost his
reputation for ever—as well as inadvertently causing the mas-
sacre of his race; he too was 'by himself destroyed'. The almost
identical refrain, sung first for herself and then for him, re-
inforces the bond between them. Through this she reveals to
herself her true feelings for him, feelings that begin in pity but
reach out into love. They express themselves first in anger: his
fate is unjust—the fault was small, the punishment far too great.
Her own brothers are hateful, their righteousness having been
only a pretext for their base cruelty. Then her thoughts move
to love: if a true impulse of love was there, as she knows it was,
can even the violation of a young girl be judged a grievous
fault? Her brothers talked of family honour—was it not an

---

[1] The *planctus* are here cited from the manuscripts, R: Roma, Vat. Reg. lat.
288, s. XII ex., fols. 63ᵛ–64ᵛ; and P: Paris, B.N. n. acq. lat. 3126, s. XII²,
fols. 88ᵛ–90ᵛ (*Planctus* VI only). I also give references to Wilhelm Meyer's
edition, *Gesammelte Abhandlungen zur mittellateinischen Rhythmik,* i (1905),
340–74.

[2] I give a text of this *planctus* in the Appendix below, p. 146.

honour too that he, a prince, should have wanted her so much as not only to possess her but to ask his kindred's leave 'to marry an alien'? Suddenly, with this thought, her love and admiration for him blossom so much that her final words extend this love and admiration to his whole people (*gens tanta*), to those whom her family had taught her to regard as 'the enemy race' (*plebs adversa*).

So too in the longest and most spectacular of the *planctus*, the lament of the girls of Israel over the death of Jephtha's daughter (III), the emotions of the protagonist (about which again the Bible tells us nothing) are set on a plane of high romance. Jephtha's daughter, who in the Bible dies in woeful obedience to her father, becomes a heroine joyfully choosing the death in which she will find glory, who almost contemptuously compels her faltering father to keep his vow, 'to be a man now in spirit as in sex, not to oppose my glory or your own'.[1] Her death takes the form of a drawn-out ritual that increasingly is made to look like a black parody of a wedding-mime; for a moment the realization of this becomes unbearable to her and she cries out against it, then at once composes herself again, to die with queenly dignity.[2]

---

[1] R fol. 64^r (Meyer, p. 349):

> Ut sexu, sic animo
> vir esto nunc, obsecro:
> nec mee   nec tue   obstes glorie . . .

I have discussed this *planctus* in detail in the article 'Medieval Poetry—I: Abélard', *The Listener*, 25 November 1965, 841–5. The late Wolfram von den Steinen has interpreted the song with a rather different emphasis: 'Die Planctus Abaelards—Jephthas Tochter', *Mittellateinisches Jahrbuch*, iv (1967, publ. 1969), esp. pp. 138–40. Cf. also von den Steinen's more general observations on Abelard's *planctus* in *CCM* ix (1966), 363–70.

[2] R fol. 64^r (Meyer, p. 351):

> Rerum pondus et ornatus
> moram virgo iam non ferens,
> lecto surgit, et repellit
> que restabant, ita dicens:
> 'Que nupture satis sunt
> periture nimis sunt!'
> Mox quem patri detulit
> ensem nudum arripit.

The independence and expressive range of the final *planctus*, David's lament over Saul and Jonathan (vi), is likewise remarkable.[1] It begins, like the biblical dirge of David, with a lament over the humiliation of Israel in battle. But where the biblical song goes on to give almost equal emphasis to Saul and Jonathan, here Saul as a person is given only three lines, Jonathan more than thirty. Saul is, in a formulaic phrase, *regum fortissime*, he is the king 'through whose lavishness the daughters of Jerusalem are clothed in purple'—nothing more. David's encounters with the king during Saul's vendetta against him—moments of high dramatic potential—are not here recalled. With Jonathan, on the other hand, David recalls not only the oneness of love they shared, but a shared agony of guilt—*que peccata, que scelera / nostra sciderunt viscera*—of which the Bible knows nothing, and which is never explained within the *planctus* itself, Where the biblical David sings of Saul and Jonathan, 'Even in death they were undivided',[2] Abelard's persona transforms this thought completely, into 'Even in death *I* could have been undivided from Jonathan'. In the longest and most moving stanzas of the *planctus* David sings to his dead friend of his wish to have died at the same moment as he, his bitter regret not to have been at his side in battle then, 'that even death would join us more than sunder us'. For to live without Jonathan 'is to die constantly'.[3]

The individual portrayal and analysis of emotions in these three *planctus* is related to, and in part due to, the reverberations that their themes had for Abelard himself. In suggesting this I do not wish to go so far as those scholars, notably Laurenzi and Vecchi, who have claimed that the *planctus* as a group 'are

[1] I give a new text, with melody, from the recently discovered manuscript P, *infra*, pp. 203 ff.

[2] II *Reg.* I. 23.

[3] Sts. 5a–b in the text below, pp. 203 ff. Von den Steinen (*CCM* ix (1966), 367) speaks of these stanzas as 'consacrés à Saül', but the tenderness and intimacy of tone show them to be addressed to Jonathan. The text of the earlier manuscript, P, which preserves sts. 4c–d in the correct order, now places the recipient of this lament beyond any doubt.

nothing more than a repetition of the whole *Historia Calami-tatum*,[1] that they 'represent the poetic synthesis of Abelard's whole sorrowful life, in biblical dress, through allegory or symbol.'[2] The symbolism in these songs seems to me subtler than that, and shows no trace of allegory; the biblical characters are not a 'dress' for Abelard—they are of the substance of the *planctus*, no mere accidents; the personal element, in so far as it is present—and in my view it colours some of the *planctus* far more and in more varied ways than it does others—grows out of a deep dramatic probing of the characters portrayed. At the same time it seems to me undeniable that the griefs and longings which here emerge with the greatest intensity, and which move furthest beyond the Old Testament narratives that the songs take as points of departure, have true, and disconcerting, counterparts in the autobiographical *Historia Calamitatum*, and in the correspondence of Abelard with Héloïse.

Most overtly in the lament of Dina: here it is in external events as much as in thoughts and feelings that art and life confront each other. From the letters we know not only the treachery of Héloïse's relatives in mutilating Abelard, but his

---

[1] F. Laurenzi, *Le poesie ritmiche de Pietro Abelardo* (Roma, 1911), p. 29. Laurenzi's ingenious attempts to see line-by-line autobiographical correspondences in the *planctus* were to a large extent fanciful and at times hilarious: e.g. of the lament of the girls of Israel over Jephtha's daughter he writes (p. 76):

'E questo canto egli [Abelardo] lo avrebbe riudito sovente e avrebbe rivisto la lunga teoria delle figlie di Francia, guidate da Eloisa, venire a deporre fiori sulla sua tomba, avrebbe udito ancora a sempre quelle voci lamentose come *odae flebiles* e quei pianti *ut cantus celebres* risonare per le valli e per i colli, "Quod sic me/semine/privet Dominus."'

Or again (p. 77), in the lament over Samson, when Abelard, 'il Sansone novello', having been 'facile vittima d'una donna', recovers his strength:

'Raccoglie tutte le sue forze e con uno scatto poderoso, lancia nel tempio della scienza il libro famoso *De Unitate et Trinitate Divina*. Il tempio della teologia tradizionale è scosso dalle fondamenta, ma Abelardo, coi nemici, ha seppellito sè stesso, perchè tra poco quelle stesse mani, che hanno scosso le colonne del tempio, getteranno alle fiamme il libro portentoso.'

[2] G. Vecchi (ed.), *Pietro Abelardo, I 'Planctus'* (Modena, 1951), p. 14.

own sense that he had made 'reparation for his fault' by offering to marry her, while she, opposing the marriage, insists that his love alone is more honour than she could ever be worthy of. In the way that Jephtha's daughter goes through with the ordeal of her ceremonial death, in her relentless courage, it is impossible not to think of Abelard's description of Héloïse taking the veil, explicitly as a sacrifice for Abelard's sake, and a sacrifice that to her was scarcely distinguishable from dying for him, voluntarily—*nunc accipe poenas, | Sed quas sponte luam!*[1] For David's lament it is more difficult to assess a subjective element with certainty or precision: there is no question of parallels of circumstance, or even of specific moments that could be paralleled from the personal prose writings. None the less, this David's strange affirmation of a shared guilt with the Jonathan who had been 'in one soul with me', his toying with what might have been, expressing the hope of a union with Jonathan beyond the grave when no union on earth was possible any more, point once more in the direction of the most ardent moments in the autobiographical writings, especially in the letters of Héloïse.[2] Once more it would be difficult to understand the imaginative innovations fully without taking this background of experience into account.

For Abelard the poet there was a fertile challenge in choosing themes to which he had a unique relation, and where the possibilities of a truly personal thematic development were latent. At the same time, as the opening of the last *planctus* suggests, his songs are *dolorum solatium*: even if they cannot 'give his laments and tears rest', they can subsume them in a creation that gives them objective dignity—no longer the private, helpless laceration of one or two human beings, but the meaningful

---

[1] *Historia Calamitatum* (ed. J. Monfrin, 2nd ed., 1962), p. 81 (*P.L.* 178, 136B). Héloïse speaks the words used by Cornelia in Lucan's *Pharsalia* (VIII. 94–8) when she promises to die for the sake of her husband, Pompey.

[2] It is worth remembering that in the twelfth century—and indeed often until the Renaissance—a similar range of loving expressions could be used without incongruity or lack of seriousness in poetry addressed to men and to women.

sorrow of the artist's persona, the dramatic creation that can
enfold the private thoughts and yet as artefact can take its place
in the outer world in its own right.

Two others among the *planctus*, Jacob's lament for his sons
(II) and David's for Abner (V), while they enrich their biblical
material, do not modify it in any essential way. Their grace-
fully stylized expressions of grief do not seem to reverberate
beyond their immediate themes. They are slighter than the
other *planctus*, lacking dramatic complexity—perhaps just because they contain no comparable personal impulse,[1] because
they do not question or transform the emotional perspectives
implied in their biblical sources, and hence do not significantly
extend these.

There remains the lament of Israel over Samson (IV), the
strangest of the six. Like the third *planctus*, the lament over
Jephtha's daughter, it is given to a chorus, not to a protagonist:
it is an exploration of a public, not an individual, sorrow. The
function of the chorus is not only to recall events but to comment on them. Thus the girls of Israel come on as mourners,
yet they also pass a judgement, or better, send out a disturbing
challenge to the audience: the heroine is 'more to be marvelled
at than mourned' (*stupendam plus quam flendam*), but the
father has acted with an insanity that degrades his whole
people:

> O mentem   amentem   iudicis,
> o zelum   insanum   principis!
> O patrem   sed hostem   generis,
> unice   quod nece   diluis![2]

[1] Laurenzi's suggestions, that Jacob is really Abelard's father Berengarius,
lamenting the misfortunes of his son (op. cit., pp. 69–71), or again that David
in the two final *planctus* is meant to be Geoffrey of Chartres (ibid., pp. 79 ff.,
cf. also Vecchi, op. cit., p. 16), seem tenuous and far-fetched.

[2] R fol. 64ʳ (Meyer, p. 352); diluit R. (A consonantally impure half-rhyme
scarcely occurs elsewhere in the six *planctus*.)

It is grammatically possible that the last two lines cited mean no more than
that Jephtha would have no grandchildren, but the parallelism of the two concluding stanzas suggests a less banal meaning. The *planctus* ends:

Oh demented mind of a judge, insane persistence of a general!
Father, but enemy of your race, whom you impair through the
death of your only one!

The chorus provokes the audience, not to accept the standpoint of father or daughter, but to reflect on the implications
of their tragedy: it asks, in effect, can a vow to God ever be holy
if it entails murder? Can such a murder ever be condoned?
Will not anyone who acquiesces in murder for allegedly religious reasons be less as a human being, 'impaired'?

In the lament over Samson, too, the last part is a judgement
by the chorus, which again forms a series of challenges to the
audience. Here, however, this 'judgement' not only takes up
a far larger proportion of the *planctus*—more than a third of the
whole—but also appears to have little to do with the substance
of the preceding lament. The narration of Samson's fate, interwoven with the mourning for it, is over; the solemn elegiac
tone ceases; by contrast, the chorus launches into a heady,
rhetorical attack on all womankind: woman has been the
downfall not merely of Samson but of all great men—beware of
her! This attack (well known as it is in connection with Samson
from other, very different contexts) seems quite incongruous
with the dignity and deep texture of the verses by which the
chorus had just evoked Samson's death. Unlike any of the
other *planctus*, this poem seems cleft into two badly fitting
halves. Is this unusual carelessness, or insensibility, on Abelard's
part, or had he a specific poetic purpose in mind? To explore
his purpose is the main concern of this study. Let us first have
the complete *planctus* before us.[1]

> Hebree,   dicite,   virgines,
> insignis   virginis   memores,
> inclite   puelle   Israel,
> hac valde   virgine   nobiles!

As the girls in the final stanza affirm that they can all be ennobled through
celebrating the nobility of Jephtha's daughter, so in the preceding one, it
seems to me, they recognize that all can be degraded through acquiescence
in the father's deed.

[1] R fol. 64^{r-v} (Meyer, pp. 369–71). This *planctus* is in the strictest form of
the 'archaic' sequence, with two perfectly symmetrical *cursus* (I and II).

I 1a Abissus vere multa
      iuditia, deus, tua.
      eo plus formidanda
      quo magis sunt occulta
      et quo plus est ad illa
      quelibet vis infirma!

Truly a great abyss
are your judgements, God,
to be feared the more
the more they are mysteries,
the more that, faced with them,
all other strengths are weak!

  1b Virorum fortissimum
     nuntiatum per angelum,
     Nazareum inclitum,
     Israelis clipeum—
     cuius cor vel saxeum
     non fleat sic perditum?

That mightiest of men
whom an angel heralded,
the renowned Nazarite,
shield of Israel—
whose heart is so like stone
it will not weep that thus he fell?

  2a Quem primo Dalida
        sacra cesarie,
     hunc hostes postea
        privarunt lumine.

Dalila robbed him first
   of his hallowed hair,
then his enemies
   robbed him of light.

  2b Exhaustus viribus,
        orbatus oculis,
     mole fit deditus
        athleta nobilis.

Drained of his strength,
   bereft of his eyes,
consigned to the mill
   is the noble champion.

  3a Clausus carcere,
     oculorumque lumine
        iam privatus,
        quasi geminis
     ad molam sudans tenebris
        est oppressus.
     Ludos marcios
     plus exercere solitos
        frangit artus.

Incarcerated,
the light of his eyes
   now plucked away,
   as if with double
darkness toiling at the mill
   he is weighed down.
He ravages the limbs
more used to exercise
   in sports of war.

  3b Hos cibario
     vix sustentans edulio
        iumentorum,
     quod—et nimius
     labor hic et insolitus—
        sumit rarum,
        crebris stimulis
     agitatur ab emulis
        ut iumentum.

Keeping those limbs
barely alive with fodder
   of beasts of burden,
   eating rarely—
and even to eat an immense
   unwonted struggle—
   with repeated goading
he is driven by his adversaries
   like a beast.

3c   Quid tu, Dalida,
    quid ad hec dicis, impia,
        que fecisti?
      quenam munera
    per tanta tibi scelera
        conquisisti?
      Nulli gratia
    per longa manet tempora
        proditori.

What do you say, Dalila,
what do you say, impious one,
    to what you have done?
What kind of recompense
for such deeds of shame
    did you seek to win?
To none is favour
shown for long, if she's
    a traitor.

II 1a Renatis iam crinibus
    reparatis viribus,
    temulentis hostibus
    lusurus inducitur,
    ut morte doloribus
    finem ponat omnibus.

Now with his locks reborn,
his strength restored,
for drunken enemies
Samson is led to play,
to set with death an end
to every pain.

1b A iocis ad seria
    fertur mens diu concita:
    tam leva quam dextera
    columpnis applicita,
    hostium et propria
    miscet dolor funera.

From sports to earnestness
the mind, long roused, is brought:
his left hand, like his right,
holding the pillars fast,
his enemies' and his own
deaths anguish joined.

2a O semper fortium
      ruinam maximam,
    et in exicium
      creatam feminam!

Oh, ever of the mighty
    supreme destruction,
for such catastrophe
    was created—woman!

2b Hec patrem omnium
      deiecit protinus
    et mortis poculum
      propinat omnibus.

She brought the father of all
    down with due speed,
and the cup of death
    she hands to everyone.

3a   David sanctior,
    Salomone prudentior
      quis putetur?
    Aut quis impius
    magis per hanc vel fatuus

Holier than David,
wiser than Solomon,
    who could be thought?
Or again, more impious—
through woman's fault—or more
    fatuous,

      repperitur?
    Quis ex fortibus

    who could be found?
Who among the mighty

non ut Sanson fortissimus	is not, like mightiest Samson,
enervatur?	unmanned?

3b   Adam, nobile   Adam, the noble

divine plasma dextere,	form made by God's right hand,
mox hec stravit:	she soon laid low;
quam in proprium	that she, whom as his own
acceperat auxilium	helpmate he had received,
hostem sensit;	he felt his foe;
ex tunc femina	woman from then on
virorum tela maxima	forged her deadliest weapons
fabricavit.	against man!

3c   Sinum aspidi   Bare your breast to the asp—

vel igni prius aperi,	bare it to fire sooner,
quisquis sapis,	wise one, whoever you are,
quam femineis	than entrust yourself
te conmittas illecebris—	to womanly wiles—
nisi malis	unless you should prefer
ad exitium	towards that catastrophe
properare certissimum	to run inexorably
cum predictis![1]	with those already named!

The story of Samson was by Abelard's time heavily weighted with figural and moral associations; the originality of Abelard's conception of Samson, compared with earlier traditional ones, throws some light upon his intentions.

The traditional figure of Samson[2]

Samson, in the last part of Abelard's *planctus*, appears in the company of Adam, David, and Solomon, as an instance of the men who were wrecked by the women they loved. It is this

---

[1] I. 3b: after I. 3c in R. I. 3b, 5 hii R; 8 agitatur et ab R. II. 1a, 4 lesurus R. II. 3a, 8 sicut Sanson R.

[2] There is a useful survey of a number of patristic and medieval views of Samson in F. Michael Krouse, *Milton's Samson and the Christian Tradition* (1949), pp. 31–62, though unfortunately this is not always reliable in its indications of the location, authorship, and content of the passages discussed: e.g. Krouse did not realize that the passage he cites from the Mozarabic Liturgy (p. 35, n. 8), with its 'exciting liturgical style', where 'every part of the action is vividly imagined and poetically expanded', is quite simply, word for word, chapter XVI of Judges in the Latin Vulgate version! So too it is

quartet of men beguiled by women that becomes as it were
standard in later medieval poetic developments of the motif.
Thus for instance in *Sir Gawain and the Green Knight* (2416-19):

> For so wat3 Adam in erde with one bygyled,
> And Salamon with fele sere, and Samson eftsone3—
> Dalyda dalt hym hys wyrde—and Dauyth þerafter
> Wat3 blended with Barsabe, þat much bale þoled.

Or in a Latin verse proverb that survives, as Walther has shown,
in 'countless manuscripts and variants':[1]

> Adam, Samsonem, si David, si Salomonem
> Femina decepit, quis modo tutus erit?

The tone and meaning lent to this topos, however, vary
remarkably across the centuries. Its first occurrence appears to
be in the pseudo-Clementine letters *Ad virgines*, long thought
to go back to the Apostolic period, though today regarded as
probably not earlier than the third century.[2] Here the purpose

important to note that when Rupert of Deutz questions Samson's worthiness
to be a figura of Christ, this is not 'a doubt which might have shaken the
framework of the entire allegorical tradition' (Krouse, p. 53): these same
doubts were voiced by Caesarius of Arles more than six centuries earlier, in
a sermon that was probably based on a lost work of St. Augustine's, and
which, notwithstanding the doubts, continues with allegoresis undeterred (see
discussion below).

[1] H. Walther, *Proverbia*, nos. 519 ff., 5026a.
[2] Cf. B. Altaner and A. Stuiber, *Patrologie* (7th ed., 1966), p. 47.

'For this is both becoming and profitable, that we should know how
many men there have been, and who [they were], that have perished
through women; and who and how many have been the women that have
perished through men, by reason of the constancy with which they have
associated with one another. . . . Hast thou not heard concerning Samson
the Nazarite, "with whom was the Spirit of God", the man of great
strength? This man, who was a Nazarite, and consecrated to God, and who
was [gifted] with strength and might, a woman brought to ruin with [her]
wretched body, and with [her] vile passion. Art thou, perchance, such a
man as he? Know thyself, and know the measure of thy strength. . . . Does
not the case of David instruct thee, whom God "found a man after His
heart", one faithful, faultless, pious, true? . . . See, then, what evils he committed because of a woman. . . . Hast thou not read concerning Amnon and
Tamar, the children of David? . . . Hast thou not read the history of Solomon, the son of David, the man to whom God gave wisdom, and knowledge, and largeness of mind, and riches, and much glory, beyond all men?

of the motif, with its examples, is to warn men and women living the ascetic life of the dangers of associating together too much, and of sleeping in the same quarters. The tone is seriously ascetic, with no trace either of humorous or of fanatic anti-feminism. Dalila herself is condemned; but the author's warnings are addressed to men and women equally, and significantly he makes no mention of Eve as having caused Adam's fall. The misadventures of Samson, David, and Solomon feature among the warnings, but these also include that of Joseph with Potiphar's wife, and that of Amnon and Tamar, where the girl was evidently wholly guiltless.

In Jerome's *Adversus Jovinianum*, where zeal, obsession, and delight in virtuosity seem inseparable,[1] the motif of 'guilt through sensuality with women' occurs of Samson, and elsewhere of David and Solomon; Jerome also dwells, in yet another passage in the work, on the guilt of Eve.[2] But—without having made an exhaustive search—I have not met in Jerome's writings the later medieval topos of Adam, Samson, David, and Solomon as a group of men who were undone by the women they desired. So too in the Latin misogynistic verse of the earlier Middle Ages: the four often occur together, yet only (it would seem invariably before Abelard) as part of a larger series of such exempla.

In the ninth century Milo of Saint-Amand, in his long poem *De sobrietate,* having told the death of John the Baptist at the wish of the 'dancing monkey' (*saltatrix simia*) Salome, goes on to a tirade against love and song and woman's beauty, 'which sends those who love it to hell':

> Hac deceptus Adam seclusus ab arbore vitae est;
> Sic Emor et Sichem Dina periere subacta;

Yet this same man, through women, came to ruin, and departed from the Lord.'
(*Ad virgines*, II. 7–12, tr. B. L. Pratten, Ante-Nicene Christian Library, xiv (1869), 388–91).

[1] Cf. David S. Wiesen, *St. Jerome as a Satirist* (1964), pp. 113 ff.
[2] *Adversus Jovinianum*, I. 23 (*P.L.* 23, 241–2); I. 24 (245); II. 4 (288); I. 27 (248).

> Hebraei mixti scortis coluere Priapum;
> Turpavit meretrix Sanson saxoque molari
> Addixit—moluisse tamen scrutare quid hoc sit![1]

Deceived by her, Adam was banned from the tree of life; thus Hemor and Sichem died when Dina was ravished; the Hebrews, mingling with harlots, worshipped Baal; a courtesan degraded Samson and consigned him to the millstone—see clearly what it is, then, to have milled!

Jacob, Joseph, David, and Solomon are added as warnings; even 'timid Peter denied Christ when a woman taunted'. The tone would seem to be one of unrelieved monastic extremism —and yet the play on a bawdy double-entendre in Samson's efforts at milling[2] indicates how much the poet is enjoying himself.

So too when Roger of Caen, in a poem *De vita monachorum*, written before 1078,[3] warns the monks at length against the vices of the flesh, one senses that he is impelled by more than a zealous asceticism. There is a joy in rhetorical tricks, witty paradox, and wordplay that suggest the aspiring man of letters more than the Desert Father:

> Femina, dulce malum, mentem roburque virile
>   Frangit blanditiis insidiosa suis.
> Femina, fax Sathanae, gemmis radiantibus, auro,
>   Vestibus, ut possit perdere, compta venit . . .
> Sed carnem foenum clamat sacer ille propheta—
>   Fac procul a foeno flamma sit ista tuo.[4]

It is in this context that Samson occurs, in the company of Lot, David, and Solomon (with a final allusion to Eve, cause of all misery), in words very close to those of the verse proverb

---

[1] *De sobrietate*, II. 212–16 (*Poetae*, iii. 651).
[2] Thus Ludwig Traube, *Poetae*, iii. 651 ad loc.
[3] For the dating and attribution, *v.* Albert C. Friend, 'Sampson, David and Salomon in the Parson's Tale', *Modern Philology*, xlvi (1948–9), 117–21.
[4] Ed. T. Wright, *SP* ii. 186–7.

already cited.[1] Even if the poet is ostensibly concerned with the
salvation of monks' souls (*Femina, mors animae* . . .), the delight
in a lighter vein of polemic is again apparent when he goes on
to paint the miseries of marriage, where the material is basically
from St. Jerome, but is couched in couplets whose tone is
almost more reminiscent of the *Remedia amoris*:

> Si quis habet sponsam turpem, fastidit et odit;
> Si pulcram, moechos anxius ille timet . . .[2]

Here, significantly, Clytemnestra is mentioned in the same
verse as Dalila. We are approaching the world of twelfth-
century humanism.

When the two most polished and learned of the poets who
composed around 1100, Hildebert and Marbod (one of whom
wrote courtly panegyric poems to ladies, the other some
touching love-poetry), take up the motif of men ruined by
their love of women, one has more than ever the sense of sheer
virtuoso delight in its unfolding. Thus Hildebert has a poem
that begins:

> Plurima cum soleant mores evertere sacros,
> Altius evertunt femina, census, honos.[3]

This opening propounds the triple theme—woman, wealth,
and ambition as the three greatest dangers to holiness—that the
poet has set himself, as if for a *quaestio disputata*, and which he
proceeds to develop with consummate craft. When Marbod

[1] Ibid. ii. 188:
> Si Loth, Samsonem, si David, si Salomonem
> Femina deiecit, quis modo tutus erit?
As Dr. Friend (art. cit., p. 120) points out, even if no manuscript of the
proverb—where Adam is included—is as early as the lifetime of Roger of
Caen, 'it is perhaps possible that the couplet was long current as a proverb
or *Merkvers* which Roger adapted and to which he thus gave the form that
we have seen translated in Frère Lorens and in Chaucer' (cf. *The Parson's Tale*,
955).
[2] Ibid. ii. 189.
[3] Printed in three separate parts by J. Werner, *Beiträge* (2nd ed., 1905),
nos. 69, 73, 75 (pp. 30–3). Cf. also P. von Moos, *Hildebert von Lavardin*
(Pariser Historische Studien III, 1965), pp. 209–10.

in his *Liber decem capitulorum*[1] plays variations on the traditional
misogynistic motifs in a chapter *De meretrice*, and then argues
in the following chapter, *De matrona*, that among all God's
gifts 'none is fairer, none better than a good woman, who is
a part of our body and we a part of hers', we are moving even
closer to the genre of the debate-poem, where the 'message'—
if it exists—is inseparable from the dialectic.

In both Hildebert's poem and Marbod's, inevitably, Samson
occurs; in both also the warning *exempla* are drawn from
classical as well as biblical legend. But it is important to observe
that, for all their dialectic *facetia*, these poems are still in a sense
within an ascetic tradition of misogyny: they are not a parody or
satire of that tradition. Hildebert closes by affirming that God's
help is needed to overcome the three temptations he has
described, Marbod even more seriously, by an image of man
crossing the ocean in Ecclesia's ship so as to reach heaven's
harbour: he must, like another Odysseus, tie himself to the
mast—the cross—to avoid the sirens' songs.[2] It is likely enough
that Abelard was acquainted with the verse of his most dis-
tinguished older poet-contemporaries in France; but his treatment of the 'cautionary Samson' motif is, I hope to show, very
different from any that had gone before it.

Apart from seeing Samson as a warning against woman's
love, the Fathers attempted both to judge his various actions
from a human standpoint and (more profusely) to interpret
them from a divine one: Samson became a *figura* of Christ, but
also of sinful man. Often one and the same writer entertains
several of these possibilities. Thus Jerome, who adduces Samson
as woman's victim in his treatise against Jovinian, can write in
his commentary on *Ezekiel* (the context is that of dedication
to priesthood):

Manue dedicated his son Samson, but his lust for Dalila smirched
the consecration of his hair, and at last the Lord abandoned him and

---

[1] Ed. W. Bulst (Editiones Heidelbergenses 8, 1947), chs. III–IV.
[2] On the earlier Christian uses of this image, cf. H. Rahner, *Griechische
Mythen in christlicher Deutung* (1945), pp. 414–86.

he was condemned to blindness, except that afterwards, when his hair grew again, he recovered his former strength, and, fore-shadowing Christ, killed many more of the aliens in his death than in life.[1]

In the same sentence Jerome is able to censure Samson humanly and to see him *in typo Christi*. Samson's resemblance to Christ in dying, here expressed with a cryptic strangeness, is explained by later authors such as Caesarius and Gregory: Christ won over, or killed the evil in, far more of mankind by his death than he had ever done by preaching in his lifetime. Jerome's disciple Philippus Presbyter († 455/6) elaborates other ways in which Samson can be seen as a type of Christ.[2] But the correspondences he makes are strained and fanciful,[3] and signifi-cantly he attempts none for those parts of Samson's story—Dalila, and his humiliation through her—where the characters of Christ and Samson diverge most sharply.

The fullest and most perceptive account of Samson in the early church is that given by St. Caesarius of Arles in his three sermons on Samson and Dalila[4] (the first of which probably draws on a lost treatise by St. Augustine).[5] Samson had his strength through God's grace, not through nature: natural strength does not leave a man when his hair is shorn. Rather, Samson's body was the vessel for a divine power, and this vessel could be both filled and drained: *Vas impleri et exinaniri potest*. What, then, are we to say of Samson the human being? Morally, he is a great enigma: *Hic si iustus est, latet valde*. As to his being vanquished by a woman, his lying with a courtesan —'perhaps we shall be able to say that these things were not sinful or damnable under the old covenant, when indeed what Samson said or did was a prefiguration. Let us then seek out

---

[1] *In Hiez.* XIII. xliv. 17/21 (Corpus Christianorum LXXV. 662).

[2] *P.L.* 26, 647.

[3] e.g. as Samson, thirsting, brought forth water to drink from the jawbone of an ass, so Christ was given to drink the faith of believers, as it were a refreshment from unclean and harsh heathendom.

[4] *Sermones*, CXVIII–CXX: *Sancti Caesarii Opera Omnia*, ed. G. Morin, i (1937), 470–82.   [5] Morin, p. 470.

what may have been the meaning of his defeat and of his victory, what the meaning of his yielding to a woman's blandishments. . . .'

Caesarius is well aware of the incongruities implicit in seeing Samson as a type of Christ, and confronts these bravely:

What was Samson? If I say, he signified Christ, I seem to myself to be speaking truth; but at once it occurs to those who think about it: was Christ overcome by a woman's wiles? How can Christ be said to have lain with a courtesan? When was Christ's head uncovered, when was he shorn, robbed of strength, bound, blinded, mocked?[1]

None the less, Caesarius upholds the figura: its meaning depends on a deeper understanding of the nature of Christ. Christ 'acted as one who is strong, suffered as one who is weak'. The 'total Christ' is both head and body: the body of which Christ is head is Ecclesia, and that body has weak limbs as well as strong. *Quaedam ergo fecit Samson ex persona capitis, quaedam ex persona corporis, totum tamen ex persona Christi.*

This recognition gives Caesarius a subtle flexibility in his figural interpretations: they can be divine ones, exemplified in Christ, and (at the same time) psychological ones, exemplified in mankind. The lion that Samson kills can be understood as heathendom, dying to its old self to become the body of Christ; or it can figure Christ's own death: out of this lion's body comes the sweet honey of redemption. Samson's betrayal by Dalila figures reason's betrayal by the flesh; but his being shorn is again ambiguous: there is a blessed, divine razor, that can shave the soul of evil, and a deadly one, which is Satan, that can mutilate our true head, Christ. The sinner is his own dark prison, his heart the millstone with which he grinds the flour of corruption to make satanic food. Dalila, again, can have not only a psychological meaning—the destructive sensuality within man—but a divine one, as Synagoga, who persecutes Christ and delivers him to death. As Synagoga, Dalila

[1] Morin, p. 471.

merges with the figure of the courtesan whom Samson visited: the escape from her house in the middle of the night is Christ's escape from the tomb; the city gates that Samson lifts and carries to the mountain-top, the gates removed in the harrowing of hell.

Gregory the Great adopts this last figura from Caesarius, and that of 'killing by dying' from Jerome,[1] but does not himself develop the interpretation of Samson in original ways, except perhaps in one detail: he sees the blinding of Samson as having a counterpart in his inner state—first through Dalila he had lost the *oculus contemplationis*.[2] It is this image that Abelard transforms into Samson's 'double darkness' (*geminis... tenebris*), an image still latent when Milton's Samson cries out against his loss both of divine and human light.

Isidore of Seville, even more than Gregory, is derivative in his interpretation of Samson. However, he provides a summary of the most popular figural parallels between Samson and Christ up to his time, and (in a far shallower way than Caesarius) tries to define the limits of the Samson–Christ juxtaposition:

Samson, formerly the Lord's Nazarite, has accomplished some things in prefiguration of Christ. First, in that his birth is heralded by an angel; then, in that he is called 'Nazarite', and himself frees Israel from her enemies; finally, in that he overthrows their temple, and many thousands of men that had mocked him died. As for the other events in his life—that a cunning woman shaved his head and delivered him to the foreigners to be mocked, that he was imprisoned, blinded, sent to the mill—in these it is not Christ who is prefigured, but those in the Church who take pride only in the mere name of Christ, and are constantly involved in wicked deeds.[3]

These sentences of Isidore's were taken over almost word for word by Hrabanus Maurus,[4] and thus became standard for the High Middle Ages. The interpretation of Samson continued—

[1] *XL Homil. in Ev.* xxi. 7 (*P.L.* 76, 1173); *Moralia,* xxix. 14 (*P.L.* 76, 491).
[2] *Moralia,* vii. 28 (*P.L.* 75, 787).
[3] *Quaest. in vet. testam., in lib. Jud.* viii (*P.L.* 83, 389–90).
[4] *Comm. in lib. Jud.* xx (*P.L.* 108, 1198).

sometimes, as with Abelard's older German contemporary
Rupert of Deutz, on an elaborate scale[1]—but principally by
the assembling and permutation of the figurae established in
the Patristic period. Even if there were no new insights to
match those of Caesarius, Samson continued to be much discussed. When Abelard came to compose his *planctus*, Samson
could be not only a crudely effective misogynistic warning, but
a compelling, many-sided symbol.

The individuality of Abelard

Examination of these traditions suggests that one aspect of
Samson had never been seen till Abelard saw it: Samson as a
man who suffered, a failure, a tragic human being. This may
seem to us so obvious a way of looking that its complete
absence before Abelard—and the uniqueness of Abelard's insight in this—could well pass unnoticed. Until then, the stress
of poets and theologians had been either on Samson as warning
or Samson as figura. Where a human comment on Samson
was made, it was an act of judgement—such as a condemnation
of his sensuality and weakness—not of understanding. No one
before Abelard attempted a compassionate penetration of the
character of Samson the man, both despairing and striving to
atone. Samson the figura was so far dominant in men's minds
that it may simply not have occurred to them that his death
was tragic: this death *meant* the deliverance of his people, the
sacrificial act by which he fulfilled his destiny, the greatest deed
in which (at least from Jerome onwards) he foreshadowed
Christ. Augustine had asked, was Samson's suicide unlawful,
and had concluded that a divine exception had been made.[2]
No one had ever asked: what drove Samson to suicide? For
Samson's death was never seen as a failure, only as a victory
through apparent defeat: thus in the flamboyant lyrical play
of Samson, composed perhaps seventy years after Abelard's
planctus,[3] the chorus concludes with a paean:

---

[1] *P.L.* 167, 1041–55.   [2] *De civ.* I. 21.
[3] i.e. *c.* 1200. Abelard's *planctus* I would tentatively put in the 1130s: there

pro tali victoria
Samson sit in gloria!¹

Abelard, by contrast, has deliberately discarded typological
thinking, and the reversal of human perspectives that it can
imply. The individuality of his *planctus* lies at least partly in
this: they reveal human problems explored from a human
standpoint, one that seems expressly to shut out theological
considerations. In the first part of the lament over Samson,
Abelard concentrates wholly on Samson the sufferer. Why this
brave man should have been humiliated and destroyed is
humanly inexplicable: it is a judgement of God, mysterious and
terrifying.² He dwells on every grim detail of Samson's helplessness and pain—he is a man reduced to the condition of a
beast. At the moment of Samson's death, *dolor* is the key-
word: his anguish is so great that he sees the summons to play
before his enemies as a chance of dying and so putting an end
to all the sufferings (II. 1*a*).³ Where in the Bible (Jud. XVI. 28)
Samson prays to God for the strength to carry out a fitting
vengeance, in the song it is *dolor*, not *ultio*, that spurs him to

seems no good reason for setting them earlier than the *Historia Calamitatum*,
composed soon after 1131 (cf. J. T. Muckle, *Mediæval Studies*, xv (1953), 47),
and—especially because of the verbal links discussed below—it seems likely
that they were near in time of composition to Héloïse's first two letters,
probably composed between 1132 and 1135 (Muckle, ibid., p. 48). Laurenzi
(op. cit., p. 20) would date the *planctus* far more precisely: 'La loro com-
posizione rimonta dunque alla metà del 1132 o ai primi mesi della seconda
metà.' But this rests on two questionable assumptions: that the *planctus* were
composed in direct reply to Héloïse's second letter, and that this letter itself
can be dated precisely, 'verso la metà del 1132' (p. 18).
¹ Text in *MÆ* xxviii (1959), 193–4. The dramatic nature of the piece is
clear: some passages can only be sung by the chorus, others only by Samson,
others by Dalila. The allocation of parts is not made explicit in the manuscripts, however, except once in the Stuttgart MS., which indicates where
Dalila's part begins.   ² I. 1*a* (the opening lines adapt Ps. xxxv. 7).
³ The notion that Samson was driven to suicide through sheer misery is,
as far as I can discover, an extremely rare one. But it occurs once more in
Chaucer's *Monk's Tale*:
But to his wyves tolde he his secree,
Thurgh which he slow hymself for wrecchednesse.
(*Cant. T.* VII. 2021–2)

bring on the multiple death by crashing the pillars. It seems he longs for his own death as much as for that of his enemies. Of victory and glory there is no trace. It is, on the surface at least, Israel's lament over Samson *sic perditum*—not Ecclesia's celebration of the Samson whose death figures a triumph.

Yet it is clear that in one or two phrases Ecclesia's image of Samson is latent: that even as we hear Israel's tragic view of him, the limitations of that view are implicitly revealed. In some of the expressions Israel uses of Samson—*nuntiatum per angelum, Nazareum inclitum*—it would scarcely have been possible for a twelfth-century audience not to recall the traditional signs of Samson as figura of Christ, likewise heralded by an angel, likewise *Nazareus*.[1] In the phrase that tells the motivation of Samson's death:

> ut morte doloribus
> finem ponat omnibus

—seemingly the most negative of motives—can one not perceive the possibility of a very different meaning, one that would be truly relevant to the figural Samson of Christendom: 'to die in order by that death to put an end to all sufferings', the Samson who can end Israel's sufferings by destroying the temple foreshadowing *Samson ille*, the harrower of hell?[2]

In that case the second part of the *planctus* begins deliberately with the theme of rebirth, physical and spiritual:

> Renatis iam crinibus
> reparatis viribus . . .

[1] The word *Nazareus* had come to be used for 'Nazarite' (i.e. a member of the Jewish sect) and for 'Nazarene' (i.e. person from Nazareth, Christ, or Christian) indifferently at least from the fourth century. Cf. Blaise, s.v.; also, for the period 800–1200, *Novum Glossarium*, s.v.

[2] Thus in a late twelfth-century sequence from Saint-Martial (ed. G. M. Dreves, *Ein Jahrtausend lateinischer Hymnendichtung*, ii. 111–12):

> Samson ille Gazam vastat
> Et in monte crucis astat
> Secum ferens spolia;
> Agnus noster portas fregit
> Infernales et subegit
> Regna mortis fortia.

A iocis ad seria
fertur mens diu concita—

and this renewal of strength out of despair leads to Samson's
voluntary death. Death, the enemy, can only be killed through
death—so Christ 'Deyde, and deth fordid',[1] and for Samson

hostium et propria
miscet dolor funera.

Samson has passed *a iocis ad seria* in a deeper sense: he has left
Dalila's world of love-sports and revelry far behind, and it is
this world that he now crushes, within his own spirit as well
as outside himself.

Again, earlier in the poem, Abelard's emphasis on Samson
the man, unique in the traditions, has led him to a momentary
identification—likewise unique, as far as I can discover—of
Samson's fate with Adam's. In Judges there is no mention of
Samson's prison fare: it is Adam, driven out of paradise, who
is cursed to the *labor insolitus* of toiling for his food and com-
pelled to eat the fodder of beasts: *in laboribus comedes ex
ea* [*terra*] . . . *et comedes herbam terrae* (Gen. III. 17–18). Behind
the second Adam is the shadow of the first; behind the perceptions of Ecclesia, the blindness of Synagoga.

The blaming of Eve

Bearing in mind the growing strength of the figural connotations of Samson's story in the opening of the second part
of the song, let us turn to the virulent anti-feminine diatribe
that follows. The two parts, seemingly so disparate, are united
by a crafty series of echoes in the language, by which Samson
and Eve are ironically played off against each other. Eve, like
Samson, has brought down (*deiecit, stravit*) a great edifice.
Samson, through death, brings an end to all pain (*morte . . .
omnibus*)—his own pain and (in so far as the *figura* of Christ
is implicit) mankind's—while Eve brings the cup of death to
all (*mortis . . . omnibus*). The Samson–Adam who chokes over

---

[1] *Piers Plowman*, B XVI. 166.

his food is complemented by this Eve who all too easily *mortis poculum propinat*.[1] The rhetorical questions addressed in the first part to a woman who is *impia* are balanced in the second by rhetorical questions about men whom Woman has made *impii*. These subtleties in the verbal texture enhance the confrontation of the two types of destruction—that wrought by Samson, and that by womankind.[2]

Are we to suppose that this grotesque of woman's destructive role represented Abelard's own feelings about women in the later part of his life? By no means. In the years when he was composing the *planctus*—at the time of his later letters to Héloïse and of the *Liber Hymnorum* that he dedicated to her—

---

[1] This phrase first occurs in an eighth-century manuscript of the early Gallican hymn *Rex aeterne domine*, of Satan

> Per pomum ligni vetiti
> Mortis propinans poculum.

These lines are missing from the great majority of manuscripts of the hymn; none the less Carleton Brown suggests that they belonged to the original text ('*Poculum Mortis* in Old English', *Speculum*, xv (1940), 390–2, cf. also G. V. Smithers, *English and Germanic Studies*, iv (1951–2), 68–75), which itself may echo Prudentius' *obliviale poclum* (*Cath.* vi. 16). It is quite possible that *Rex aeterne domine* was one of that very group of ancient Gallican hymns whose textual uncertainties (*confusio*) Abelard deplores to Héloïse in the preface to his own *Liber Hymnorum* (*P.L.* 178, 1771–2).

[2] One further possibly meaningful echo is worth considering, in Abelard's use of the 'right hand' image (from *tam leva quam dextera* in the first part to *divine plasma dextere* in the second). The detail of the two pillars seized one by each hand is biblical (*alteramque earum dextera, et alteram laeva tenens*, Jud. XVI. 29). It was not, to my knowledge, given allegorical significance. None the less right hand and left have definite associations in the tradition of biblical allegory: the right is associated with Christ and divine grace, with justice, righteous action, and eternal life (Hrabanus Maurus, *Allegoriae in Sacram Scripturam*, *P.L.* 112, 909), the left with earthly life, adversity, and the wicked deeds both of angels and men (ibid. 1055). Later, for Chrétien (*Perceval*, 39 ff.), the left hand signifies 'la vaine gloire / Qui vient de fausse ypocrisie', the right, 'Carité'. Abelard, after mentioning Samson's two hands, proceeds to his twofold deed—his enemies' death, and his own. Is there an implicit correspondence—the vengeance righteous, the suicide 'sinister'? Whether or not this is latent, it is clear that Samson's twofold act of destruction is balanced in the second part by a twofold act of creation: where God with his right hand created Adam, Eve—or Woman—created (*fabricavit*) the weapons to destroy Adam.

we can see in his religious writings an exceptional theological exaltation of womankind. He is to my knowledge the first theologian to suggest that 'the creation of woman surpasses that of man by a certain dignity, since she was created within paradise, but man outside it'; he argues that 'inasmuch as woman is physically the weaker sex, to that extent her virtue is more acceptable to God and more worthy of honour'; Christ asks the Samaritan woman at the well for a drink of water 'to indicate plainly that women's virtue is the more pleasing to him in that they are weaker in person'; the saints who are virgin martyrs have achieved 'a perfection of virtue that we know to be rare in men but frequent in women'. Abelard's groups of liturgical hymns *in commune sanctarum mulierum* and *in commune virginum* repeat these thoughts in poetic form.[1]

Again, did Abelard ever feel in any way that Héloïse was responsible for his undoing? Far from it. Throughout the *Historia Calamitatum* he insists that he alone was to blame—the autobiography contains not one word of censure or reproach for Héloïse. Recriminations such as those launched by Milton's Samson against his Dalila are quite foreign to him.

Where close examination shows the writing in the rest of this poem to be so intense and subtle, can we then assume that the climax is no more than an insensitive application of traditional moral dogma? An alternative conclusion seems to me inescapable: Abelard is using the misogynistic literary topoi parodistically, to achieve an entirely individual poetic effect. Parodistic uses of these topoi become common from the thirteenth century—in the fabliaux, in Jean de Meun, and later in Chaucer—but in contexts of satire and comedy, where their poetic function is unmistakable. In Abelard's *planctus* their function remains enigmatic: to show even the presence of this

---

[1] *P.L.* 178, 243B (compare the difference between Abelard's own emphasis and that of Ambrose in the passage he cites!), 245A, 248A, 250A (ed. J. T. Muckle, *Mediæval Studies*, xvii (1955), 268–75); *A.H.* xlviii. 215 ff. On Abelard and the *Adversus Jovinianum*, see the Appendix below, p. 147.

element of parody convincingly, requires first a plausible account of the whole poetic motivation of this part.

I submit there is a twofold motivation, subjective and objective. The first is illuminated by certain passages in the letters, showing us the viewpoint not of Abelard but of Héloïse. Though Abelard tried time and again to convince her of the contrary, Héloïse was immovable in holding herself responsible for Abelard's fall from glory. She had known St. Jerome's anti-feminine arguments against marriage, and had herself used them in trying to prevent Abelard from marrying her.[1] When Abelard none the less insisted on the marriage, she obeyed, but ever afterwards saw her assent in this as the cause of the tragic humiliation of Abelard that followed. So it is she, not Abelard, who uses the old topical arguments against woman seriously: Abelard, she thinks, had been great, like the Old Testament patriarchs, and like them was brought low through a woman's fault (however blameless she knew her own intention had been):

O summam in viros summos et consuetam feminarum perniciem! Hinc de muliere cavenda scriptum est in Proverbiis. . . . Prima statim mulier de paradiso virum captivavit et, quae ei a Domino creata fuerat in auxilium, in summum ei conversa est exitium. Fortissimum illum Nazaraeum Domini et angelo nuntiante conceptum Dalila sola superavit, et eum inimicis proditum et oculis privatum ad hoc tandem dolor compulit ut se pariter cum ruina hostium opprimeret. Sapientissimum omnium Salomonem sola quam sibi copulaverat mulier infatuavit. . . .[2]

Oh supreme, familiar disaster that women bring to the greatest men! Because of this it is written in *Proverbs* to beware of woman. . . . The first woman at once drove man from paradise: she, who had been created by the Lord as man's helpmate, turned into his supreme undoing. That mightiest Nazarite of the Lord, whose conception was heralded by an angel, Dalila alone vanquished, and when he was betrayed to his enemies and robbed of his eyes, the agony at length drove him to make an end of himself together with the destruction

[1] *Historia Calamitatum* (ed. Monfrin), pp. 76–9 (*P.L.* 178, 130–2).
[2] Ed. J. T. Muckle, *Mediæval Studies*, xv (1953), 79 (*P.L.* 178, 195).

of his enemies. A woman alone, with whom he had united, made foolish Solomon, the wisest of all men. . . .

The verbal echoes of this letter in the *planctus* are unmistakable. It is Héloïse who had assigned Samson the desperate motive for his death, sheer grief; for her the seriousness of this fall, and of the other woman-caused falls she links with it, cannot be doubted. Is it possible, then, that Abelard is deliberately using lightly what she had said in bitterest earnest?

On one plane—that of private poetry—I believe he is doing just that. If we consider this *planctus* as written first and foremost for Héloïse,[1] then it must be interpreted as his answer to her letter. It is a subtle and sensitive answer, though achieved by way of a contrast, one of whose elements is unsubtle and crude. In the first part of the *planctus* Abelard shows that imaginatively he understands all the grimness of Samson's fate: he too can see in Samson's mode of death an urge to end pain that had become intolerable, he too can see the full extent of Dalila's baseness (I. 3c). But it is folly to generalize from this to the necessary guilt and fatefulness of all womankind. To comfort Héloïse and show her that her despairing outburst was groundless, Abelard now exaggerates it and takes it *ad absurdum*. He begins (II. 2a) with an exclamation that exactly matches hers. It appears to be serious, and yet the moment one looks at it theologically—woman was 'created for the purpose of destruction'—it is clearly outrageous. While Abelard seems to

[1] As Vecchi has suggested (op. cit., p. 20), Abelard probably refers to the *planctus*, designating them *sequentiae*, in the letter to Héloïse (*P.L.* 178, 379) in which he dedicates his collection of sermons to her, 'libello quodam hymnorum vel sequentiarum a me nuper precibus tuis consummato'. This passage would then imply that the *planctus*, like the hymns, were written in response to Héloïse's instigation. It is possible, however, that Abelard is using *sequentiae* loosely here, as an alternative designation for the hymns. While the hymns were clearly meant for liturgical purposes (cf. Abelard's preface to the *Liber Hymnorum*, *P.L.* 178, 1771–4), it seems to me far likelier that the *planctus* were paraliturgical (notwithstanding the fact that the newly-found text of VI occurs amid a group of liturgical sequences in a Nevers prosarium—cf. M. Huglo, *Ephemerides Liturgicae*, lxxi (1957), 18). If my assumption is right, it is easier to understand why the *planctus* were able to be poetically of a far more intimate nature than anything in the *Liber Hymnorum*.

go on to reproduce Héloïse's own series of examples in support, he shows them preposterous by outdoing them. To say that David and Solomon were women's dupes can be serious, to say that no great man was not unmanned by a woman cannot; to say that Eve was no true friend to Adam can be meant gravely, to say that every woman since Eve has spent her time fabricating the worst weapons to attack men can only be a joke.[1] The very rapidity of the action—*protinus . . . mox . . . ex tunc*—prevents one from following it too seriously. The song concludes *con brio* with Abelard's high-spirited warning against women's wiles: where Solomon, warning against adultery, had said 'Who can carry fire in his breast without singeing his clothes?' (Prov. VI. 27), Abelard caps this by 'Sooner clasp an asp than trust a woman!' All this he addresses to the woman he trusts supremely, teasing her out of the bitter implications for herself that she had seen in Samson's fate. So too in one of the most beautiful of the ninth-century *planctus*, Notker's lament for Rachel, a voice questions Rachel's grief and tries to relieve her pain by a gentle teasing:

> Quid tu, virgo
> mater, ploras,   Cuius vultus
> Rachel formosa,   Jacob delectat?
>
> Ceu sororis aniculae   Lippitudo eum iuvet!
>
> Terge, mater,   Quam te decent
> fluentes oculos!   genarum rimulae?—[2]

Why do you weep, maiden mother, lovely Rachel, whose face gives Jacob delight? As if your older sister's bleary-eyedness would

---

[1] The military associations of the language—*stravit, hostem, tela maxima*—giving the sense of woman as Amazon, again underline the preposterous nature of the invective. Compare the tone and imagery of Chaucer's envoy to *The Clerk's Tale* (*Cant. T.* IV. 1202–6):

> For though thyn housbonde armed be in maille,
> The arwes of thy crabbed eloquence
> Shal perce his brest, and eek his aventaille.
> In jalousie I rede eek thou hym bynde,
> And thou shalt make hym couche as doth a quaille.

[2] Ed. W. von den Steinen, *Notker der Dichter* (1948), ii. 86.

attract him! Lady, dry your streaming eyes—how do you think your
tear-cracked cheeks become you?

The differences are considerable: not only in tone, but in the
dialectic of Notker's sequence, which works through dialogue,
and in its symbolism—it is in her figural role as Ecclesia, rather
than humanly, that this Rachel's sorrows for her children are
causeless.[1] Yet the possibility that the tragic elements of a
planctus can be seen less tragically, that even within its fabric
humour can play a part in showing a sorrow to be unfounded,
is clearly present already in one of the earliest extant lyrical
laments of the Middle Ages.

The *objective* effect of Abelard's use of misogyny, and the
poetic justification for his strange conjunction of lament and
parody, seem to me to follow from his twofold presentation
of Samson. As I tried to show, while the first part of the poem
recreates Israel's view of Samson, in some phrases a contrasting
view, Ecclesia's view, is implicit. Here there is no dialogue, as
in Notker's *Rachel*: the contrast cannot be established as simply
as between Rachel and the voice she hears. It can only be a
summons to the audience, latent in certain expressions that they
hear, to reflect critically on what they are hearing: can it all
be taken unquestioningly, or does it call out for another
measure by which to be judged?

For the Israelites, who are lamenting, it is clear that Samson
is no hero: what they sing of is a man's destruction through a
woman, his degradation, and his escape through suicide (it
seems almost incidental to them that this suicide also results in

---

[1] While Notker clearly knows and in part relies on the figural association
of Rachel with Ecclesia, I hesitate to equate them completely here (as Wolfram
von den Steinen did, *Notker*, i. 399 ff., followed by Dag Norberg, *Manuel
pratique de latin médiéval* (1968), p. 177). Ecclesia the bride of Christ does not
mourn the death of her martyrs, nor does Ecclesia the institution. Rather, it
is the human helplessness of Rachel that is stressed: as 'maid and mother' she
is the *dolorosa*, not only Mary, but any girl or woman who has thought passionately about the loss of one she loved. Whose is the voice that challenges
her grief? Is she won over by its pleas and proofs? With sublime tact Notker
leaves these questions unanswered.

the death of his enemies). It is hardly an exaggeration to say that they show a contempt for Samson—in his fall he is like one who has been unmanned, *enervatur*—and a contempt for womankind; as the opening shows, the tragedy is meaningless to them, they are afraid because they do not understand God's purpose. A few expressions, however, seem to hint at a very different vantage-point, from which Samson's life and death were divinely ordained—a sacrifice foreshadowing a greater sacrifice. If this perspective is not forgotten towards the end of the poem, some surprising things emerge. An expression such as *mortis poculum propinat omnibus* can be taken in two ways: in a flippant, misogynistic sense, such as 'a woman always brings a man to his grave', or in a theological sense: all mankind must die because of a woman's primordial guilt. But this is precisely what Ecclesia knows is no longer true: the new Samson *has* delivered his people. David and Solomon, Samson and Adam may have been duped by women and led by them into sin; Israel may believe that this brought them to eternal death—but Ecclesia knows it did not. So too at the close: *exitium certissimum* may refer humorously to the catastrophe of enslavement to a woman, which—the poet wryly admits— some men enter by choice; but if the import is theological— that the patriarchs went to an inexorable death because of their sins with women—then once more this can only be Israel's imperfect view, not Ecclesia's.

The two halves of the poem are related as two extreme conceptions that in their one-sidedness complement each other. As the first part, saying 'Samson was a suicide and a tragic failure', summons the reply 'But his destiny was not meaningless: his life was divinely foretold, and his death more than a desperate escape from degradation'—so the second half, saying 'Nothing of the catastrophe was Samson's fault, it was all Dalila's, *così fan tutte*', summons another reply: 'If Samson had been no more than a woman's gull, his sufferings could not be seen as tragic; his ruin would be mere bad luck (as of a man fleeced by a nightclub-hostess and then put in jail), it could not be a great man's destiny. To put all the fault with Woman is perverse: this cannot be one of the abysses of God's judgement, only a mockery of God's purposes. It is Samson's own weakness, and his realization of it, that give his destruction a tragic dignity and are inseparable from his grandeur and strength.' I have put my own response to the poem into words not as in any way a definitive one, but to indicate the *kind* of challenge that it sets. To a large extent the possible reaction remains open: the poet attempts to provoke thought, not to offer a ready substitute for thought.

A modern analogy may clarify further what I take to be Abelard's intention and technique in this *planctus*. In the twentieth century it has been a dramatic poet, Brecht, who has tried to sketch for the drama a 'non-Aristotelian' way of representing character and action, a way that 'strives to make possible, indeed to prompt, in the spectator, a critical, or it may be an opposing, attitude to the events portrayed, as well as to the way they are portrayed'.[1] 'The non-Aristotelian dramatic technique is for the presentation of contradictions and for the appreciation of these contradictions.'[2] 'The events must not follow each other imperceptibly, but one's judgement must be able to intervene.'[3] Thus Brecht rejects the concept of emotional identification (*Einfühlung*) with the characters, but shows that this does not imply a rejection of emotion itself in the drama. It is a task of his drama to show that 'the common aesthetic assumption, that emotions can be aroused only by way of identification, is false'.[4] At the same time, the emotions arising from his drama and embodied in it 'must always be subjected to criticism'. Thus Brecht gives an example: a sister mourns that her brother is going to war; it is the Peasants' War, and he is fighting on the peasants' side:

Shall we identify ourselves wholly with her grief? Or not at all? We must be able both to identify ourselves with her grief and not

---

[1] Bertolt Brecht, *Schriften zum Theater*, iii (1963), 29.
[2] *Schriften zum Theater: Über eine nicht-aristotelische Dramatik* (1957), p. 212.
[3] Ibid., p. 166.   [4] *Schriften*, iii (1963), 25.

to do so. The way we are truly moved will arise through the re-cognition and sensation of this discordant process.[1]

This comment seems to me of great relevance to the two *planctus* in which Abelard has used a chorus. As Abelard has presented Jephtha and his daughter, we cannot, strictly, identify with either of them: we can admire her heroism, but deplore the waste and the murder; we can see the torment that his sense of duty causes him, and at the same time with the chorus see that the root of this torment is insane. The one thing we can no longer do after experiencing Abelard's *planctus* is to accept the biblical narrative of the event without questioning its implications.[2]

So too we cannot fully accept as ours Israel's thoughts and feelings in either half of the Samson *planctus*: each offers an imperfect, distorting image of the subject Abelard has chosen; each reflects a view that cannot reckon with the event that Samson's death prefigures. But a Christian audience, by being aware of this, can confront both Israel's mourning and her derision critically: these are at one in the defect of partial vision. The lamentation is shown, by some of the very phrases it employs, to be ultimately misguided; the misogynistic tirade, by reaching into what is theologically preposterous, is itself satirized.

Abelard is not afraid to insert crude elements, so as to make something that is not itself crude; to use one-sided attitudes,

---

[1] *Schriften* (1957), p. 212.

[2] It is not surprising that, to achieve the kinds of effect described above, Brecht, like Abelard here, should at times use a technique of juxtaposing scenes that contrast violently in tone and manner: so, for instance, in his *Leben des Galilei*, in which the April Fools' Day episode in the market-place (scene 10), where Galileo's ideas are burlesqued by the ballad-singer and populace, is followed by the scenes (11-12) in which he is summoned to the Inquisition, and where the Inquisitor gives a different travesty of Galileo's thought, as grim as the first had been lighthearted. Or again, at the close of *Der gute Mensch von Sezuan*, the heroine's despairing plea to the gods is followed at once by their rejection of her, expressed through the comically high-flown, complacent song with which they disappear. Here the way in which the ending is a chal-lenge to the audience is made explicit by the player's epilogue.

so as to bring the hearer to an attitude that is not one-sided. In his conjunction of *planctus* and satire he has widened the boundaries of both. So too, some thirty years later, the Archpoet was to write a poem, *Lingua balbus, hebes ingenio*,[1] that is simultaneously a sermon on the death of Christ and a self-mocking begging-poem. Through the Archpoet's fusion of these, the boundaries of religious meditation and of personal parody were permanently widened; without such a widening, much of Villon's verse would scarcely have been possible. Like Abelard in this *planctus*, the Archpoet keeps his audience on the alert: he challenges them to guess his real intention behind what he presents at any moment. Neither his witty begging nor his sermonizing are to be accepted unquestioningly; out of the interweaving of the two comes an effect that is far greater than either could be separately—greater, that is, in so far as the audience can make the intellectually agile response required of them. This is true in a more limited way of Abelard's *planctus*: the enigmatic technique is not yet as highly developed, the fusion of disparates is still far from perfect. But it is an experiment in the same direction. While in fullness of achievement it cannot be compared with the lament over Jephtha's daughter, it attempts a range of effects different from those in any of the other *planctus*, and different, to the best of my knowledge, from anything in medieval poetry before its time. The originality and independence of the *planctus* as a group is clear—but this may well be the most experimental poem among them.

[1] Ed. H. Krefeld and H. Watenphul, *Die Gedichte des Archipoeta* (1958), no. 1 (pp. 47–52).

APPENDIX

Planctus Dine Filie Iacob (R fol. 63ᵛ, Meyer, pp. 366–7):

Abrahe proles,   Israel nata,
patriarcharum   sanguine clara,

Incircumcisi   viri rapina
hominis spurci   facta su*m* preda,

Generis sancti   macula summa,
plebis adverse   ludis illusa.
    Ve mihi misere   per memet prodite!

Quid alienigenas   iuvabat me cernere?
Quam male sum cognita   volens has cognoscere!
    Ve mihi misere   per memet prodite!

Sichem, in exicium   nate tui generis,
nostris in obprobrium   perpes facte posteris!
    Ve tibi misero   per temet perdito!

Frustra circumcisio   fecit te proselitum,
non valens infamie   tollere prepucium.
    Ve tibi misero   per temet perdito!

Coactus me rapere,   mea raptus spetie,
quovis expers venie   non fuisses iudice!
Non sic, fratres,   censuistis,   Symeon et Levi,
in eodem   facto nimis   crudeles et pii!
Innocentes   coequastis   in pena nocenti,
Quin et patrem   perturbastis: ob hoc execrandi!

Amoris impulsio,   culpe satisfactio,
quovis sunt iudicio   culpe diminutio!
Levis etas   iuvenilis   minusque discreta
ferre minus   a discretis   debuit in pena.
Ira fratrum   ex honore   fuit lenienda,

quem his fecit   princeps terre   ducta peregrina.
    Ve mihi,   ve tibi,   miserande   iuvenis:
    in stragem   communem   gentis tante   conc*i*dis!

4 sunt R   30 conditis R

Abelard and the Adversus Jovinianum

There are three important places in Abelard's writings that reflect
something of Jerome's discussion of women and marriage in the
treatise against Jovinian. The first (see above p. 138) is Abelard's
report in the *Historia Calamitatum* of what Héloïse had said to dis-
suade him from marriage. This must be a stylized rather than wholly
remembered account of Héloïse's arguments some fifteen years
earlier (1117–18). The second is his discussion of the pagan ideal of
continence in the *Theologia Christiana*, composed *c.* 1124—that is,
perhaps five years after Abelard's castration and a decade before the
planctus. These passages have been discussed by Ph. Delhaye, 'Le
dossier anti-matrimonial de l'*Adversus Jovinianum* et son influence
sur quelques écrits latins du XIIe siècle', *Mediæval Studies*, xiii (1951),
70–5. A third (not mentioned by Delhaye) is in the *Carmen ad
Astralabium Filium*, composed by Abelard towards the end of his
life.

The *Theologia Christiana*, arguing that the pagan philosophers had
intimations of the Christian Trinity, attributes to them a high ideal
of purity of life 'which the Jews did not comprehend' (*P.L.* 178,
1195A): 'the woman swiftly bewitched the man in Paradise, and
longing for a woman brought Samson, the Lord's Nazarite, whose
birth had been announced by an angel, to his death; David, greatest
of prophets and kings . . . was so ensnared by one glance at Bath-
sheba that, killing the most valiant and loyal Uria, he became guilty
both of adultery and murder, that is, of the greatest betrayal. And
wantonness degraded Solomon, greatest of wise men, even as far
as idolatry. . . .' Then, having quoted some of Solomon's dicta and
of Jerome's, Abelard continues (1197D): 'Spurred by these and suchlike reasons philosophers have resolved on a life of continence for
themselves.' Here the arguments of 'philosophers' (Jerome, and his
citations from Theophrastus) loom large. But the import of these
arguments is here not misogynistic: Abelard stresses 'it is clear that
this power of continence, or love of modesty, has not been lacking
in those women who have been outstanding in their philosophical
and literary endowment' (1201B). He goes on to show 'with what
great reverence, with what wholesome love the pagans too strove
to keep the faith of marriage intact' (1202B), and here again most
of his examples, culled from Valerius Maximus as well as Jerome,

are of women. It is because God delights in continence in every race that he gave the Sibyls the gift of prophecy, and performed a miracle to protect the vestal virgin Claudia from the suspicion of guilt (1202C). In these passages the tone is very different from that in the analogous places in *Adversus Jovinianum* (i. 41–9; *P.L.* 23, 270 ff.): where Jerome's chief emphasis is on the denigration of marriage as an inferior state, Abelard's is on the reverent admiration for outstanding women.

The only place in Abelard's works that would appear to show traces of a more 'straight' use of misogynistic matter is in the very late *Carmen ad Astralabium* (ed. B. Hauréau, *NE* XXXIV. ii (1895), 157- 86). This contains the passage (p. 172):

> Ne te blanditiis seducere Dalila possit,
> Quae tecum dormit, sit tibi cura vigil.
> Non est vicino tutum dormire colubro;
> Anguem transcendit femina nequitia.
> Nequitia similem serpens sibi credidit Evam,
> Et cito persuasit credere nequitiae;
> Hinc, prius hanc aggressa, virum tentavit in illa,
> Facta per hanc omnis causa caputque mali.

The poem also includes a vigorous warning against *meretrices* (p. 163). At the same time the poet recognizes (p. 162):

> Nil melius muliere bona, nil quam mala peius;
> Omnibus ista bonis praestat, et illa malis.

And in praise of women Abelard affirms (p. 176), as he had done in his letters and hymns:

> Quanto plus fragilis muliebris sexus habetur,
> Tanto eius virtus praeminet in meritis.

There is likewise a passage (p. 167), often quoted, of great gentleness and insight, about Héloïse herself.

The long verse tract to Astralabe, with the exception of a small number of evidently personal lines (most perceptively discussed by Georg Misch in his *Geschichte der Autobiographie*, III. i (1959), 692 711), is for the most part a compilation of conventional proverbial 'wisdom', which Abelard assembles in Polonius' fashion. As such, it is matter drawn from very diverse traditional sources: e.g. it is presumably not the young Astralabe personally, beginning his studies for the priesthood, who is advised to whip his servants (p. 162), to choose his woman sleeping-partner carefully (p. 172), or, more cynically, 'Si nequeas caste, ne spernas vivere caute' (p. 173)—all this along with many more predictable injunctions towards Christian piety. But in any case the poem as printed by Hauréau is highly problematic: it is garbled, largely haphazard in form, with repetitions that often seem like interpolations. Despite Brinkmann's work on the text (*Münchner Museum*, v (1932), 168–201), it is still difficult to imagine what the original version may have looked like, to what extent Abelard may have aimed at no more than a helter-skelter assemblage of *sententiae*, and indeed how much of the text in Hauréau may be by Abelard himself. A critical edition, which will bring new light to these questions, is an urgent need.

V

HILDEGARD OF BINGEN AS POETESS
AND DRAMATIST

TOWARDS the middle of the twelfth century, in her convent at Disibodenberg, where she had lived since she was eight years old, Hildegard of Bingen was writing the words and music of her songs. Not long after 1150 she collected them together and formed them into a complete lyrical cycle, which she called her 'symphony of the harmony of heavenly revelations' (*symphonia armonie celestium revelationum*).[1] Saint Hildegard became famous for her visionary writings, for her correspondence with Saint Bernard, with popes and with emperors; her medical and scientific treatises have attracted ever-increasing attention in the present century; only her lyrical and dramatic poetry has been to an astonishing degree neglected.[2] The songs have never

---

[1] This dating emerges from two testimonies: in the preface to her *Liber Vitae Meritorum* (Pitra, pp. 7–8), referring to the beginning of this book in 1158, Hildegard mentions the *Symphonia* as one of a number of writings completed between 1151 (when she finished *Scivias*) and 1158. At the same time, Odo of Soissons's letter of 1148 (see below) makes it certain that Hildegard's poetic activity reached back at least into the forties. It is not quite accurate to say that 'Dichtung und Komposition der Symphonia breiten sich wohl über die ganze Zeit der schriftstellerischen Tätigkeit Hildegards aus' (*Echtheit*, p. 21): we have no evidence that Hildegard was composing the *Symphonia* between 1158 and her death in 1179.

[2] In the introduction to his facsimile of the 'Riesenkodex' text of the *Symphonia* (1913), Josef Gmelch attributed this neglect to a defect in the poetry itself: 'Es fehlt ihnen die schulmäßige, künstlerische Form. Und deswegen werden sie, wie sie bisher vergessen waren, wohl auch in Zukunft wenig Beachtung finden' (p. 27). Clearly Gmelch could not envisage principles of poetic form beyond the conventional ones of regular metre and rhyme. F. J. E. Raby (*Christian-Latin Poetry*, p. 294) dismissed her poetry in a single phrase: 'Hildegarde, the famous mystic, whose sequences are in prose'; so too Karl Langosch (*Reallexikon der deutschen Literatur*, ii (2nd ed., 1965), 383) recently described her songs as 'nur Entwürfe in Prosa', adding the absurd

yet been critically edited,[1] never yet with reference to the oldest manuscript, written in Hildegard's lifetime at her own convent on the Rupertsberg near Bingen, where she moved with her nuns in 1150. The music of only a handful of the songs has been transcribed; they have received virtually no literary discussion. Yet I believe these songs contain some of the most unusual, subtle, and exciting poetry of the twelfth century. Similarly, Hildegard's play, the *Ordo Virtutum*, is not even mentioned in the standard works on medieval drama, such as those of Karl Young and E. K. Chambers.[2] Yet this play seems to me to be, together with its renowned contemporaries the *Mystère d'Adam* and the *Ludus de Antichristo*,[3] at the summit of twelfth-century dramatic achievement, and to be as original in conception as they. To attempt a concise literary introduction to Hildegard's poetic and dramatic compositions, and to begin to substantiate the high poetic claims that I would make for them, will be the purpose of this chapter.

The *Symphonia* in its final form consisted of some seventy compositions—sequences and hymns, antiphons and responsories—appropriate to a wide range of liturgical occasions, both

comment 'da sie des Lateins nur wenig, der Form gar nicht mächtig war'. (On the scope of Hildegard's knowledge of Latin, see especially H. Liebeschütz, *Das allegorische Weltbild der heiligen Hildegard von Bingen* (1930), pp. 159 ff., and *Echtheit*, pp. 180 ff.) In the same year as Langosch, however, Josef Szövérffy gave Hildegard a more fitting place in his *Annalen der lateinischen Hymnendichtung*, ii. 139–42, with several quotations and most helpful bibliography.

[1] The best printed text is that in Pitra (pp. 441–65); but, like other editors, Pitra did not use the earlier, Dendermonde manuscript.

[2] *The Drama of the Medieval Church* (2 vols., 1933); *The Medieval Stage* (2 vols., 1903); nor again, most recently, does Hildegard's play receive mention in O. B. Hardison's *Christian Rite and Christian Drama in the Middle Ages* (1965).

[3] I am assuming a date not far from 1150 for all three plays. I cannot agree with Otto Ursprung's suggestion (*Miscelanea en homenaje a Mons. H. Anglès*, ii (1958–61), 944) that the epilogue of Hildegard's play *derives from* a chapter in her late *Liber Divinorum Operum*, composed between 1163 and 1170: the assumption that the passage in the prose context necessarily precedes the dramatic one is arbitrary. If, as I believe, Hildegard planned the play as an intrinsic part of her *Symphonia*, then the play too would fall in the period before 1158.

on the greater Church feasts and on days of less known, locally celebrated saints. For all the cycle the music is extant. Thus in its size and scope the *Symphonia* is most nearly comparable to the great liturgical cycle of an earlier period, Notker's *Liber Hymnorum* (composed chiefly between 860 and 870), though Hildegard's compositions are less frequently attached to specific liturgical days than Notker's are. In the Wiesbaden 'Riesen-kodex' (R), in which Hildegard's theological writings and letters were collected and edited, the *Symphonia* concludes with the lyrical play, *Ordo Virtutum*. This collection was made in the decade following her death, probably by her nephew Wezelin, Provost of Sankt Andreas in Cologne.[1] In the earlier manu-script at Dendermonde, which today is fragmentary, the play and nineteen of the songs are missing, but it contains two short lyrical pieces that are omitted from the 'Riesenkodex' and thus have remained unpublished.[2] The Dendermonde manuscript was almost certainly copied under Hildegard's personal super-vision,[3] and I have used it wherever possible as the basis of my texts. For seventeen of the songs, and for a portion of the play, it is conceivable that they began as poetic passages in Hilde-gard's prose writings and were set to music subsequently.[4] The

---

[1] R: Hessische Landesbibliothek, Wiesbaden, cod. 2, written at the Ruperts-berg *c.* 1180–90 (cf. *Echtheit*, pp. 154–79).

[2] One leaf has been cut away between fols. 155^v and 156^r, and one between fols. 164^v and 165^r. One or more leaves—perhaps a complete gathering of eight—have been lost before fol. 153^r. The fragmentary nature of the Dender-monde manuscript (D), and the fact that it contains pieces not found in R (fol. 155^r *O frondens virga*; fol. 157^r *Laus trinitati*), have not previously been observed. I hope to publish shortly, as a separate article, a comparative analysis of the *Symphonia* in its two manuscripts, together with an attempt to recon-struct the contents of the lost portions in D. In their discussion of D in *Echtheit*, the authoresses date it after 1163 (p. 21), probably around 1175 (p. 194).

[3] Cf. *Echtheit*, pp. 18, 49–51.

[4] Sisters Schrader and Führkötter write: 'Von den 70 Liedern, die R über-liefert, sind 41 den übrigen Werken Hildegards entnommen' (p. 21). But this is misleading: this figure includes twenty-four songs that recur in the epilogue to the life of Saint Rupert (Pitra, pp. 358–65); these, however, were clearly not written for this epilogue, to which they bear no intrinsic relation. They were songs written for the *Symphonia*, and subsequently accommodated,

priority of the lyrical or the prose context, however, seems to me impossible to determine with certainty; and in any case, a letter to Hildegard from Odo of Soissons, which can be dated in 1148, shows that she was already praised for her lyrical compositions (*modos novi carminis*) at a time when her first visionary prose work, the *Scivias*, was not yet complete.[1]

What is it that is new in Hildegard's songs? Most immediately striking, perhaps, is the directness and daring of particular images:

> O rubor sanguinis
> qui de excelso illo fluxisti
> quod divinitas tetigit,
> tu flos es
> quem hyemps de flatu serpentis
> numquam lesit.[2]

> Redness of blood
> which flowed from that high place
> touched by divinity,
> you are a flower
> that winter with its serpent blast
> has never harmed.

This is a brief antiphon for the feast of Saint Ursula and her maidens. It is a meditation less on their particular martyrdom than on the essence of martyrdom. The blood that the martyr sheds is instantly sanctified—it is as though it were flowing from heaven from the very first; on earth, this blood of the martyr becomes a flower, it is divinely endowed with beauty and immutable life. This immortal flower, the martyr's testament, is an exemplar for mankind: it does not suffer winter like other flowers, it remains unhurt by the *flatus serpentis*—

rather awkwardly, in the prose setting of the epilogue. (For details of the songs that occur elsewhere, see L. Bronarski, *Die Lieder der heiligen Hildegard* (1922), p. 15; Gmelch's information, op. cit., pp. 18–22, is not always reliable.)

[1] *P.L.* 197, 352A: 'Dicitur quod elevata in caelestibus multa videas, et multa per scripturam proferas, atque modos novi carminis edas, cum nihil horum didiceris.' For the date of this letter, see *Briefwechsel*, p. 42. The *Scivias*, begun in 1141, was not finished till 1151 (*Briefwechsel*, p. 31).

[2] R 471vb.

the phrase suggests not only the cruel, serpent-toothed winds of winter, but the breath of the serpent Satan, which can destroy the divine flowers that begin to burgeon in human hearts.

These are mere indications of what may lie behind so compressed an image. Other associations too are possible: cannot the blood which flows 'de excelso illo' evoke also 'where Christs blood streames in the firmament'? Hildegard anticipates Marlowe in an image I have not met elsewhere in the Middle Ages in so vivid a form. The martyr's sacrifice is thus implicitly linked with that of Christ. The blood that becomes a flower on earth may have a more literary association as well: the 'flos dive Veneri gratus Adonis' (to quote from a contemporary secular lyric)[1]—for Adonis' blood, when it becomes a flower on earth, is likewise immortal in its yearly renewal. While for the reflecting mind this association deepens the meaning of the poem, the principal impulse behind the image is—I am sure—intuitive rather than literary. It is the most immediate links: blood—flower—winter—serpent, that give the image its prime effect and force.

In a hymn of Hildegard's to the Holy Spirit, the opening and close are dense with arresting, even violent, images of fire and music, wounds and jewels:

> O ignee spiritus, laus tibi sit
> qui in timpanis et citharis operaris!
> Mentes hominum de te flagrant . . .

> Unde omnes creature que de te vivunt te laudant,
> quia tu preciosissimum ungentum es
> fractis et fetidis vulneribus,
> ubi illa in preciosissimas gemmas convertis.[2]

> Fiery Spirit, praise be to you
> whose music sounds in tympana and lutes!
> The minds of men are ablaze through you . . .

---

[1] *Ver prope florigerum*, l. 7 (*MLREL* ii. 374).

[2] D 157ᵛ–158ʳ (De spiritu sancto Ymnus); R 473ʳᵇ⁻ᵛᵇ (Ymnus de spiritu sancto). Complete text from R in Pitra, pp. 450–1.

So all creatures that have life from you praise you,
for you are the most precious ointment
for broken and fetid wounds,
which you transform into most precious jewels.

Between these stanzas develops a long meditation, more
austere in language and for the most part abstract, on the
nature and motivation of human evil. But certain overtones
of the dominant opening images, fire and music, are still to be
heard here. The fire of the Spirit is both light and warmth:
when present in the human mind, it can be the lantern of desire
(*eius lucerna est desiderium*); but when a mist (*nebula*) darkens
will and desire, the fiery Spirit becomes a scorching heat, burning evil away: *tu eum cicius in igne comburis, cum volueris* ('swiftly
you consume it in your flame, when you will'). The music
likewise has a twofold aspect: when the human intellect calls
upon the Spirit, it is in the sweetest sound, implicitly the sound
of the *cithara—Intellectus te in dulcissimo sono advocat*. But when
human reason (*racionalitas*) declines into evil, the Spirit when
it wills makes that reason taut and batters it, as if using it as its
own tympanum: *Tu eam cum vis stringis et confringis*.

The poem's final image is again one of transformation: as
divinity made human blood into a flower, so here the ointment
of the Spirit makes human wounds, fetid with evil, into jewels.
The repetition of 'most precious' might be criticized on poetic
grounds (the excessive use of superlatives, as well as of voca-
tives and exclamations, are perhaps the most obvious flaws in
Hildegard's poetic diction, the obverse side to its mystical
intensity); yet I think the repetition has also a specific poetic
purpose: it is to underline the final kinship between the trans-
muting Spirit and what it has transmuted, to bring out more
vividly the force of the phrase 'all creatures that have life from
you'. Christ's wounds had been symbolically identified with
jewels since the early Christian *sphragis*-imagery: the word
sphragis itself could mean both gem and wound.[1] Again, in

[1] Cf. F. J. Dölger, *Sphragis* (Studien zur Geschichte und Kultur des Alter-
tums, v, fasc. 3–4, 1911).

medieval lapidaries, as in Hildegard's own *Physica*, a number
of jewels were regarded as crystallizations of liquid substances.[1]
Here in the poem the human jewels, the virtues of the soul, are
a fusion of mortal blood and the Spirit's ointment, crystallized
together.

Hildegard again strives to make the operations of the Spirit
palpable in her antiphon *O virtus Sapientie*, in an image of sur-
realist fantasy, but weighty with meaning:

O virtus Sapientie,	You power of Wisdom
que circuiens circuisti	that circled circling
comprehendendo omnia	and embracing all
in una via que habet vitam,	in a course that is filled with life—
tres alas habens—	you have three wings:
quarum una in altum volat,	one soars into the heights,
et altera de terra sudat,	another has moisture from the earth,
et tercia undique volat—	the third flies everywhere.
laus tibi sit sicut te decet,	All praise be to you, Wisdom,
o Sapientia![2]	as is your due!

In the *Scivias* (III. 5), Hildegard describes a vision of the
'ardour of God' (*zelum dei*), a figure that likewise has three
wings, 'white as a dazzling cloud'. But there these wings are
allegorized as three stages in the Redemption and mankind's
victory over Satan: the interpretation is strained, it remains
unclear why these stages should be imagined as the three wings
of the ardour of God, or what significant difference there
might be between the three stages or wings. In the antiphon,
by contrast, Hildegard avoids allegory and relies on the evocative power of the winged image itself: the three wings, cen-
trally pinned, instantly convey a sense of revolving flight, a
circling motion that complements the opening image. This
circular movement (which since the *Timaeus* had been regarded

[1] Cf. especially Hildegard's Praefatio to Book IV of her *Physica*, 'De Lapidibus' (*P.L.* 197, 1247c ff.).   [2] R 466rb.

as the motion of the World-Soul),[1] while it may comprehend the cosmos and be the moving force of the life within it, is none the less a self-sufficient movement, a perpetual contemplative motion unconcerned with the earth itself. But, unlike the World-Soul, Hagia Sophia did more than play in the presence of the Creator, harmonizing all things: her delight was to be with the children of men.[2] Thus Hildegard completes her first image by a second, more complex, picture of motion: while with one wing Sophia flies heavenward, another reaches down to the earth, sharing the earth's moisture and fertility. *Sudat* is a favourite word of Hildegard's, and is often used in conjunction with her favourite imagery of greenness, flowering, and perfumes: for her *sudare* has the associations not of the sweat of effort but of the distillation of a perfume, a heavenly quality, out of anything that is fertile or beautiful on earth. These two motions, the upward flight and the descent to rest on earth, find their completion in the third (which is also that of the opening image), the omnipresent circling.

Perhaps the fullest and most memorable celebration of the Holy Spirit as a cosmic principle, as the inherent life of the universe, occurs in Hildegard's sequence *O ignis spiritus paracliti*. In the hymn and the antiphons so far discussed, Hildegard was composing in a poetic *Kunstprosa*, or 'free verse', in which the rhythmic patterns are adjusted to the demands of the music but are otherwise autonomous. In a song such as *O ignis spiritus paracliti*, however, Hildegard was also making a distinctive contribution to the sequence form, a contribution that has not yet been recognized. She does not follow the form that was almost universal in her own day, the sequence in which each pair of versicles showed complete regularity of metre and rhyme; instead, she turns to older forms such as were used by Notker and others in the ninth century. (With her sequence to the Holy Spirit in particular, a direct knowledge of Notker's masterpiece *Sancti spiritus*[3] seems to me highly probable).

---

[1] *Timaeus* 34 b.   [2] Prov. VIII. 30-1.
[3] Ed. W. von den Steinen, *Notker der Dichter und seine geistige Welt* (1948),

Hildegard does not, on the other hand, simply copy Notker in his mostly strict syllabic and melodic symmetry in pairs of versicles. She makes each pair melodically similar, at times almost identical, yet a trace of asymmetry always remains. So too, while certain lines in a pair of versicles may correspond syllabically as in Notker, others will vary considerably. (The only analogies I know to this occur in a group of Mozarabic Latin sequences, from the ninth century to the eleventh, which were first noticed in 1951 by Dom Louis Brou).[1]

Hildegard's innovation has nothing capricious or careless about it: she establishes in the music a pattern of echo and modification which is beautifully reflected in the thematic development of the poetry: in each pair of versicles, the images and meaning of the second both mirror and carry forward those of the first.

Thus, for instance, in the fourth pair in the sequence to the Holy Spirit,[2] who is defined at the beginning as 'life of life in every creature', *vita vite omnis creature* (a phrase that echoes the closing invocation in the Hermetic *Asclepius*: *Vitae vera vita*),[3] the Spirit is characterized first as an irresistible force that penetrates the universe from without; then, in the complementary half-stanza, as the source of motion and fertility within the natural world. When the pervasive power has moved from the circumference of the cosmos right through to its centre, it becomes the centre-point from which new elemental life radiates:

> (4*a*) O iter fortissimum
>   quod penetravit omnia
>   in altissimis et in terrenis
>   et in omnibus abyssis—
>   tu omnes componis et colligis:

---

ii. 54–7. Ed. with melody H. Husmann, *Die mittelalterliche Mehrstimmigkeit* (Arno Volk-Verlag, Köln, n.d.), pp. 16–17.

[1] *Hispania Sacra*, iv (1951), 27–41; cf. also my study 'The Beginnings of the Sequence', *PBB* (Tübingen) lxxxvii (1965), 52–3.

[2] *O ignis spiritus paracliti* (text from R, Pitra, p. 450).

[3] *Asclepius*, 41 (*Corpus Hermeticum*, ed. Nock–Festugière, ii. 355).

(4*b*) De te nubes fluunt,
ether volat, lapides
humorem habent,
aque rivulos educunt,
et terra viriditatem sudatt.[1]

(4*a*) Most mighty course
that penetrated all things
in the heights and in the world
and in all the abysses—
you harmonize and gather up all:

(4*b*) From you the clouds stream out,
the pure air flies, the stones
have their moisture,
through you the waters dilate their brooks,
and the earth floods with greenness.

The threefold action in the first of these versicles recalls the
functions of the three wings of the *virtus Sapientie*, as well as
perhaps the Neoplatonic triad of *processio, conversio,* and *reditus*:[2]
the divine force descends and enters into all things, it harmonizes
them, and draws them to itself. If here the language associates
the powers of the Holy Spirit with those of the Anima Mundi,
in the second versicle it links them with those of the goddess
Natura: there the motifs strikingly anticipate those of two
stanzas in Alan of Lille's invocation to Natura in the *De*

---

[1] D 158ʳ⁻ᵛ (Sequentia); R 473ʳᵃ⁻ʳᵇ (Sequentia de spiritu sancto). 4*a* 2
omnia—corr. out of *omniũ* D; 5 *omnes* corr. out of *omnis* D; 4*b* 5 *sudatt*—
sic D.

[2] Hildegard's acquaintance with learned sources still poses extensive problems (cf. Bertha Widmer, *Heilsordnung und Zeitgeschehen in der Mystik Hildegards von Bingen* (1955), pp. 22 ff.). The absence of specific allusions or citations
(other than biblical), and the extreme rarity of echoes, remain startling. One
must, however, reckon with the possibility that Hildegard had met with such
a concept as the triadic cosmic process in e.g. Boethius' *O qui perpetua mundum
ratione gubernas* (*Cons. Phil.* III, m. 9).

planctu.[1] At the same time, these functions, cosmic and terrestrial, complement each other; the movement of the thought and that of the music are shaped by the same symmetrical-asymmetrical pattern, the undulation of parallelism and contrast.

In her sequences in honour of the saints Hildegard could allow herself a greater freedom of imaginative treatment than was possible or permissible with the theme of the Holy Spirit. It is among these that she achieves her most individual and spectacular poetic effects. The three outstanding instances, in my opinion, are the sequences to Saint Ursula, Saint Rupert, and Saint Maximinus. While in the Maximinus sequence[2] Hildegard again uses her special parallelistic form, in those to Saint Ursula and Saint Rupert, which I shall discuss here, she takes up the traditional but rare form of the repetitionless sequence, of which we find probably the earliest surviving examples in Notker (eight among his forty sequences), and which was scarcely used after the tenth century. Musically, the essentially free and linear development of this type, in which the strophic sections are bound together only by the modified recurrence of musical topoi, was ideally suited to Hildegard's poetic treatment of Saint Ursula's martyrdom, in which a progressing, though allusive, narrative is interwoven with lines of mystical reverie.

A hagiographic *Passio* from the later tenth century, and another from the eleventh, preserve the legend of Saint Ursula, the English princess who, reluctantly betrothed to a pagan

---

[1] *De planctu Naturae* (ed. T. Wright, *Anglo-Latin Satirical Poets*), ii. 458:

> Cui favet caelum, famulatur aer,
> quam colit tellus, veneratur unda,
> cui velut mundi dominae tributum
>   singula solvunt . . .
>
> Cuius ad nutum iuvenescit orbis,
> silva crispatur folii capillo,
> et sua florum tunicata veste
>   terra superbit.

[2] Text and melody in my book *The Medieval Lyric* (1968), pp. 233–5; transl. and discussion ibid., pp. 75–8.

prince, delayed her marriage by a three-year pilgrimage to
Rome, with a retinue of eleven thousand maidens, all of whom
on the return journey were martyred by the Huns at Cologne.
This legend, which had relied on little more than the tenuous
support of a fourth-century inscription at Cologne com-
memorating some unnamed women martyrs, captured people's
imagination afresh when in 1106 a mass of bones was found
buried not far from the church of Saint Ursula.[1]

Of the three versions of the legend that Hildegard could have
known and taken as a point of departure for her sequence,[2]
only one, the eleventh-century *Passio*, contains a few phrases
that suggest a direct connection.[3] Yet these phrases are insignifi-
cant beside the unfettered imaginative grandeur of Hildegard's
development of the theme. With her the legend sheds all that
is trivial or grotesque, merely anecdotal or merely edifying:
everything is concentrated towards making the legend a symbol
of that love-death, that *mors osculi*, which the mystical tradition
had surmised in the opening verse of the Song of Songs,
Osculetur me osculo oris sui . . .

1 Ecclesia, your eyes are sapphire-like,
    your ears are as the mountain of Bethel,

---

[1] Cf. W. Levison, 'Das Werden der Ursula-Legende', *Bonner Jahrbücher*,
cxxxii (1927), 1–164, cxxxix (1934), 227–8. Levison's outstanding discussion
unfortunately does not mention Hildegard's contribution. Cf. also S. Sudhof,
'Ursula und die elftausend Jungfrauen', *Die deutsche Literatur des Mittelalters,
Verfasserlexikon*, v (1955), 1105–9.

[2] It is chronologically possible for Hildegard to have known, besides the
two *Passiones*, Geoffrey of Monmouth's version of the legend (*Historia regum
Britanniae*, chs. 87–8, ed. E. Faral, *Les Légendes arthuriennes* iii. 162–3). It is
unlikely that at the time of writing the *Symphonia* she knew the *Liber revelationum de sacro exercitu virginum Coloniensium* of her younger contemporary
and friend Elisabeth of Schönau (ed. F. W. E. Roth, *Die Visionen der heiligen
Elisabeth* (1884), pp. 123–38, 157–60). The writing of these visions can be
dated 1156–7 (cf. K. Köster, 'Elisabeth von Schönau', in *Schönauer Elisabeth
Jubiläum* (1965), p. 27); in content they are quite unrelated to Hildegard's
lyrical compositions.

[3] e.g. *Passio* (ed. J. Klinkenberg, 'Studien zur Geschichte der Kölner
Märterinnen', *Bonner Jahrbücher*, xciii (1892), 154–60, ch. 2, ll. 12–16; ch. 4,
l. 7; ch. 14, l. 10; ch. 15, l. 17; ch. 17, l. 1.

your nose is as a mountain of myrrh and incense,
and your mouth is like the roar of many waters.

2 With the vision of true faith
Ursula loved the son of God
and left behind bridegroom and world alike
and gazed into the Sun
and cried out to the young and fairest one:

3 'With great longing
I have longed to come to you,
to sit beside you at heaven's wedding-feast,
to race towards you by an unfamiliar way,
as a cloud races in the purest air,
sapphire-like.'

4 When Ursula had spoken thus
it was noised abroad among all peoples,
so that men said
'What simple, girlish ignorance!
She does not know what she is saying.'

5 And they began to play with her
amid great bursts of music—
until the burden of fire
fell upon her.
Then all could see
that setting the world at naught is like the mountain of Bethel.

6 Then too they were aware
of the most fragrant scent of myrrh and incense,
for setting the world at naught transcends all perfumes.

7 Then Satan rushed into his minions,
and they destroyed those bodies
in all their womanly grace.

8 And all the elements heard
the piercing sound,
and before the throne of God they cried:

9 'Wach! the red blood of the innocent lamb
is shed on her wedding-day!

10 Let all the heavens hear it,
and in consummate music
praise the divine lamb—
for in these pearls
of the substance of God's word
the throat of the serpent of old
lies strangled.'[1]

Hildegard begins with an astonishing composite image, laden with prophetic and mystical associations from the Old Testament. In her visions in *Scivias*, and in the illuminations made under her supervision to accompany them, Ecclesia is seen as larger than life, but still as a recognizable womanly figure. Here Ecclesia is a figure of cosmic dimensions, and Hildegard does away with the last traces of realism. The sapphire of her eyes evokes the throne in Ezekiel's vision of the Son of Man; her ears, the *porta caeli* of Jacob's dream, where earth and heaven seemed nearest to each other; her nose, the fragrant place where the lover in the Song of Songs waits for his bride; her mouth evokes that roar of waves which, coming from the wings of the four living creatures, seemed to Ezekiel *quasi sonum sublimis dei*.[2]

The next image is of Ursula herself, turning away from her earthly lover and directing her cry of longing to the divine lover. She begins in the traditional mystical terms coloured by the Song of Songs, but concludes with the sparkling image of her spontaneous, air-borne run towards him, by a way that is 'alien' to the human body:

> velut nubes que in purissimo aere
> currit, similis saphiro.

This was prepared by an earlier image—it was by gazing 'in solem' that she beheld her heavenly beloved—as well as by the associations of Ezekiel's sapphire. The divine Sun has the

[1] Text and melody are given in the Appendix below, pp. 202 ff.
[2] Ez. I. 24–6 (cf. also Apoc. XIX. 6); Gen. XXVIII. 17; Cant. IV. 6.

sapphire of heaven as his throne; the cloud, hastening towards the sun, can become *similis saphiro*.

Now Hildegard takes up the narrative, introducing remarkable innovations. The two *Passiones* mention Ursula and her maidens playing games together on board their ships—a charming but inconsequential detail.[1] Hildegard develops the context of these games: other people discover the girl's longing for her death into divine love, they do not comprehend, they tease her for it, try to bring her back to 'normality' with the help of games and music. But then, suddenly, comes the moment when she is confronted with martyrdom. It is not light and sublime as she had imagined—a racing cloud made radiant by the sun; it is a painful experience, as of being weighed down and scorched—*ignea sarcina*. But her example in confronting death has a sublime effect on those who had mocked her longing for martyrdom before: the effect is expressed in the same words as in the opening image of Ecclesia, some of which recur now almost like a refrain: all at once they see Ursula's *contemptus mundi*, which they had thought mere foolishness, as something more than humanly beautiful: they smell the scents of Ecclesia's nostrils, see the arduous heights of Bethel that are her ears: the immense and unfathomable figure of Ecclesia has become real for them in the figure of this girl.

For a brief moment, in stanza 7, Hildegard returns to the narrative and records the moment of death of these maidens, stressing the human beauty and graciousness, *nobilissimos mores*, that went to waste. Then she projects the martyrdom into a cosmic vision, with a strangeness and grandeur that matches the vision of Ecclesia at the beginning. It is not the saints and angels, but the elements, the ultimate principles of the natural universe, that sing the martyrs' praises and summon the heavens to hear. *Wach!*, the German exclamation of amazement and anger, gives a deliberately stark and outlandish effect to their cry. Deliberate, too, is the ambiguity in *sanguis innocentis agni*, by which the maiden's sacrifice is fused with that of Christ,

[1] Levison, art. cit., pp. 149–50; Klinkenberg, art. cit., p. 157.

and her union with Christ in dying as well as in the mystic
marriage is conveyed.

The elements summon the spheres to music, to praise the
victory over Satan that this multiple martyrdom signifies. The
sequence ends with their summons, in an image of the same
haunting, almost barbarous, visionary power as the opening
one: as Ursula in death becomes united and even identified
with the divine lamb, so too, in this final image, her eleven
thousand companions become pearls made of the substance of
the divine Word. And these pearls form themselves into an
immense necklace that is drawn tight around the throat of the
serpent Satan, so tight that life is choked out of him.

Hildegard's longest and most elaborate sequence is dedicated
to Rupert, the saint whose relics lay on the mountain where she
founded her new convent. It was she who restored the church
that Rupert, an eighth-century Rhenish nobleman who died
at the age of twenty, had built there,[1] she who furthered his
cult by writing his life[2] as well as by her lyrical poetry. While
in Hildegard's sequence to Saint Ursula the images are related
to one another through a thematic and visionary unity that
underlies them, in that to Saint Rupert she works by a series
of contrasts, and echoes within contrasts. Here the images of
the saint are set against images of the heavenly Jerusalem, the
unity is that of a collage. The vision of Jerusalem is the back-
cloth for a kind of reverie, not so much on the life of the saint
—his biography is scarcely relevant[3]—as on the eschatological
meaning of holiness.

   1 Jerusalem, city of gold, graced with royal purple,
      building of utmost bounty, you never-darkened light,
      you are lovely in the dawn, and in the sunlight's blaze.

   2 Blessed childhood, sparkling in the dawn,
      superb time of youth, burning in sunlight—

---

[1] See *Lexicon für Theologie und Kirche*, ix. 104, s.v. Rupert von Bingen.
[2] *P.L.* 197, 1083–92.
[3] In the *Vita* Hildegard does, however, stress the many signs of Rupert's
spiritual precocity from earliest childhood to adolescence.

in these, noble Rupert, you were bright as a gem,
so you cannot be eclipsed by foolish men:
the valley cannot hide the mountain.[1]

The image of Jerusalem in the first stanza is unusual in the
way it speaks of dawn and sun. The city of Saint John's vision
has God and the Lamb as its sole illumination.[2] Jerusalem in
this sequence, therefore, is not the completed city of the end of
time, set in a new heaven and earth: it is the city still growing
and being built in time, still related to the *primum caelum et
prima terra*. That is why, in the second stanza, that same dawn
and sunlight can irradiate and warm not only the heavenly
Jerusalem but the childhood of a saint on earth. This childhood
is the dawning of Jerusalem's light in an individual being, and
in his spiritual growth that inner sun climbs to its zenith. Then
he shines *sicut gemma* (the phrase points forward to the moment
when he will become part of the fabric of the divine city);
already he stands out among mankind as a mountain among
valleys—the simile seems to contain a playful allusion to the
spiritual aspirations of Hildegard's own 'Rupertsberg'.

[1] D 164ᵛ (Sequentia); R 476ᵛᵃ–477ʳᵇ (De Sancto Ruperto); complete text
and melody in the Appendix below, pp. 202 ff.

1 O Ierusalem, aurea civitas,   ornata regis purpura,
   o edificatio summe bonitatis,   que es lux numquam obscurata,
   tu enim es ornata   in aurora   et in calore solis.

2 O beata puericia,   que rutilas in aurora,
   et o laudabilis adolescentia,   que ardes in sole! [D-text ends]
   Nam tu, o nobilis Ruperte,   in his sicut gemma fulsisti,
   unde non potes abscondi   stultis hominibus,
   sicut nec mons valli   celatur.

3 Fenestre tue,   Ierusalem,
   cum topazio   et saphiro   specialiter* sunt decorate.
   In quibus dum fulges, o Ruperte,   non potes abscondi
   tepidis moribus, sicut nec mons valli,
   coronatus rosis, liliis et purpura,
   in vera ostensione.

      * spelialiter R

[2] Apoc. XXI. 23.

3 Jerusalem, your windows are framed
  wondrously with topaz and sapphire.
  As your brightness, Rupert, is caught in them,
  it cannot be eclipsed by men's apathy—
  the valley cannot hide the mountain—
  crowned with roses, with lilies and purple,
  in a true vision.

The third stanza again sets an image of Jerusalem against one
of the saint; again they are related, this time through a conceit:
the radiance of the saint is caught and reflected in the windows
of the city. For the saint himself, the mountain-image recurs,
now passing into the 'true vision' of flowers, a crown for the
human being and the mountain-top alike. The echo of 'purpura'
from the opening line of the poem suggests that already on
earth the saint has something of the regality of the heavenly
city.

4 O tener flos campi   et o dulcis viriditas pomi,
  et o sarcina   sine medulla
  que non flectit pectora   in crimina!
  O vas nobile   quod non est pollutum
  nec devoratum   in saltatione
  antique spelunce,   et quod non est maceratum
  in vulneribus   antiqui perditoris—

5 In te symphonizat spiritus sanctus,
  quia angelicis choris   associaris,
  et quoniam in filio dei ornaris,
  cum nullam maculam habes.

6 Quod vas decorum tu es! . . .

  Tender flower of the field, and sweet green of the apple,
  fruit with no bitter core,
  enticing no hearts into crimes;
  noble urn, that remains untarnished,
  not drunk to the dregs in the dance
  in the ancient cave, nor destroyed
  in the attacks of the ancient ravager—

The Holy Spirit makes music over you,
for you belong to the dances of angels,
and are filled with the beauty of the Son of God,
and have no flaw.

What a beautiful urn you are! . . .

The flower-images of the third stanza point forward to the
buoyant stream of associative imagery in the two that follow,
with their joyful celebration of innocence: the *flos campi* of the
Song of Songs is conjoined with the image of an apple still
growing to its perfection in Eden, not yet 'the fruit of that
forbidden tree'. The last emblem of the saint's innocence is the
urn (a metaphor for the angels in the pseudo-Dionysius),[1]
which is here evoked by a contrasting double image: polluted
in an orgiastic rite of dance and music, in a cavern dedicated
to a pagan cult; and again, dedicated to a blessed, heavenly rite,
in which angels dance to a divine music.

The last part of the sequence is an extended image of Jerusalem, which begins:

7 O Ierusalem, fundamentum tuum
positum est cum torrentibus lapidibus,
id est cum publicanis et peccatoribus . . .

Jerusalem, your foundations
are built of fiery stones,
of publicans and sinners . . .

The growing celestial Jerusalem of Hildegard's vision is a
human building, its walls gleam with living stones (*vivis lapidibus*). The blessed become both *ornamenta dei* and *ornati*—both
fabric of the city and its inhabitants—and (the last stanza makes
the link explicit) Saint Rupert is one of these.

For a last insight into Hildegard's individual mind, I should
like to discuss the originality of conception and achievement

---

[1] *De caelesti hierarchia*, ch. 15 (in Scotus Eriugena's translation, *P.L.* 122,
1067C, 'geometrica et tectonica vasa').

in her play, the *Ordo Virtutum*.[1] It is by more than a century our earliest surviving morality-play.[2] While Hildegard's contemporary, the author of the *Ludus de Antichristo*, included in his huge cast of human characters five personified figures—the queens Ecclesia, Synagoga, and Gentilitas, and the two consorts of Antichrist, Heresis and Hypocrisis—in the *Ordo Virtutum*, except for its prologue, all the characters are personifications, and the dramatic action consists wholly of encounters between personified forces. Yet the play is by no means a dramatized *Psychomachia*, if by this we understand Prudentius' limited and thematically simplified conception. Indeed the play shows no perceptible debt to Prudentius either in language or in details of content (though I think it unlikely that Hildegard should have had no acquaintance at all with Prudentius' poem). In the *Psychomachia* the combats themselves, and who will win them, are predictable, the possibility of dramatic excitement is virtually excluded. In the *Ordo Virtutum* nothing is predictable:

[1] A complete text is given below, pp. 180–92.

[2] E. K. Chambers's reference, when writing of the *Ludus de Antichristo*, to 'two unprinted and little-known French plays, also of the twelfth century', on the theme of the debate between the Four Daughters of God (*The Medieval Stage*, ii. 152), unfortunately rests on a misunderstanding. The two pieces are the *De Salvatione Hominis Dialogus* (ed. F. Michel, *Libri Psalmorum* (1860), pp. 364–8), which is attributed in one manuscript to Stephen Langton (cf. ibid., p. xxi); the other, a similar dialogue in the first part of the *Vie de Tobie* attributed to a Norman clerc Guillaume (ed. R. Reinsch, *Archiv für das Studium der neueren Sprachen*, lxii (1879), 380–96). Neither of these dialogues, which are largely verbally identical, is dramatic, for they have a narrative *continuo*: the dialogue is both preceded and concluded by narrative, narrative is resumed between speeches, and the speeches themselves invariably contain words such as 'she said' (*fet ele*) in their opening lines. According to A. Langfors, in *Notices et Extraits*, xlii (1933), 139–290, the *Vie de Tobie* is early thirteenth century, and probably incorporated the debate of the Four Daughters from the *Dialogus*.

So too, Otto Ursprung's suggestion (art. cit., p. 945) that Hildegard's dramatization of allegorized virtues goes back to Hrotsvitha's play *Sapientia* is erroneous: in Hrotsvitha's play the mother Sapientia and her daughters Fides, Spes, and Karitas are *not* personifications: as Hrotsvitha's own preface makes explicit, they are four women who were persecuted (and the three daughters put to death) by a Roman emperor (Diocletian in the preface, but Hadrian in the course of the play).

this story of Anima, Diabolus, and the Virtutes is essentially new, the audience could not know what would happen next, so that dramatic tension and sudden reversals of expectation were possible; there is an interest in motives, in the sources of emotion and in the workings of a particular human mind that leaves the world of Prudentius far behind.

The sixteen Virtutes and their queen, Humilitas, are on raised *sedes* at the back of the playing-space. Their costumes, if we can go by the contemporary illuminations depicting the Virtutes in Hildegard's *Scivias*,[1] must have been spectacular, in glowing colours. There, for instance, Caritas has a dress the colour of the heavens, with a golden stole reaching down to her feet; Fides, a scarlet dress, a token of martyrdom. Obedientia wears a hyacinth colour, and has silver fetters on her throat and hands and feet; Timor Dei has a dark mauve dress (the text simply calls it *umbrosum indumentum*)[2] on which many closed eyes are painted in silver—as if all her attempts at seeing God had been dazzled by the excess of his light.

At the foot of the steps leading up to the *sedes* is Diabolus. While all the other players sing their lines, Diabolus only speaks, or shouts:[3] he is set off against the rest as deliberately as Bassa Selim against the protagonists in Mozart's *Entführung* (I know of no parallel in twelfth-century drama). Diabolus is in chains, and the chains rattle when he moves or speaks.

The brief lyrical prologue, in which a chorus of patriarchs and prophets, walking up the steps, gaze in wonderment at the Virtutes above them, establishes the frame of imagery within which the play takes shape. The patriarchs and prophets sing:

Who are these, who are like clouds?[4]

[1] Cf. the fine reproductions in Maura Böckeler's translation, *Wisse die Wege* (3rd ed., 1955), especially plate 29.

[2] *P.L.* 197, 654A.

[3] i.e. his words are not set to music in the manuscript, and his first speech is introduced by the phrase 'Strepitus Diaboli'.

[4] The phrase is from Is. LX. 8 ('Qui sunt hi, qui ut nubes [volant, et quasi columbae ad fenestras suas]?'). Pitra (p. 457) prints the complete verse in his text, but the manuscript gives no indication in support of this.

The Virtutes answer:

> You holy ones of old, why do you marvel at us?
> The Word of God grows bright in the shape of man,
> and thus we shine with him,
> building up the limbs of his beautiful body.

From this the ancient ones recognize:

> We are the roots, and you, the boughs,
> fruits of the living eye,
> and we grew up in its shadow.[1]

The two basic images are that of the divine light, too bright to reach the earth direct, but streaming down by way of the clouds, the Virtutes; and the cosmic tree, growing up out of the created world into the divine. The divine is still being created by mankind—the Virtutes are 'building the limbs of the beautiful body' of the Logos. Hildegard unites the two images, light and tree: the Old Testament patriarchs and prophets are the roots of the cosmic tree, and they grew up in the shadow of the divine light: they belong to the world of *umbra* and *figura*. The Virtutes are the fruits of that tree, but also fruits ripened by the full divine sunlight, *fructus viventis oculi*. (How distinctively Hildegard's unconventional expressiveness is revealed in such a phrase; for her, thinking directly

---

[1] R 478va–481vb (Incipit ordo virtutum):
    [Prologue]
  Patriarche et Prophete:
    Qui sunt hi, qui ut nubes?
  Virtutes:
    O antiqui sancti, quid admiramini in nobis?
    Verbum dei clarescit in forma hominis,
    et ideo fulgemus cum illo,
    edificantes membra sui pulcri corporis.
  Patriarche et Prophete:
    Nos sumus radices et vos rami,
    fructus viventis oculi,
    et nos umbra in illo fuimus.

in taut images—images that, however complex, remain sharp—
seems to have become almost second nature.)

At the opening of scene I the word *umbra* recurs with a
different meaning, a Platonic–dualistic one: a chorus of souls
lament that they have fallen from their royal, heavenly state
into exile on earth, *in umbram peccatorum*, and long to be
restored to their true home. This longing is expressed with
particular intensity by the 'happy soul', Felix Anima, who
becomes the central character in the play:

> Oh sweet divinity, oh gentle life,
> in which I shall wear a radiant robe,
> receiving that which I lost in my first manifestation,
> I sigh for you, and invoke all the Virtues . . .

She is sighing for the return of that blissful state which she
lost in the fall of Adam. Is hers the true Christian longing for
the eternal, the true *contemptus mundi*? The Virtues answer her,
'multum amas'—echoing the words Christ used of the woman
who anointed his feet.[2] But this love can be directed in diverse
ways: once more Anima expresses her longing, and the Virtutes answer her, more sternly this time, that more than an
ecstatic impulse is needed:

> Oh let me come to you joyfully,
> that you may give me the kiss of your heart!
> We must fight together with you, royal daughter.[1]

With this rebuff, this warning of a harder task on earth than
merely pining for heaven, Anima grows depressed (*gravata*):

---

[1] [Scene 1]

> Felix Anima:
>> O dulcis divinitas, et o suavis vita,
>> in qua perferam vestem preclaram,
>> illud accipiens quod perdidi in prima apparitione,
>> ad te suspiro, et omnes Virtutes invoco! . . .
>>
>> O libenter veniam ad vos,
>> ut prebeatis michi osculum cordis!
> Virtutes:
>> Nos debemus militare tecum, o filia regis. . . .

[2] Luke VII. 47.

she is too impulsive to sew her immortal dress patiently:

> I don't know what to do
> or where to flee.
> Woe is me, I cannot complete
> this dress I have put on.
> Indeed I want to cast it off!

She rejects the Virtutes' remonstrances with the laconic retort, appealing to Nature for justification:

> God created the world:
> I'm doing him no injury—
> I only want to enjoy it!

Soon after this we hear the *strepitus Diaboli*: his chains clank, and he calls out to Anima:

What's the use of hard effort, foolishly, foolishly? Look to the world: it will embrace you with great honour![1]

Encouraged by this, Anima goes out into the world: perhaps she runs through the audience and leaves by the main door of the church. As she departs, the Virtutes lament: they recognize that Anima's longing for the divine had contained an element of hubris, and concealed a largely sensual desire for bliss. It is a tragic irony that she who is initially innocent and in her feelings most apt for divine love cannot pass through the next stage of spiritual development without a fault of the will.

---

[1] [Scene 1 *cont.*]

> Infelix, Anima:
> > O nescio quid faciam,
> > aut ubi fugiam!
> > O ve michi, non possum perficere
> > hoc quod sum induta.
> > Certe illud volo abicere! . . .
>
> > Deus creavit mundum:
> > non facio illi iniuriam,
> > sed volo uti illo!
>
> Strepitus Diaboli ad Animam illam:
> > Fatue, fatue, quid prodest tibi laborare? Respice mundum,
> > et amplectetur te magno honore.

She is a Psyche who impetuously wants to see the divine Eros
before the God is ready to reveal himself:

> Is this not a plangent voice, of utmost sorrow?
> Ah, a certain wondrous victory already
> rose in that soul, in its wondrous longing for God,
> in which a sensual delight was secretly hidden,
> alas, where previously the will had known no guilt
> and the desire fled man's wantonness.[1]

The scene concludes with a hostile exchange between the
Virtutes and Diabolus: he taunts them not only with their
failure to prevent Anima's escape, but with their own inade-
quacy, the taunt that he will fling at them throughout the play:
nescitis quid sitis, you do not know what you are. In an important sense this is true: the Virtutes' whole lives have been
eternally in conformity with God; they have never asserted
themselves, never expressed a personality or will of their own
as distinct from God; therefore they have no nature of their
own, as Satan has.

Queen Humilitas answers that she can see through him: he
was the dragon whom God flung in the abyss; and the other
Virtutes join her, singing 'As for us, we dwell in the heights'.
But they have not, or not yet, answered Satan's specific
charge; and one remains with the feeling that Satan has won
this round.

In the long lyrical second scene the Virtutes dance, both
singly and together, singing words that reveal their nature and
their relation to the human and the divine. Satan continues to
harass them—*nescitis quid colitis!* But at the close of the dance

----

[1] [Scene 1 *cont.*]

> Virtutes:
> O plangens vox est hec maximi doloris!
> Ach, ach, quedam mirabilis victoria
> in mirabili desiderio dei surrexit,
> in qua delectatio carnis se latenter abscondit,
> heu, heu, ubi voluntas crimina nescivit
> et ubi desiderium hominis lasciviam fugit. . . .

Queen Humilitas defines the Virtutes from another vantage-point, which seems to answer Satan:

> Daughters of Israel, God raised you from beneath the tree,
> so now remember how it was planted.
> Therefore rejoice, daughters of Jerusalem.[1]

They are the heirs to the Old Testament patriarchs, sprung from the same root. Despite Satan's efforts, the divinely planted cosmic tree is still growing, and this is a cause for joy.

Nevertheless, the Virtutes continue to lament, because Anima has not returned. At the beginning of the third scene she comes back, repentant, but still too weak and lacerated to mount the steps that lead up to the Virtutes. She calls out to them again and again, but they remain aloft and remote, singing *curre ad nos*, which unaided she simply cannot do. Finally, she invokes Humilitas, who is more understanding than the rest: she does not simply summon her to come up, but entreats her companions to descend and carry her:

> All you Virtues, lift up this mournful sinner,
> with all her scars, for the sake of Christ's wounds,
> and bring her to me . . .
>
> Oh unhappy daughter, I want to embrace you:
> the great surgeon has suffered harsh and bitter wounds for you.

As the Virtutes descend, they sing in joyful praise of the *felix culpa*:

> Living fountain, how great is your sweetness . . .
> Rejoice then, daughter of Jerusalem,
> For God is giving you back many
> whom the serpent wanted to sunder from you,

---

[1] [Scene 2]
    ⟨Humilitas⟩:
       O filie Israhel, sub arbore suscitavit vos deus,
       unde in hoc tempore recordamini plantationis sue.
       Gaudete ergo, filie Syon!

> who now gleam in a greater brightness
> than would have been their lot before.[1]

But the joy of the Virtutes is premature: the sound of their descent rouses Satan, lurking at the foot of the steps, who roars and hurls himself on Anima. Now for the first time Anima resists and struggles against him. She cries out to Humilitas for help, and the queen, issuing commands from above, sends the Virtutes, led by Victoria, to hunt Diabolus. They catch him and, if we can go by the illumination in *Scivias*,[2] they truss him up in his own chains and lay him flat, face upwards. Castitas, at this moment symbolically identified with the Virgin Mary, triumphantly places her heel on his head: she sees this gesture as a re-enactment at this moment, in the victory on behalf of this particular Anima, of the same moment as it is eternally present in the mind of God, and as it was temporally present in the Incarnation:

> In the mind of the Highest, Satan, I trod on your head,
> and in a virgin form I nurtured a sweet miracle
> when the son of God came into the world;
> therefore you are laid low, with all your plunder;
> and now let all who dwell in heaven rejoice,
> because your belly has been confounded.

Once more the call to joy is premature. Satan, though bound,

---

[1] [Scene 3]

> Humilitas:
>> O omnes Virtutes, suscipite lugentem peccatorem,
>> in suis cicatricibus, propter vulnera Christi,
>> et perducite eum ad me. . . .
>> O misera filia, volo te amplecti,
>> quia magnus medicus dura et amara vulnera
>> propter te passus est.
>
> Virtutes:
>> O vivens fons, quam magna est suavitas tua . .
>> unde gaude, filia Syon,
>> quia deus tibi multos reddit
>> quos serpens de te abscidere voluit,
>> qui nunc in maiori luce fulgent
>> quam prius illorum causa fuisset.

[2] *Wisse die Wege*, plate 17.

can still play his trump card, his appeal to Nature, a more formidable appeal than Anima's in her quest for happiness. Taking up Castitas' own taunt, *venter tuus confusus est*, he says:

You don't know what you are nurturing, for your belly is devoid of the beautiful form received from a man; in this you transgress the command that God enjoined in the sweet act of love; so you don't know what you are![1]

It is both a human and a theological attack: anyone who does not know sexual love knows nothing of Nature, nothing of life; Castitas is a mere child. At the same time he is saying, if she gave birth as Virgin, then it is unnatural and unhuman: then the birth of Christ has nothing to say to humanity. She answers, saying that his mind pollutes the virgin birth: he thinks that anything which is unknown to Nature must be unnatural; in fact this birth was greater than Nature, and gathered human nature towards itself: *Unum virum protuli, qui genus humanum ad se congregat.*

The finale takes up this theme of reintegration once more, but in terms of images related to those of the prologue: the re-creation of the divine on earth, the restoration of the primordial *viriditas*, the perfect blossoming, the divine eye whose glance makes whole. Those who sing are mankind: the chorus of souls from the opening scene, and the Virtutes (who, we might say, borrowing Plotinus' phrase, are 'the soul at its divinest'); they are all who are still striving for the divine in the created world, in the midst of sufferings and setbacks—but also it is

---

[1] [Scene 4]

⟨Castitas⟩:
  In mente altissimi, o Satana, caput tuum conculcavi,
  et in virginea forma dulce miraculum colui,
  ubi filius dei venit in mundum;
  unde deiectus es in omnibus spoliis tuis,
  et nunc gaudeant omnes qui habitant in celis,
  quia venter tuus confusus est.

Diabolus:
    Tu nescis quid colis, quia venter tuus vacuus est pulcra forma
    de viro sumpta—ubi transis preceptum quod deus in suavi
    copula precepit; unde nescis quid sis!

Christ who here appeals to the Father; it is the cosmic Adam, who is not yet whole, whose beautiful limbs are still, laboriously, being formed on earth:

> In the beginning all creation was verdant,
> flowers blossomed in the midst of it;
> later, greenness sank away.
> And the champion saw this and said:
> 'Now remember
> that the fullness which was made in the beginning
> need not have grown dry,
> and that then you resolved that your eye would never fail
> until you saw my body full of jewels.
> For it wearies me that all my limbs are exposed to mockery:
> Father, behold, I am showing you my wounds.'
> So now, all you people,
> bend your knees to the Father,
> that he may reach you his hand.[1]

The *Ordo Virtutum* is a morality-play by its theme, the fight for a soul, but its language often reaches out into mysticism. It is a highly individual language, at times awkward and at times unclear; the adjectives can be repetitious and limited in range, the interjections excessive. It is the language not of a polished twelfth-century humanist but of someone whose

---

[1] [Finale]

⟨Virtutes et Anime⟩:
In principio omnes creature viruerunt,
in medio flores floruerunt;
postea viriditas descendit.
Et istud vir preliator vidit et dixit . . .
'Nunc memor esto,
quod plenitudo que in primo facta est
arescere non debuit,
et tunc in te habuisti
quod oculus tuus numquam cederet
usque dum corpus meum videres plenum gemmarum.
Nam me fatigat quod omnia membra mea in irrisionem vadunt.
Pater, vide, vulnera mea tibi ostendo.'
Ergo nunc, omnes homines,
genua vestra ad patrem vestrum flectite,
ut vobis manum suam porrigat.

unique powers of poetic vision confronted her more than once with the limits of poetic expression.

At its finest, however, Hildegard's poetry faces these limits triumphantly, and achieves a visionary concentration and an evocative and associative richness that set it apart from nearly all other religious poetry of its age. With only isolated exceptions such as Abelard's *planctus*, twelfth-century Latin religious lyric is poetry of the Fancy: the corpus of Victorine sequences, the hymns of Walter of Châtillon, and Abelard's own *Liber Hymnorum*, with all their formal and rhetorical skill, and their subtle play with Old Testament figurae and a patristic heritage of symbolism, their poetic art tends towards an ingenious and cerebral construction rather than an imaginative unity of themes and images, a cohesion going beyond the conceptual dimension. It is this that we find so strikingly in Hildegard's *Symphonia*: it is a poetry of the Imagination; it reveals a remarkable degree of 'esemplastic power'. While it cannot often match Notker's *Liber Hymnorum* in the perfection of organizing words and images in a totally harmonious and coherent structure, there is an exuberance in her imagery, a sense of mercurial play in her use of language, a visionary daring, which can achieve poetic effects in their way as extraordinary as those achieved by Notker's limpid control. Though of very different temperaments, the ninth-century poet and the twelfth-century poetess show some true affinities: in their conception of a unified cycle of liturgical lyric, in their choice of lithe, flexible forms bound not by rhyme but by associations springing out of the words and the melodies; above all, in their never jaded poetic sensitivity, *vas nobile quod non est pollutum*.[1]

[1] It was only after the completion of this chapter that I was able to obtain M. Immaculata Ritscher's article 'Zur Musik der heiligen Hildegard', *Colloquium Amicorum: Joseph Schmidt-Görg zum 70. Geburtstag* (1967), pp. 309–26. Dr. Ritscher for the first time observes the fragmentary nature of MS. D (pp. 313–14), though without analysing its contents in detail. She gives valuable documentation for the liturgical use of Hildegard's songs (pp. 311–12). Unfortunately, like all previous scholars, she assumes the invariable priority of Hildegard's prose to her poetry: 'Im ganzen sind 43 Liedtexte Hildegards Werken entnommen' (p. 315).

THE TEXT OF THE *ORDO VIRTUTUM*[1]
(R 478va–481vb)

Incipit Ordo Virtutum.

⟨PROLOGUE⟩

Patriarche et Prophete

Qui sunt hi, qui ut nubes?

Virtutes

O antiqui sancti, quid admiramini in nobis?
Verbum dei clarescit in forma hominis,
et ideo fulgemus cum illo,
edificantes membra sui pulcri corporis.

Patriarche et Prophete

Nos sumus radices et vos rami,
fructus viventis oculi,
et nos umbra in illo fuimus.

Title: *sic* R; Incipit ordo virtutum de patriarchis et prophetis A   1 Cf.
Is. LX. 8. Pitra, p. 457 completes the verse, but the absence of music for the
remainder makes it unlikely that Hildegard intended this   6 nos rami A
6–8 Pitra omits manuscript direction 'Patriarche et prophete' and so gives these
lines to the Virtutes.

[1] A new text of the *Ordo Virtutum* seems desirable, as none of the three works
in which it has been printed is easily accessible today. The earliest text, in
F. W. E. Roth's *Geschichtsquellen des Niederrheingau's*, iii (1880), 450–6, is in
many places garbled, and I do not record its readings here; more valuable are
the editions by Cardinal Pitra, *Analecta Sacra*, viii (1882), 457–65, and Maura
Böckeler, *Der hl. Hildegard von Bingen Reigen der Tugenden* (1927), containing
a transcription of the music and a German translation. Pitra's text contained
some ten misreadings that affect the sense; all of these were successfully
eliminated by Böckeler, but she in turn departed from the manuscript in nine
new places—departures that were intended as corrections of Hildegard's text,
but that seem to me unnecessary. My text is based on Josef Gmelch's photo-
graphic facsimile of the *Symphonia* in R, and on a microfilm most generously
presented to me by the Hessische Landesbibliothek. I was not able, as I was
for the lyrical pieces, to collate R personally. I have collated the copy of the
Ordo Virtutum made for Trithemius in 1487, in the manuscript that today is
B.M. Add. 15102, fols. 207^r–221^r. I give all variants, other than purely ortho-
graphic, from this manuscript (A), which has not been used by the earlier
editors. Line-arrangement, capitalization of the names of characters, and
punctuation are my own.

⟨SCENE I⟩

Querela Animarum in carne positarum
  O nos peregrine sumus.
  Quid fecimus, ad peccata deviantes?   10
  Filie regis esse debuimus,
  sed in umbram peccatorum cecidimus.
  O vivens sol, porta nos in humeris tuis
  in iustissimam hereditatem quam in Adam perdidimus!
  O rex regum, in tuo prelio pugnamus.

Felix Anima
  O dulcis divinitas, et o suavis vita,
  in qua perferam vestem preclaram,
  illud accipiens quod perdidi in prima apparitione,
  ad te suspiro, et omnes Virtutes invoco.

Virtutes
  O felix Anima, et o dulcis creatura dei,   20
  que edificata es in profunda altitudine sapientie dei,
  multum amas.

Felix Anima
  O libenter veniam ad vos,
  ut prebeatis michi osculum cordis.

Virtutes
  Nos debemus militare tecum, o filia regis.

Sed, gravata, Anima conqueritur
  O gravis labor, et o durum pondus
  quod habeo in veste huius vite,
  quia nimis grave michi est contra carnem pugnare.

Virtutes ad Animam illam
  O Anima, voluntate dei constituta,
  et o felix instrumentum, quare tam flebilis es   30
  contra hoc quod deus contrivit in virginea natura?
  Tu debes in nobis superare diabolum.

9 Querelae *Pitra* (reading R); Querele A   11 regni *Pitra*   23 Anima
felix A   30 debilis *Pitra*

Anima illa

Succurrite michi, adiuvando, ut possim stare!

Scientia Dei ad Animam illam

Vide quid illud sit quo es induta, filia salvationis,
et esto stabilis, et numquam cades.

Infelix, Anima

O nescio quid faciam,
aut ubi fugiam!
O ve michi, non possum perficere
hoc quod sum induta.
Certe illud volo abicere!   40

Virtutes   .

O infelix conscientia,
o misera Anima,
quare abscondis faciem tuam coram creatore tuo?

Scientia Dei

Tu nescis, *nec* vides, nec sapis illum qui te constituit.

Anima illa

Deus creavit mundum:
non facio illi iniuriam,
sed volo uti illo!

Strepitus Diaboli ad Animam illam

Fatue, fatue quid prodest tibi laborare? Respice mundum, et
amplectetur te magno honore.

Virtutes

O plangens vox est hec maximi doloris!   50
Ach, ach, quedam mirabilis victoria
in mirabili desiderio dei surrexit,
in qua delectatio carnis se latenter abscondit,
heu, heu, ubi voluntas crimina nescivit
et ubi desiderium hominis lasciviam fugit.
Luge, luge ergo in his, Innocentia,

33/4 animam illam sciencia dei adiuvat A   39 quo *Pitra*   44 quec
R; nec A   48 Fatua! fatua! *Böckeler*   56 Euge, euge *Pitra*

que in pudore bono integritatem non amisisti,
et que avariciam gutturis antiqui serpentis ibi non devorasti.   58

Diabolus

Que est hec potestas, quod nullus sit preter deum? Ego autem
dico, qui voluerit me et voluntatem meam sequi, dabo illi omnia.
Tu vero, tuis sequacibus nichil habes quod dare possis, quia etiam
vos omnes nescitis quid sitis.

Humilitas

Ego cum meis sodalibus bene scio   63
quod tu es ille antiquus dracho
qui super summum volare voluisti—
sed ipse deus in abyssum proiecit te.

Virtutes

Nos autem omnes in excelsis habitamus.

⟨SCENE 2⟩

Humilitas

Ego Humilitas, regina Virtutum, dico:
venite ad me, Virtutes, et enutriam vos
ad requirendam perditam dragmam   70
et ad coronandum in perseverantia felicem.

Virtutes

O gloriosa regina, et o suavissima mediatrix,
libenter venimus.

Humilitas

Ideo, dilectissime filie,
teneo vos in regali talamo.

Karitas

Ego Karitas, flos amabilis—
venite ad me, Virtutes, et perducam vos
in candidam lucem floris virge.

59 praeter Dominum *Pitra*; R has 'preter me', corrected by the same hand
to 'preter deum'. Syntax and meaning are difficult: possibly an original assertion by Satan of his universal might—*quod nullus sit preter me*—was changed
into a rejoinder made by Satan to the Virtutes: they bid Innocentia mourn
that she has not destroyed Satan, and he replies 'What is this power—as if
there were no one but God?'   71 coronandam *Böckeler*

Virtutes

O dilectissime flos, ardenti desiderio currimus ad te.

Timor Dei

Ego, Timor Dei, vos felicissimas filias preparo　　　　　80
ut inspiciatis in deum vivum et non pereatis.

Virtutes

O Timor, valde utilis es nobis:
habemus enim perfectum studium numquam a te separari.

Diabolus

Euge! euge! quis est tantus timor? et quis est tantus amor? Ubi
est pugnator, et ubi est remunerator? Vos nescitis quid colitis.

Virtutes

Tu autem exterritus es per summum iudicem,
quia, inflatus superbia, mersus es in gehennam.

Obedientia

Ego lucida Obedientia—
venite ad me, pulcherrime filie, et reducam vos
ad patriam et ad osculum regis.　　　　　　　　　90

Virtutes

O dulcissima vocatrix,
nos decet in magno studio pervenire ad te.

Fides

Ego Fides, speculum vite:
venerabiles filie, venite ad me
et ostendo vobis fontem salientem.

Virtutes

O serena, speculata, habemus fiduciam
pervenire ad verum fontem per te.

Spes

Ego sum dulcis conspectrix viventis oculi,
quam fallax torpor non decipit—
unde vos, o tenebre, non potestis me obnubilare.　　　　100

82 valide *Pitra*　　　　87 morsus *Pitra*　　　　100 obumbrare A

Virtutes

O vivens vita, et o suavis consolatrix,
tu mortifera mortis vincis
et vidente oculo clausuram celi aperis.

Castitas

O Virginitas, in regali thalamo stas.
O quam dulciter ardes in amplexibus regis,
cum te sol perfulget
ita quod nobilis flos tuus numquam cadet.
O virgo nobilis, te numquam inveniet umbra in cadente flore!

Virtutes

Flos campi cadit vento, pluvia spargit eum.
O Virginitas, tu permanes in symphoniis supernorum civium: 110
unde es suavis flos qui numquam aresces.

Innocentia

Fugite, oves, spurcicias Diaboli!

⟨Virtutes⟩

Has te succurrente fugiemus.

Contemptus Mundi

Ego, Contemptus Mundi, sum candor vite.
O misera terre peregrinatio
in multis laboribus—te dimitto.
O Virtutes, venite ad me
et ascendamus ad fontem vite!

Virtutes

O gloriosa domina, tu semper habes certamina Christi,
o magna virtus, que mundum conculcas,   120
unde etiam victoriose in celo habitas.

Amor Celestis

Ego aurea porta in celo fixa sum:
qui per me transit
numquam amaram petulantiam in mente sua gustabit.

101 et suavis A   110 uirginintas R   123 transiit A

Virtutes

O filia regis, tu semper es in amplexibus quos mundus fugit,
O quam suavis est tua dilectio in summo deo!

⟨   ⟩

Ego sum amatrix simplicium morum qui turpia opera nesciunt;
sed semper in regem regum aspicio
et amplector eum in honore altissimo.

Virtutes

O tu angelica socia, tu es valde ornata   130
in regalibus nuptiis.

Verecundia

Ego obtenebro et fugo atque conculco
omnes spurcicias Diaboli.

Virtutes

Tu es in edificatione celestis Ierusalem,
florens in candidis liliis.

Misericordia

O quam amara est illa duricia que non cedit in mentibus,
misericorditer dolori succurrens!
Ego autem omnibus dolentibus manum porrigere volo.

Virtutes

O laudabilis mater peregrinorum,
tu semper erigis illos,   140
atque ungis pauperes et debiles.

Victoria

Ego Victoria velox et fortis pugnatrix sum—
in lapide pugno, serpentem antiquum conculco.

Virtutes

O dulcissima bellatrix, in torrente fonte
qui absorbuit lupum rapacem—

127 Speaker's name erased in R, erasure illegible on microfilm and facsimile.
Pitra inserts 'Castitas', Böckeler 'Disciplina'. A has *Caritas* (but she, like Castitas,
has already declared herself).   128 rege regum *Pitra*   129/30 Virtus A
143 pugna RA, *em.* pugnans *Pitra*, pugno *Böckeler*. The virtue is victorious
like David (cf. *I Reg.* xvii. 50), and like the second Eve (cf. *Gen.* iii. 15).

o gloriosa coronata, nos libenter
militamus tecum contra illusorem hunc.

Discretio

Ego Discretio sum lux et dispensatrix omnium creaturarum,
indifferentia dei, quam Adam a se fugavit per lasciviam morum.

⟨Virtutes⟩

O pulcherrima mater, quam dulcis et quam suavis es,   150
quia nemo confunditur in te.

Pacientia

Ego sum columpna que molliri non potest,
quia fundamentum meum in deo est.

Virtutes

O firma que stas in caverna petre,
et o gloriosa bellatrix que suffers omnia!

⟨Humilitas⟩

O filie Israhel, sub arbore suscitavit vos deus,
unde in hoc tempore recordamini plantationis sue.
Gaudete ergo, filie Syon!

⟨SCENE 3⟩

Virtutes

Heu, heu, nos Virtutes plangamus et lugeamus,
quia ovis domini fugit vitam!   160

Querela Anime penitentis et Virtutes invocantis

O vos regales Virtutes, quam speciose
et quam fulgentes estis in summo sole,
et quam dulcis est vestra mansio—
et ideo, o ve michi, quia a vobis fugi!

Virtutes

O fugitive, veni, veni ad nos, et deus suscipiet te.

149 in differentia RA *Pitra*, indifferentia *Böckeler*. I cannot translate 'in
differentia' here, and suspect that Discretio (whether she means discernment,
or prudence) is being linked with God's impartiality, rather than with
his diversity.   149/50 Virtutes A   160/1 Querele A   165 fugitiva
Böckeler. Hildegard seems to treat both 'fugitivus' and 'peccator' (176, 189) as
common rather than masculine in gender.

Anima illa

> Ach! ach! fervens dulcedo absorbuit me in peccatis,
> et ideo non ausa sum intrare.

Virtutes

> Noli timere nec fugere,
> quia pastor bonus querit in te perditam ovem suam.

Anima illa

> Nunc est michi necesse ut suscipiatis me,   170
> quoniam in vulneribus feteo
> quibus antiquus serpens me contaminavit.

Virtutes

> Curre ad nos, et sequere vestigia illa
> in quibus numquam cades in societate nostra,
> et deus curabit te.

Penitens Anima ad Virtutes

> Ego peccator qui fugi vitam:
> plenus ulceribus veniam ad vos,
> ut prebeatis michi scutum redemptionis.
> O tu omnis milicia regine,
> et o vos, candida lilia ipsius, cum rosea purpura,   180
> inclinate vos ad me, quia peregrina a vobis exulavi,
> et adiuvate me, ut in sanguine filii dei possim surgere.

Virtutes

> O Anima fugitiva, esto robusta,
> et indue te arma lucis.

Anima illa

> Et o vera medicina, Humilitas, prebe michi auxilium,
> quia superbia in multis viciis fregit me,
> multas cicatrices michi imponens.
> Nunc fugio ad te, et ideo suscipe me.

---

166 me et ideo A (*om.* in peccatis)   171 q̄uo R; quomodo A
176 peccatrix quae *Böckeler*   177 plena *Böckeler*   179 i.e. 'All you
host of Queen Humility'; Pitra's emendation ('militiae regina') seems unnecessary.

Humilitas

O omnes Virtutes, suscipite lugentem peccatorem,
in suis cicatricibus, propter vulnera Christi,   190
et perducite eum ad me.

Virtutes

Volumus te reducere et nolumus te deserere,
et omnis celestis milicia gaudet super te—
ergo decet nos in symphonia sonare.

Humilitas

O misera filia, volo te amplecti,
quia magnus medicus dura et amara vulnera
propter te passus est.

Virtutes

O vivens fons, quam magna est suavitas tua,
qui faciem istorum in te non amisisti,
sed acute previdisti   200
quomodo eos de angelico casu abstraheres
qui se estimabant illud habere
quod non licet sic stare;
unde gaude, filia Syon,
quia deus tibi multos reddit
quos serpens de te abscidere voluit,
qui nunc in maiori luce fulgent
quam prius illorum causa fuisset.

SCENE 4

Diabolus

Que es, aut unde venis? Tu amplexata es me, et ego foras
eduxi te. Sed nunc in reversione tua confundis me—ego autem
pugna mea deiciam te!   211

189 peccatricem *Böckeler*   191 eam *Böckeler*   199 ff. The thought
of these syntactically difficult lines seems to be, that God has not rejected the
gaze of sinners, but has foreseen (through the redemptive process) how to divert
them from a fall such as the angels had: the angels who fell thought that they
possessed a thing (divine sovereignty) which cannot lawfully subsist thus
(among created beings).   206 abscindere *Böckeler*

Penitens Anima

> Ego omnes vias meas malas esse cognovi, et ideo fugi a te.
> Modo autem, o illusor, pugno contra te.
> Inde tu, o regina Humilitas, tuo medicamine adiuva me!

Humilitas ad Victoriam

> O Victoria, que istum in celo superasti,
> curre cum militibus tuis
> et omnes ligate Diabolum hunc!

Victoria ad Virtutes

> O fortissimi et gloriosissimi milites, venite,
> et adiuvate me istum fallacem vincere.

Virtutes

> O dulcissima ⟨bellatrix, in torrente fonte   220
> qui absorbuit lupum rapacem—
> o gloriosa coronata, nos libenter
> militamus tecum contra illusorem hunc.⟩

Humilitas

> Ligate ergo istum, o virtutes preclare!

Virtutes

> O regina nostra, tibi parebimus,
> et precepta tua in omnibus adimplebimus.

Victoria

> Gaudete, o socii, quia antiquus serpens ligatus est!

Virtutes

> Laus tibi, Christe, rex angelorum.

⟨Castitas⟩

> In mente altissimi, o Satana, caput tuum conculcavi,
> et in virginea forma dulce miraculum colui,   230
> ubi filius dei venit in mundum;

214 anima illa (before *inde*) R   219/20 Virtus A   227 sociae *Böckeler*
228 Christe angelorum A   228/9 Castitas A

unde deiectus es in omnibus spoliis tuis,
et nunc gaudeant omnes qui habitant in celis,
quia venter tuus confusus est.

Diabolus

    Tu nescis quid colis, quia venter tuus vacuus est pulcra forma
de viro sumpta—ubi transis preceptum quod deus in suavi copula
precepit; unde nescis quid sis!

Castitas

    Quomodo posset me hoc tangere
quod tua suggestio polluit per immundiciam incestus?
Unum virum protuli, qui genus humanum   240
ad se congregat, contra te, per nativitatem suam.

Virtutes

    O deus, quis es tu, qui in temetipso
hoc magnum consilium habuisti,
quod destruxit infernalem haustum
in publicanis et peccatoribus,
qui nunc lucent in superna bonitate!
Unde, o rex, laus sit tibi.
O pater omnipotens, ex te fluit fons in igneo amore:
perduc filios tuos in rectum ventum velorum aquarum,
ita ut et nos eos hoc modo perducamus   250
in celestem Ierusalem.

⟨FINALE⟩

⟨Virtutes et Anime⟩

    In principio omnes creature viruerunt,
in medio flores floruerunt;
postea viriditas descendit.
Et istud vir preliator vidit et dixit:
'Hoc scio, sed aureus numerus nondum est plenus.
Tu ergo, paternum speculum aspice:
in corpore meo fatigationem sustineo,

---

236 sumpta est *Pitra*   248 virtutes (before *O pater*) RA   256 *Pitra*
inserts 'Hoc [tempus] scio', but I think *hoc* here refers to the statement *viriditas
descendit*.   258 fastigacionem A

parvuli etiam mei deficiunt.

Nunc memor esto, quod plenitudo que in primo facta est   260
arescere non debuit,
et tunc in te habuisti
quod oculus tuus numquam cederet
usque dum corpus meum videres plenum gemmarum.
Nam me fatigat quod omnia membra mea in irrisionem vadunt.
Pater, vide, vulnera mea tibi ostendo.'
Ergo nunc, omnes homines,
genua vestra ad patrem vestrum flectite,
ut vobis manum suam porrigat.[1]

---

[1] In his preface to B.M. Add. 15102, Trithemius lists the works of Hildegard known to him, among them *cantica plurima*—this presumably includes the *Ordo Virtutum*, even though it is not specified. Then, alluding to R, he continues (fol. 1ᵛ):

Hec omnia scripta habentur in maximo quodam volumine et valde precioso, de quo opinio vulgi est quod manu sancte Hildegardis sit conscriptus. Vidi librum, grande ut dixi volumen, in predicto monasterio sancti Ruperti. De quo hec omnes que sequuntur epistole licet cum festinacione scripte sunt, anno domini millesimo cccc° octogesimo septimo, per quendam monachum sancti Benedicti de cenobio Spanheim iubente me eiusdem monasterii abbate licet indigno.

Trithemius is explicit only about the Epistles: he does not say that the *Ordo Virtutum* was copied, either directly or exclusively, from R. While we cannot rule out the existence of a further exemplar of the *Ordo Virtutum* at the Rupertsberg in his time, one no longer traceable today, the most reasonable assumption is that A is copied from R. The seemingly independent wording in A of the direction over 34, *animam illam sciencia dei adiuvat*, is almost certainly due to the copyist's misreading of R (fol. 479ʳᵃ), where *animam illam* is superscript. Thus the copyist assumed that these words came first, and that the *ad*, coming last, was incomplete. (So too, in the same column of R, where R has *Felix anima* with *anima* superscript, A has written *Anima felix*.) For the rest, the variants in A seem to be either minor scribal errors (e.g. 6 *nos* for *vos*, 228 *Christe angelorum* for *Christe rex angelorum*, 258 *fastigacionem*), or attempts at minor improvements (e.g. 9, 161 *Querele* for *Querela*, 44 the correction to *nec*), or attempts to assign a speaker when omitted in R (e.g. 127 *Caritas*, 150 *Virtutes*, 229 *Castitas*). None of the variants in A suggests to me that A had any source in addition to R.

VI

EPILOGUE · PATHS OF FURTHER INQUIRY

I SHOULD like to conclude my study with a brief indication of the relevance of the small group of texts I have discussed to a wider discussion of medieval poetry. Here only the barest sketch is possible, to mark some of the trails it would be exciting to pursue.

The four works explored in the previous chapters—*Ruodlieb* and *Semiramis*, Abelard's *Planctus* and Hildegard's *Symphonia*—disparate as they are, can be seen to have one important trait in common. Each has shown certain aspects of the poet's symbolic power—in the widest sense, his power of meaning more than he says. To some scholars such a notion of the symbolic in medieval poetry has seemed, and may still seem, dangerous and perhaps anachronistic:[1] while the allegorical and figural are universally acknowledged as present in medieval literature, to speak of the symbolic there—in any of the ways this has been poetically important in the last hundred years—may still appear to be historically questionable, to be 'reading into' the poetry something that is not there. There is little in the theoretical works from the eleventh century to the thirteenth, for instance, that explicitly relates to a poet's concern with unconfined meaning as against fixed signification, with

[1] Cf. for instance the observations of C. S. Lewis, *The Allegory of Love* (1936), pp. 46–7:

'But of course the poetry of symbolism does not find its greatest expression in the Middle Ages at all, but rather in the time of the romantics: and this, again, is significant of the profound difference that separates it from allegory. I labour the antithesis because ardent but uncorrected lovers of medieval poetry are easily tempted to forget it. Not unnaturally they prefer symbol to allegory; and when an allegory pleases them, they are therefore anxious to pretend that it is not allegory but symbol.'

the evocative and enigmatic as against the sphere of fixed correspondences. Yet it seems to me certain that from the beginnings of Christian literature there have always been at least some remarkable and gifted writers who were drawn to express themselves in a symbolic mode, whose images and visions and narrations are rich with meaning precisely because that meaning has deliberately been left unexplained and unconfined.

Thus, it is not possible to say in so many words what the round dance of Christ and his disciples on the eve of his death (*Acts of John*, 94 ff.)[1] *stands for*—and the evocative strength of

[1] The lines in the hymn where the dance-image occurs directly are:
  Grace is dancing.
12 'I want to play the flute—
  all of you, dance.' 'Amen.'
13 'I want to make a lament—
  all of you, make the gestures of mourning.' 'Amen.' . . .
15 'The twelfth number
  dances aloft.' 'Amen.'
16 'To the whole
  does the dancer belong.' 'Amen.'
17 'Whoever does not dance, does not understand
  what is coming about.' 'Amen.' . . .
28 'But when you follow the motions
  in my dance,
29 see yourself
  in me, who am speaking . . .
31 You who dance, understand
  what I am doing, for it is yours,
32 this suffering of the man,
  that I shall suffer . . .
35 You who saw what I suffer,
  as a sufferer yourself, you saw me,
36 and as you saw, you did not stand still
  but quite dissolved into motion . . .
45 I want holy souls
  to be brought into rhythm, following me . . .
49 I have leapt,
  but you must know the whole,
50 and when you have known it, say:
  glory to you, Father!'

Transl. from M. Bonnet, *Acta Apostolorum Apocrypha*, ii. 1 (1898), 193–9, with reference to E. Hennecke–W. Schneemelcher, *Neutestamentliche Apokryphen* (3rd ed., 1964), ii. 154–6. I adopt the arrangement of Hennecke-

the image is bound up with that undefined potential. In the song in the *Acts of Thomas* (108 ff.),[1] even if we are right to interpret the journey of the child from the East allegorically, what is the pearl he must bring back from his quest, what the sealed royal letter that becomes a speaking eagle? Will not any attempts, however ingenious, to devise fixed and explicit 'meanings' for these, diminish the poetry and show themselves inadequate to its rich suggestiveness? Even if one granted that the meaning of the *De ave phoenice*, with its account of the

Schneemelcher, and the emendations suggested there for 16, 28, 35, 45. Cf. also M. Pulver, 'Jesu Reigen und Kreuzigung nach den Johannesakten', *Eranos-Jahrbuch*, ix (1942), 141 ff.

[1]
    1 When I was a little child
       and lived in the realm, in the house of my father,
    2 and was serene in the wealth and luxury
       of those who nurtured me,
    3 from the East, our homeland,
       my parents sent me, with provisions for the journey,
    4 and out of the wealth of our treasury
       they had long since bound up a load for me.
    5 It was great, but so light
       that I could carry it alone . . .
    11 And they made an agreement with me
       and wrote it in my heart, lest I forget it:
    12 'If you go down into Egypt
       and carry off the one pearl
    13 that is in the sea,
       encircled by the loud-breathing dragon,
    14 you shall put on your light-ray robe again,
       and your toga, that covers it,
    15 and with your brother, who is next to us,
       you shall be heir in our kingdom.' . . .
    49 And my letter was one
       that the king had sealed with his right hand,
    50 against the wicked, the people of Babel
       and the tumultuous demons of Sarbûg.
    51 It flew in the form of an eagle,
       king of all birds,
    52 it flew and alighted beside me
       and became entirely speech.

Transl. after Hennecke–Schneemelcher, ii. 349–51, and A. F. J. Klijn, *The Acts of Thomas* (1962), pp. 120–3, with reference to the Greek text of M. Bonnet, *Acta*, ii. 2 (1903), 219–22.

bird's self-immolation and renewal, could be 'fixed' as allegorizing Christ's resurrection, or the spiritual rebirth of man—or indeed both—what of the abundance of narrative details? The spices on the funeral pyre, the phoenix's flight, bearing its own ashes, in a cortège of other birds—the poet gives us no guidance with these. This is not, I think, because he was too careless to give such details definable meanings; rather, because he wanted them to work in ways different from the definable. When Perpetua in her visions sees 'a white-haired man sitting in shepherd's dress, vast, milking sheep . . . who gave me a mouthful of the cheese he was milking' (*Passio SS. Perpetuae et Felicitatis*, IV), nearly all who have discussed the passage[1] identify this shepherd with Christ, and the cheese with the sacrament. But is this not to disregard all that is here unusual (the age and size and posture of the shepherd, the milking that produces not milk but cheese) in order to reduce it to the banal, to turn the evocative and individual into the known?[2] Is not *this* the anachronism, reading into the text what the writer has not intended, in order to comply with modern notions of the medieval?

However much less we may know about their functions than about those of allegory and figura, the existence of 'unfixed' meanings must be reckoned with. From the very first, the literary world of Christendom was a world that inherited and furthered symbolic modes of expression. While these are clearly not to be found in every medieval literary text, and not necessarily in every text that is imaginatively outstanding, to exclude the possibility of their presence would be to falsify historically.

---

[1] E. R. Dodds, *Pagan and Christian in an Age of Anxiety* (1965), p. 51, an outstanding exception.

[2] So too, to mention only one later instance, with the attempts to make Dante's Vergil stand for Reason, or some other concept, his Beatrice for Theology, or some other concept—cf. the important comments of Erich Auerbach in his essay 'Figura', *Scenes from the Drama of European Literature* (1959), pp. 67–76, and of Bruno Nardi in his *Dal 'Convivio' alla 'Commedia'* (1960), pp. 118 ff.

In the four works treated here, I have tried to show the presence of symbolic modes in diverse ways. In *Ruodlieb* it was primarily in the symbolic shaping of aspects of the narrative. Many details were found to be there not simply for a delight in narrative elaboration, but for the sake of a further contribution to the poetic fabric, a contribution that could often only be suggested, not stated outright. At times—*agna vetus cupide vas lingit salis amore*—a simple symbolism that the poet had ready to hand in a homely proverb could give rise to a thematic development that pervades and enriches the whole of a narrative situation.

In *Semiramis* I would suggest a symbolic technique is present in two ways: in the poet's way of weighting descriptive detail with mysterious and exotic associations, and in his ambiguous treatment of the heroine. His world is concocted largely out of the more fabulous elements in the ancient texts that he knew, yet it can by no means be reduced to these. The details are selected for their suggestive power, for making every aspect of that world seem heavy with hidden meaning. In the last resort the mystery here, the macabre fantasy, is only an escapism —this world does not, even implicitly, grow into or contrast with a waking reality it could illuminate. Only in the enigma of the heroine, achieved by the presentation of contrasting views of her, do we arrive at something more compellingly symbolic, something that goes beyond the simple juxtaposition of opposing statements, suggesting possibilities of understanding that cannot be readily defined.

It is this symbolic juxtaposition of conflicting attitudes that Abelard brings to a new degree of subtlety in his Samson lament. The conflicting attitudes point towards a meaning they cannot themselves express, they are like searchlights from different directions cast on the central enigma of the hero and the divine judgement revealed in him. With Hildegard, finally, we observed repeated attempts to project the symbolism of an inner vision: some of her strangest images—the three wings of Sapientia, the surreal features of Ecclesia—showed great evocative power, and were indeed able to convey meaning beyond what could be abstractly expressed. At the opening and close of her play come images of growth—the cosmic tree, the body of Adam-Christ—in which it is deliberate that the human and divine 'components' can no longer be conceptually separated; the image here becomes a necessity, in order to 'say the unsayable'.

The works I have discussed are in many ways unparalleled. Their individuality, too, is bound up with the question of their symbolism, with their particular ways of meaning more than they say. Yet this need not imply that discussion of them has no significance beyond these works themselves. They are, in one sense, a pointer backwards—they allow us to glimpse the kinds of imaginative richness on which these authors must have been nourished—but even more, they can be seen as a pointer forwards. The problems they raise link with ones that are crucial in the understanding of later poetry, sometimes bringing one back to questions that have long been asked, sometimes, too, prompting new questions or new ways of asking old ones.

Questions about the poet's symbolic shaping of his narrative can lead further into some of the subtlest achievements in the narrative art of the later Middle Ages. To look closely for a moment at one instance: like parts of *Ruodlieb*, Chaucer's *Merchant's Tale* attains dense poetic texture by the symbolic use of divergent aspects of a theme, what might be called the 'Solomonic' theme. Almost every medieval connotation of Solomon (his sorcery apart) is made relevant to Chaucer's fabliau: Solomon the sinful idolater, the cynically wise philosopher–misogynist, but also the woman's dupe, and the builder of the temple, and the resplendent lover in the Song of Songs. There is parody of Solomon the pessimistic philosopher in the effusive praise of wives at the opening; Placebo, the yes-man, perverts another point of Solomon's wisdom as he passes from *Wirk alle thyng by conseil* to *youre owene conseil is the beste*; it is Solomon's maxim *Omnia tempus habent* that gives ironic 'authority' to the heroine's resolve towards adultery (1972). The *gardyn enclosed*, and its *welle*, for all the pagan associations with which Chaucer decks them, are the *hortus conclusus* and *fons* of the Song of Songs; Januarie lures May there with Solomon's own passionate words (2138 ff.), which have here become *olde lewed wordes*. The patriarch's most misogynistic utterance is cited by Pluto, ravisher of Proserpina (2242 ff.), while she, an 'idol', condemns the lechery and idolatry of Solomon *in his elde*, by appeal to the *verray God*. May's mortal longing for the pears (2330–7) parodies the languishing bride in the Canticle, about to be visited by her Solomon (*stipate me malis, quia amore langueo*). At the opening and close, straightforward parody; between them, a bitter re-enactment of the one 'canonized' scene of sexual joy, whose climax here becomes a divine intervention, in which the idols are armed with the words and deeds of the idolater—such are the instruments of the symbolic shaping of Chaucer's tale. What does this contribute to the fable of sexual deceit? By way of Solomon, a spectrum of perceptions against which that fable demands to be measured: Januarie, like the ageing king, is both *a lecchour and an ydolastre* and a dupe; but is not the philosophic Solomon, with his caricature of women, just as blind and inadequate in his attitude? What image of fidelity and chastity has the man—Solomon or Januarie—to offer that would qualify him to mould a *yong thyng* like *warm wex*? As Proserpina points out (2291 ff.), it is but a step from the 'wise' observer—with all his façade of respectability, temple-building, and wealth—to the foolish victim. At the same time, the Song of Songs contributes a motif that evokes both understanding and pity for the sour-sweet contrasts it establishes: how tarnished and distorted a reflection this escapade gives of the love in that first, radiant *hortus conclusus*, and how deeply the man is to blame!

As for the symbolic weighting of descriptive detail, to conjure up an imagined, mysterious world—a close examination of the ways by which the poets achieve this can be fruitful in approaching, for instance, both Wolfram's world of the grail

o

and Dante's earthly paradise. Does not the strangeness of these
fabled realms prompt a further inquiry: to what extent is the
poet presenting something deliberately enigmatic? Does he
want us to accept the new realm unquestioningly, or to attempt
to judge it? In what way is the beauty of that earthly paradise
imperfect? Is the grail earth's finest image of the immutable—
and is the immutable inevitably that which turns to stone,
which deadens, draining warm life away?

The problems of enigma and judgement are equally engross-
ing in the sphere of persons and their actions, as with Abelard's
Samson. How are we to regard, for instance, Sigune in *Titurel*,
when she sends her beloved Schionatulander on the quest for
the hound's leash? Or Piers Plowman, when he tears up the
Pardon? Is it not possible that what is enigmatic in such
moments may be deliberately so, that the poet is demanding
of his audience not the simple acceptance of the situation as he
tells it to them, but a response that embraces it as intrinsically
problematic?

The problems of the projection of inner vision, finally, can
touch every kind of attempt at embodying in images some
aspect of the intelligible, immaterial world. Thus in the twelfth
century alone the inquiry could extend to visions of very
different kinds: in Hildegard's own mystical prose writings,
we should have to ask, how and why do the visions she relates
nearly always suggest so much more than her own allegoresis
of them can express? So, too, with the prophetic visions of
a Joachim of Flora: in what ways are his images—such as those
in the *Liber Figurarum*—able to reach beyond abstract con-
cepts? And with the allegorical visions of the twelfth-century
Platonists: what can be expressed by allegory can also in principle be expressed conceptually, yet do not these visions at
moments reach the limits of allegorical statement? Where
Bernard Silvestris, for instance, requires three goddesses, each
with her own equipment, for the fabrication of man,[1] or Alan
of Lille conjures up four spheres, each showing the relation

[1] *De mundi universitate*, II. xi–xii (ed. C. S. Barach–J. Wrobel, pp. 56 ff.).

between matter and form in a different light,[1] is this merely the allegorist's playfulness, multiplying entities beyond necessity, or are these, too, attempts at saying what could not be said any other way, at using allegorical constructs as if they were myths, to extend the range of conceptual statement? Here at least are one or two of the many paths along which the study of poetic individuality in the Middle Ages can lead.

[1] *Sermo de sphaera intelligibili* (ed. M.-Th. d'Alverny, *Alain de Lille, Textes inédits* (1965), pp. 297 ff.).

APPENDIX

MELODIES OF PETER ABELARD
AND HILDEGARD

A note on the transcriptions

THERE is nothing in the original notation of the following three pieces to indicate the way in which they should be rhythmically performed. (The notation consists of neumes on a four-line staff.) Nevertheless, Abelard's *Planctus* is here presented in regular rhythmic patterns, whereas the two sequences by Hildegard are transcribed in a rhythmically non-committal form: in stemless noteheads. The reason for this difference lies partly in the nature of the melodies, partly in that of the versification. Abelard's *Planctus* is (at least for stanzas 3–5) largely syllabic: that is, it sets one note—only occasionally two—to each syllable. Because of this it is possible to select a rhythmic mode that reflects the stress-pattern of the verse, which tends for the most part to alternate stressed and unstressed syllables. With one exception, the first rhythmic mode seemed the most suitable.

Hildegard's melodies, by contrast, are melismatic: a syllable may have as many as eleven notes set to it, and the length of melisma does not mirror the degree of stress of a syllable. A stressed syllable may well have only one note and its succeeding unstressed one a melisma of three or four notes. (It is for this reason that the first stanza of Abelard's *Planctus* has been presented in the second rhythmic mode, which, being iambic, allows more time for melisma in the weak part of the beat.) If these two melodies are set into a strictly modal framework, by either of the methods most commonly used by scholars, the result is artificial. Moreover, the syllabic structure of Hildegard's poetry is flexible, its lines variable in length. A compromise modal rendering, sensitive to the rhythm of the poetry, is certainly feasible, but at the same time would be highly speculative. The present transcriptions are thus clinical; they leave aside problems of rhythmic interpretation, and with them an integral part of the melodies themselves.

IAN BENT

(i) Abelard, *Planctus 'Dolorum solatium'*

1a	Do - lo	rum	so	la - ti - um,
1b	Nunc quo	ma	- ior	do - lor est
1c	Stra - ges	mag	- na	po - pu - li,
1d	Du - cum	de - so	la - ti - o,

la - bo - rum re	— me - di - um
ius - ti - or - que	me - ror est
re - gis mors et	fi - li - i,
vul - gi des - pe -	ra - ti - o

me - a	mi - chi	ci - tha - ra.
plus est	ne - ces - sa - ri - a.
hos - ti - um vic - to - ri - a,
luc - tu	re - plent om - ni - a.

2a	A - ma - lech	in - va - lu	- it
2b	In - sul - tat	fi - de - li	- bus
2c	In - sul - tan - tes	in - qui	- unt
2d	Quem pri - mum	his	pre - bu	- it

Is - ra - hel	dum co - ru	- it,
in - fi - de - lis	po - pu - lus:
'Ec - ce, de	quo gar - ri	- unt?
Vic - tus rex	oc - cu - bu	- it:

in - fi - de - lis iu - bi - lat
in ho - no - rem ma - xi - mum
qua - li - ter hos pro - di - dit
ta - lis est e - lec - ti - o

Phi - lis - te - a, dum la - men - tis
plebs ad - ver - sa, in de - ri - sum
de - us su - us, dum a mul - tis
de - i su - i, ta - lis con - se

ma - ce - rat se Iu - de - a.
om - ni - um fit di - vi - na.
oc - ci - dit diis pro - stra - tus.
cra - ti - o va - tis mag - ni!'

3a Sa - ul re - gum for - tis - si - me,
3b Qua - si non es - set o - le - o
3c Plus fra - tre mi - chi Io - na - tha,
3d Ex - per - tes, mon - tes Gel-bo - e,

vir - tus in - vic - ta Io - na - the—
con - se - cra - tus do - mi - na - co,
in u - na me - cum a - ni - ma,
ro - ris si - tis et plu-vi - e,

3a, 3b contd.

3a qui vos ne – qui – vit vin-ce – re
3b sce – les – te ma – nus gla-di – o

per – mis-sus est oc – ci – de – re.
iu – gu-la – tur in pre-li – o.

3c, 3d contd.

3c que pec – ca-ta, que sce – le – ra
3d nec ag – ro-rum pri –mi – ci – e

nos – tra sci – de – runt vis-ce – ra!
ves – tri suc – cres – cant in – co – le!

4a Ve, ve ti – bi, ma – di – da
4b U – bi chris – tus do – mi – ni
4c Planc – tum, Si – on fi – li – e,
4d Tu mi – chi, mi Io – na – tha,

tel – lus ce – de re – gi – a,
Is – ra – hel – que in – cli – ti
su – per Sa – ul su – mi – te,
flen – dus su – per om – ni – a—

qua et te, mi Io – na – tha,
mor – te mi – se – ra – bi – li
lar – go cu – ius mu – ne – re
in – ter cunc – ta gau – di – a

ma – nus stra – vit im – pi – a,
sunt cum su – is per – . di – ti.
vos or – na – bant pur – pe – re.
per – pes e – rit la – cri – ma.

5a He – u cur con – si – li – o
5b Vi – cem a – mi – ci – ci – e
5c In – faus – ta vic – to – ri – a

ad – qui – e – vi pes – si – mo,
vel u – nam me red – de – re
po – ti – tus in – te – re – a,

ut ti – bi pre – si – di – o
o – por – te – bat tem – po – re
quam va – na, quam bre – vi – a

non   es - sem   in   pre - li   o?
sum - me   tunc   an - gus - ti - e:
hinc   per - ce - pi   gau - di - a!

vel   con - fos - sus   pa - ri - ter
tri - um - phi   par - ti -. ci - pem
quam   ci - to   du - ris - si - mus

mo - re - rer   fe - li - ci - ter,
vel   ru - i - ne   co - mi - tem
est   se - cu - tus   nun - ti - us

cum   quid   a - mor   fa - ci - at
ut   te   vel   e - ri - pe - rem
quem   in   su - am   a - ni - mam

ma - ius   hoc   non   ha - be - at,
vel   te - cum   oc - cum - be - rem,
lo - cu - tum   su - per - bi - am

et   me   post te vi – ve – re
vi – tam   pro te fi – ni – ens
mor – tu – is   quos nun – ti – at

mo – ri   sit as – si – du – e,
quam sal – vas – ti to – ci – ens,
il – la – ta mors ag – gre – gat,

nec ad vi – tam a – ni – ma
ut et mors nos iun – ge – ret
ut do – lo – ris nun – ti – us

sa – tis sit di – mi – di – a.
ma – gis quam dis – iun – ge – ret.
do – lo – ris sit so – ci – us.

6a Do qui – e – tem fi – di – bus—
6b Le – sis pul – su ma – ni – bus,

vel – lem ut et planc -ti – bus—
rau – cis planc – tu vo – ci – bus,—

si pos - sem et
de - fi - cit et

fle - - ti - bus!
spi - - ri - tus.

(ii) Hildegard of Bingen, *De undecim milibus virginum*

D 168v–169r (Sequentia); R 477 ra-vb (De undecim milibus virginum)

1. O——— Ec - - cle - si - - a,

o - - cu - li tu - i si - mi - les

sa - phi - ro——— sunt,———

et——— au - res tu - e mon -ti Be - -

thel,——— et na - sus——— tu - us est

si - cut mons mir - - re—— et——

thu - ris, et os—— tu - um qua - - si

so - nus a - - - qua - rum——

mul - - ta - - - rum.——

2. In——vi - - si - - o - ne ve -

re fi - - - - - - - - -de - - - - - - - i

Ur - - - - su - - - la fi - li - - -

um—— de - i—————— a - -

ma - - vit—— et—— vi - - rum——

et—— in—— ce - les - - ti - bus

nup - ti - is—— te - - cum——

se - - de - - re, — per a - li-

e - nam vi - am ad te cur - - - rens,——

ve - - lut—— nu - bes que in pu - ris-

- si - mo a - e - re cur - -

rit,—— si - mi - lis sa - - - - - -

phi - - ro.'

4. Et—— post - quam——————

Ur — — — — su - la sic di-

xe - rat,—— ru - - mor—— is - te

per om - nes—— po - - pu - los e-

xi - - - - - - - - - - it, et—— di-

xe - runt 'In - no - cen - - - ti - - a

pu - - - el - la - ris ig -

no - ran - ti - e nes - - - - - cit

quid di - - - - - - - cit!'

5. Et—— ce - - - pe - runt lu - - de - re

cum—— 'il - - - la   in——————— mag -

na   sim -   pho - ni - - - - - a,   us -

que dum   ig - ne - a   sar - ci -

na   su - - per   e - am   ce -

ci - - - - - dit; —   un - - - - de

om - nes cog - nos - - - ce -   bant

qui - - - a   con - temp -

tus——   mun - di——   est——   si -

cut —— mons——   Be - - - - -thel.

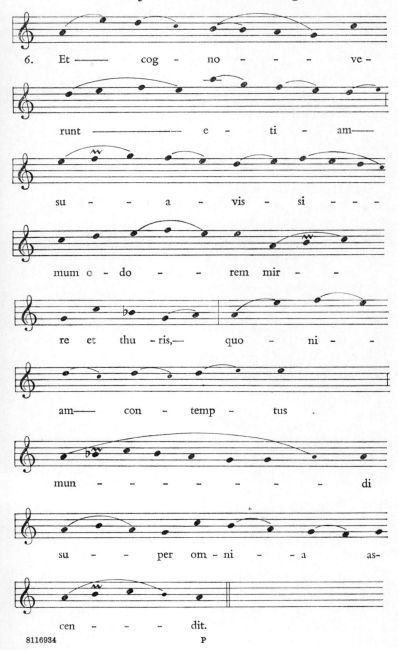

6. Et —— cog - no - - - ve -

runt —————— e - ti - am——

su - - a - vis - si - - -

mum o - do - - rem mir - -

re et thu - ris,—— quo - ni - -

am—— con - temp - tus .

mun - - - - - - - di

su - - per om - ni - - a as-

cen - - - dit.

P

7. Tunc di - a - bo - lus mem - bra

su - a in - va - - sit, que

no - - bi - lis - si - mos mo - res in—

cor - po - ri - bus——— is -

tis oc - ci - - - de - runt.

8. Et hoc in al - ta vo - - ce

om - ni - - a e - le - men-

ta—— au - di - - e - runt, et

an - - te—— thro-num de - i

di – xe – – runt:

9. 'Wach, ————— ru – bi – cun –

dus san – guis —— in – – no –

cen – – tis ag – – ni in

de – spon – sa – ti – o – ne

su – a ef – – fu – sus

est!————————

10. · Hoc——————— au – di – ant

om – nes —— ce – – – – li, ——

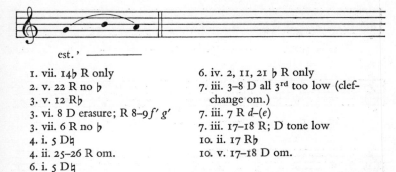

est. '

1. vii. 14♭ R only
2. v. 22 R no ♭
3. v. 12 R♭
3. vi. 8 D erasure; R 8–9 *f' g'*
3. vii. 6 R no ♭
4. i. 5 D♮
4. ii. 25–26 R om.
6. i. 5 D♮

6. iv. 2, 11, 21 ♭ R only
7. iii. 3–8 D all 3rd too low (clef-change om.)
7. iii. 7 R *d–(e)*
7. iii. 17–18 R; D tone low
10. ii. 17 R♭
10. v. 17–18 D om.

[The first Arabic numeral indicates the stanza; the Roman numeral indicates the phrase (whether marked off by a full or half barline); the final Arabic numeral the note within that phrase. Letters in lower-case italic denote pitch names.]

(iii) Hildegard of Bingen, *De Sancto Ruperto*

D 164ᵛ (Sequentia); R 476ᵛᵃ–477ʳᵇ (De Sancto Ruperto)

num-quam ———— ob - scu - ra — — ta,

tu e - nim—— es or — —

na — — ta in au - ro - ra et

in ca - lo - re so — — lis.

2. O be - a - ta pu - e - ri - ci -

a, ———— que ru - ti - las in

au - ro - ra, et o lau - da - bi-

lis a - do - les - cen - ti - a,————

que ar - des in ———— so — —

- - - - - - - - - - - le!

nam tu, o no - bi - lis Ru - per -

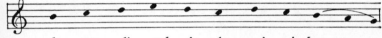

te, ———— in his sic - ut gem -

ma ful - sis - ti, un - de non po - tes

ab - scon - di stul - tis ho - mi - ni - bus, ————

sic - ut nec mons val - - li

ce - - la - - - - tur.

3. Fe - nes - tre——— tu - e, Ie-

ru - sa - - - - - lem,

cum to - pa - zi - o et sa - phi -

ro ——————— spe - ci - a - li -

ter ——— sunt— de - co - - ra - te.

In qui - bus dum ful - ges, o Ru -

per - - te, non po - tes abs-

con - - di te - pi - dis mo - ri - bus,

sic - ut nec mons val - - li, co - ro - -

na - tus ro - sis, li - li - is et pur -

pu - ra, in ve - ra os - ten - - -

si - o - ne.

4. O te - - - ner flos cam -

pi et o dul - cis vi - ri - di-

tas ——— po - mi, et o sar - ci-

na si - - ne me-dul - - la que

non flec - tit pec - to - ra

in cri - - mi - - na!

O vas ——————— no - bi - le

quod non est pol - lu - - tum— nec de-

vo - ra - - - tum —— in sal - ta-

ti - o - ne—— an - ti - - que —

spe - - - - - - lun - ce,

et quod non est ma - ce - - - ra -

tum —— in vul - ne - ri - bus an-

ti - qui per - di - -to - - ris:

5. In —— te sym - pho - ni - zat spi - ri - tus

sanc - tus, qui - a an - ge - li-

cis cho - ris as - so - ci - a - ris, et

um an - he - las - ti, in ti - mo-

re — de — i et in am-ple-

xi - o - ne ca - ri - ta -

tis, et in sua - vis - si - mo o -

do - re — bo - no - rum — o-

pe - - rum.

7. O Ie - ru - sa - - lem, —

fun - da - men - tum — tu - um

po - si - - tum — est

8. De - in - de mu - ri —

tu - - i — ful - mi -

nant vi - vis — la - pi - di - - -

bus — qui per sum - mum stu - di - -

um bo - ne vo - lun - ta - tis — qua - si —

nu - - - bes in ce - lo —

— vo - la - ve - - runt.

9. Et i - ta tur - res —

tu - i, — o Ie-

ru - sa - lem, ——— ru - ti - - lant

et can - dent per — ru - - - bo -

rem et per can - do - rem ————— sanc-

to - rum, et per

om - ni - a or - na - men-

ta ——— de - - i que ti - bi non-

de - sunt, o —— Ie - ru - sa - lem.———

10. Un - - de vos, ——— o —— or -

- - - na - ti et o co - ro-

na - - - ti —— qui ha - bi - ta-

tis in Ie - ru - sa - - lem,

et o tu —— Ru - - - - per -

te, qui —— es—— so - - ci-

- - us —— e - o-rum in hac

ha - bi - ta - - ti - o - ne, suc-

cur - ri - te no - bis fa - mu - lan - ti-

- - bus et in e - xi - li - o

la - bo - ran - ti - - - bus!

1. ii. 7–11 R *e–f–g, a–(g)*   2. iii. 14 R *g–f*   2. iv. 1 R *g*

Text, spelling, and melody of Abelard's *planctus* 'Dolorum solatium' follow the manuscript P (see above, p. 114 n. 1), with three exceptions: 2*d*, 1 Quos P; 5*c*, 11 sit nuntius P; 6*b*, 1 Lelis (*fort.* Celis [chelys]) P. In 3*d*, 4, P's *vestri* can be construed as a pronominal genitive (cf. Hildegard, *De Sancto Ruperto* st. 9: *turres tui*), or corrected to *vestro*.

Since these pages have been in proof, two other editions of these melodies have been announced: Lorenz Weinrich, 'Dolorum solatium' *Mittellateinisches Jahrbuch* V (1968 [1969]), 59–78, has promised a full transcription of the *planctus* (from P, R, and a later manuscript, Bodley 79) in a forthcoming issue of *The Musical Quarterly*. Otto Müller Verlag, Salzburg, have announced an edition of Hildegard, *Lieder*, by P. Barth, M. I. Ritscher, and J. Schmidt-Görg. This new interest in one of the most neglected aspects of medieval monody is to be warmly welcomed.

INDEX